S0-ARL-316

LOCATION OF VIDEONOTES IN THE TEXT

Chapter 1
Creating a World and Adding Objects, p. 19
Moving the Camera in 3D Space, p. 34
Creating the Snowy World, p. 54

Chapter 2
Adding Instructions to an Alice World, p. 62
Using the Program Design Cycle, p. 82
Creating Simultaneously Executed Instructions, p. 98
Creating the Scene from *Alice's Adventures in Wonderland*, p. 109

Chapter 3
Creating and Using a Variable, p. 116
Creating a Set Instruction for a Variable, p. 118
Calling an `ask user` Function, p. 122
Using Math to Avoid Collisions, p. 132
Creating the Miles Per Gallon World, p. 146

Chapter 4
Creating an `If/Else` Instruction, p. 156
Using a Relational Operator, p. 165
Testing an Object's Color Property, p. 169
Using a `While` Instruction to Make an Object Vanish, p. 182
Using the `While` Instruction to Move an Object, p. 186
Creating the Dragon Guardian World, p. 191

Chapter 5
Creating a Class-Level Method, p. 196
Passing Arguments to a Method, p. 211
Writing a Class-Level Function, p. 221
Creating the Exercise Competition World, p. 243

Chapter 6
Handling Key Press Events, p. 254
Handling a Mouse Click Event, p. 261
Creating the Jumping Fish World, p. 276

Chapter 7
Creating a List and Using the `For all in order` and `For all together` Instructions, p. 285
Using the `Let the mouse move <objects>` Event, p. 305
Creating an Array and a Loop that Steps Through It, p. 311
Creating the School of Fish World, p. 320

Chapter 8
Creating a Recursive Method, p. 327
Creating the Recursive Weightlifting Jock World, p. 339

STARTING OUT WITH

Second Edition

Alice

STARTING OUT WITH

Second
Edition

Alice

A Visual Introduction to Programming

Tony Gaddis

Haywood Community College

Addison-Wesley

Boston   Columbus   Indianapolis   New York   San Francisco
Upper Saddle River   Amsterdam   Cape Town   Dubai   London   Madrid   Milan
Munich   Paris   Montreal   Toronto   Delhi   Mexico City   Sao Paulo   Sydney
Hong Kong   Seoul   Singapore   Taipei   Tokyo

Vice President/Editorial Director: Marcia Horton
Editor-in-Chief: Michael Hirsch
Editorial Assistant: Stephanie Sellinger
Vice President of Marketing: Patrice Jones
Marketing Manager: Yezan Alayan
Marketing Coordinator: Kathryn Ferranti
Vice President, Production: Vince O'Brien
Managing Editor: Jeff Holcomb
Production Project Manager: Kayla Smith-Tarbox
Senior Operations Supervisor: Lisa McDowell
Art Director: Linda Knowles
Cover Designer: Suzanne Harbison
Cover Image: © Gail Shumway/Getty Images
Media Editor: Dan Sandin
Project Management: Peggy Kellar, Aptara®, Inc.
Composition and Illustration: Aptara®, Inc.
Printer/Binder: R.R.Donnelley—Willard
Cover Printer: Coral Graphics

Library of Congress Cataloging-in-Publication Data
Gaddis, Tony.
   Starting out with Alice/Tony Gaddis.—2nd ed.
     p. cm.
   Includes index.
   ISBN-13: 978-0-321-54587-9
   ISBN-10:   0-321-54587-7
   1. Alice (Computer program language) 2. Computer games—Programming. 3. Three-dimensional display systems. I. Title.
   QA76.76.C672G28 2011
   794.8'1526—dc22
                                      2010034087

10 9 8 7 6 5 4 3 —DOW—14 13 12

Addison-Wesley
is an imprint of

www.pearsonhighered.com

ISBN 13: 978-0-32154587-9
ISBN 10:   0-321-54587-7

Brief Contents

Preface   xiii

Chapter 1   **Introduction to Alice and Objects**   1

Chapter 2   **Programming in Alice**   57

Chapter 3   **Variables, Functions, Math, and Strings**   113

Chapter 4   **Decision and Repetition Structures**   151

Chapter 5   **Methods, Functions, and More about Variables**   195

Chapter 6   **Events**   249

Chapter 7   **Lists and Arrays**   281

Chapter 8   **Recursion**   323

Appendix A   **Installing Alice**   343

Appendix B   **Answers to Checkpoints**   347

     Index   355

Contents

Preface   xiii

Chapter 1 **Introduction to Alice and Objects   1**

1.1 What Is a Computer Program? 1
1.2 Algorithms and Programming Languages 2
1.3 Learning to Program with Alice 5
TUTORIAL 1-1: Opening and playing an Alice world .6
1.4 Objects 13
1.5 Classes and the Alice Galleries 16
TUTORIAL 1-2: Creating a world and adding objects 19
1.6 3D Objects and the Camera 31
TUTORIAL 1-3: Moving the camera in 3D space 34
TUTORIAL 1-4: Manipulating objects in 3D space 40
TUTORIAL 1-5: Manipulating subpart objects .43
Review Questions 51

Chapter 2 **Programming in Alice   57**

2.1 Writing Methods 57
TUTORIAL 2-1: Adding instructions to an Alice world 62
TUTORIAL 2-2: Exploring additional primitive methods 67
2.2 Naming Conventions 73
2.3 Designing a Program 77
TUTORIAL 2-3: Using the program design cycle .82
2.4 Comments 88
TUTORIAL 2-4: Inserting comments 89
2.5 Tips for Setting Up an Initial Scene 90
2.6 Executing Instructions Simultaneously 97
TUTORIAL 2-5: Creating simultaneously executed instructions 98
2.7 Exporting Your Code for Printing 104
2.8 Exporting an Alice World to Video 105
Review Questions 106

ix

Chapter 3   Variables, Functions, Math, and Strings   113

3.1   Variables 113
TUTORIAL 3-1: Creating and using a variable 116
TUTORIAL 3-2: Creating a set instruction for a variable 118
3.2   Using Functions 120
TUTORIAL 3-3: Calling an `ask user` function 122
TUTORIAL 3-4: Using a proximity function 127
3.3   Creating Math Expressions 130
TUTORIAL 3-5: Using math to avoid collisions 132
3.4   Working with Strings and Text 138
TUTORIAL 3-6: Converting a Number variable to a string 141
Review Questions 144

Chapter 4   Decision and Repetition Structures   151

4.1   Boolean Values 151
4.2   The `If/Else` Decision Structure 153
TUTORIAL 4-1: Creating an `If/Else` instruction 156
4.3   Relational Comparisons and Logical Operators 163
TUTORIAL 4-2: Using a relational operator 165
TUTORIAL 4-3: Testing an object's color property 169
4.4   The `Loop` Instruction 174
TUTORIAL 4-4: Using the `Loop` instruction 175
4.5   The `While` Instruction 180
TUTORIAL 4-5: Using a `While` instruction to make an object vanish 182
TUTORIAL 4-6: Using the `While` instruction to move an object 186
Review Questions 189

Chapter 5   Methods, Functions, and More about Variables   195

5.1   Writing Custom Class-Level Methods 195
TUTORIAL 5-1: Creating a class-level method 196
5.2   Saving an Object to a New Class 199
TUTORIAL 5-2: Saving an object to a class 200
5.3   Stepwise Refinement 203
TUTORIAL 5-3: Completing the *WorkOut* world 207
5.4   Passing Arguments 209
TUTORIAL 5-4: Passing arguments to a method 211
5.5   Using Class-Level Variables as Properties 215
TUTORIAL 5-5: Adding a property to an object 217
5.6   Writing Class-Level Functions 220
TUTORIAL 5-6: Writing a class-level function 221

5.7   World-Level Methods and Variables 226
5.8   Using Clipboards 229
5.9   Tips for Visual Effects and Animation .230
Review Questions 241

Chapter 6   **Events   249**

6.1   Responding to Events 249
6.2   Handling Key Press and Mouse Events .253
TUTORIAL 6-1: Handling key press events .254
TUTORIAL 6-2: Handling the while a key is pressed event 258
TUTORIAL 6-3: Handling a mouse click event 261
6.3   Using Events in Simulations and Games 264
6.4   Tips for Games and Simulations 268
Review Questions 275

Chapter 7   **Lists and Arrays   281**

7.1   Lists 281
TUTORIAL 7-1: Creating a list and using the *For all in order*
and *For all together* instructions 285
TUTORIAL 7-2: More complex list processing 291
TUTORIAL 7-3: Using the Let the mouse move <objects> event 305
7.2   Arrays 308
TUTORIAL 7-4: Creating an array and a loop that steps through it 311
TUTORIAL 7-5: Randomly selecting an array element 317
Review Questions 319

Chapter 8   **Recursion   323**

8.1   Introduction to Recursion 323
TUTORIAL 8-1: Creating a recursive method 327
8.2   Problem Solving with Recursion 330
TUTORIAL 8-2: Recursive problem solving in animation 331
TUTORIAL 8-3: Writing a recursive mathematical function 336
Review Questions 338

Appendix A   **Installing Alice   343**

Appendix B   **Answers to Checkpoints   347**

Index   355

Preface

This book teaches computer programming using Alice, a revolutionary software system that is freely available from Carnegie Mellon University. Alice is a three-dimensional graphical system that can be used to create animations and computer games. With Alice, students build virtual worlds inhabited by objects from the real world, such as people, animals, cars, airplanes, and more. The virtual worlds that students create, and the objects they place in them, can be programmed to perform actions. While learning to program in Alice, students learn the same fundamentals that are taught with traditional languages such as Java, C++, or Visual Basic.

Changes in the Second Edition

This book's pedagogy, organization, and clear writing style remain the same as in the previous edition. Many improvements have been made, which are summarized here:

- **Online Video Notes**
  An extensive series of online video notes have been developed to accompany this text. Throughout the book, video note icons alert the student to videos that explain many of the book's hands-on tutorials. Additionally, one programming exercise at the end of each chapter now has an accompanying video note explaining how to develop the problem's solution. The videos are available at www.pearsonhighered.com/gaddis.

- **Updated for Alice 2.2**
  This book has been updated for compatibility with Alice 2.2.

- **Exporting an Alice World to Video**
  Chapter 2 discusses the process of exporting an Alice world to video.

- **Expanded Coverage of Decision Structures**
  Chapter 4, Decision and Repetition Structures, has a new section on testing the value of an object's property with an If/Else instruction, a new tutorial on testing an object's color property.

- **Expanded Coverage of Repetition Structures**
  Chapter 4, Decision and Repetition Structures, has a new tutorial on using a While instruction to repeatedly manipulate an object's opacity property.

- **Additional Programming Problems**
  Additional programming problems have been added to Chapters 1, 2, 4, and 5. Many of these new problems are designed to focus on a small set of topics from their chapter, and can be completed in a short period of time.

Why Use Alice to Teach Programming?

With Alice, Abstract Concepts Become Concrete

Many students have trouble learning computer programming because the concepts are so abstract. This is where Alice comes to the rescue! Alice brings abstract concepts down to earth, and makes them more concrete. For example, objects take on the form of physical entities, such as people, buildings, animals, and cars, which can be seen on the screen. When an object's methods are called, they cause the object to perform actions that can be observed. The student gets the sense that he or she is working with a real, tangible object. This experience prepares the student to understand the more abstract object-oriented principles that he or she will encounter when studying traditional programming languages.

Alice Eliminates Syntax Errors

For many beginning students, learning the syntax of a programming language can be a daunting task. Precious time that should be devoted to learning the fundamentals of programming is often spent tracking down missing semicolons or unbalanced braces.

Syntax errors in Alice are never a problem because they never happen! The student builds a program by dragging and dropping tiles into an editor. The tiles represent programming instructions and method calls. When values or expressions are needed for variable assignments or as arguments for methods, pop-up menus appear allowing the student to select the needed value or expression.

Runtime errors can still occur, of course, because the student can use the wrong instruction, or get instructions out of order. But, because syntax is not an issue, the student devotes his or her time to developing and debugging algorithms.

Alice Is Motivating

Perhaps the most compelling reason to use Alice is the fact that students enjoy it so much. Rather than writing programs that perform calculations and display text on the screen, students use Alice to create rich animations and computer games. The time that students spend with Alice is productive because they learn the fundamentals of programming while creating virtual worlds.

Alice in the Classroom

Alice is used in a variety of ways in the classroom, and this text is designed to accommodate all of them. The following are a few examples:

- This text can be used with Alice for the first part of an introductory programming course before moving to a traditional programming language. Depending on the amount of time devoted to Alice in such a course, the entire book can be covered, or some of the later chapters can be omitted.
- This text can be used with Alice for a brief introduction to programming in a computer concepts course or an introduction to technology course. Later chapters can be omitted to fit the amount of time available.
- This text can be used in a semester-long course that uses only Alice to teach programming fundamentals.
- This text can be used in short courses or summer programs in which Alice is used to teach programming or virtual world building.

Brief Overview of Each Chapter

Chapter 1 Introduction to Alice and Objects

Chapter 1 explains what an algorithm is and why we use programming languages. The Alice software is introduced and the student learns about objects and three-dimensional graphical environments.

Chapter 2 Programming in Alice

In Chapter 2 the student learns about primitive methods in Alice and how to write instructions that call them. The program design cycle is introduced and the student learns to use it to develop a program.

Chapter 3 Variables, Functions, Math, and Strings

Chapter 3 introduces variables and their data types. The student also learns about functions and how to call them. Math expressions are introduced and the student learns to use functions that work with strings.

Chapter 4 Decision and Repetition Structures

Chapter 4 first discusses Boolean expressions. Then the student learns to write decision structures using the `If/Else` instruction, and repetition structures using the `Loop` and `While` instructions.

Chapter 5 Methods, Functions, and More about Variables

In Chapter 5 the student learns to write class-level methods in objects, create new properties in objects, and save objects as new classes. Stepwise refinement is discussed and the student learns to divide a large problem into several methods.

Chapter 6 Events

Chapter 6 introduces event-driven programming. The student learns how to handle various events in Alice, with a special emphasis given to developing games.

Chapter 7 Lists and Arrays

Chapter 7 introduces lists and arrays as data structures. The student learns how to create lists and arrays and how to process items stored in them.

Chapter 8 Recursion

Chapter 8 introduces recursion and discusses how to use recursion in problem solving. Examples that use recursion for animation and for calculations are demonstrated.

Appendix A Installing Alice

Appendix A presents step-by-step instructions for installing the Alice software.

Appendix B Answers to Checkpoints

Appendix B provides the answers to all of the Checkpoint questions that appear throughout each chapter. Students can use these answers to check their own progress as they work through the text.

Features of the Text

Concept Statements

Most major sections of the text start with a concept statement. This statement concisely summarizes the main point of the section.

Example Worlds

The text has an abundant number of complete and partial example worlds, each designed to highlight the topic currently being studied.

Tutorials

Each chapter has several hands-on tutorials that lead the student through the process of developing or completing an Alice world. These tutorials give the student experience performing the tasks discussed in the chapters.

VideoNote

Video Notes

A series of online videos, developed specifically for this book, are available for viewing at www.pearsonhighered.com/gaddis. Icons appear throughout the text alerting the student to videos that accompany specific tutorials and programming problems.

Notes

Notes appear throughout the text. They provide short explanations of interesting or frequently misunderstood points relevant to the topic at hand.

Tips

Tips appear throughout the text and advise the student on the best techniques for approaching different programming or animation problems.

Checkpoints

Checkpoints are questions placed at intervals throughout each chapter. They are designed to query the student's knowledge quickly after learning a new topic.

Review Questions

A thorough set of multiple choice and short answer questions appear at the end of each chapter.

Exercises

At the end of each chapter, following the review questions, appears a set of exercises for developing Alice worlds. These exercises are designed to solidify the student's knowledge of the topics presented in the chapter.

Supplements

Student Resource CD

This CD includes:

- A copy of the Alice software
- A set of example Alice worlds

If you cannot locate your CD, many of these resources are also available at http:// www.aw.com/cssupport

Instructor Resources

The following supplements are available to qualified instructors:

- Completed Alice worlds for the tutorials
- Answers to all of the review questions
- Solutions for the exercises
- PowerPoint presentation slides
- Test bank

Please visit the Addison-Wesley Instructor Resource Center (http://www.aw.com/irc) or send an e-mail to computing@aw.com for information on how to access these resources.

Acknowledgments

There have been many helping hands in the development and publication of this text. I would like to thank the following faculty reviewers:

Carol Buse
Amarillo College

Scott A. Hood
Kennebec Valley Community College

Jim McDonald
Monmouth University

W. Brett McKenzie
Roger Williams University

Laurie J. Patterson
University of North Carolina Wilmington

Charles Payne
Northern High School

Charlotte Young
South Plains College

I would also like to thank everyone at Addison-Wesley for making the *Starting Out With* series so successful. I am extremely fortunate to have Michael Hirsch as my editor, and Stephanie Sellinger as editorial assistant, guiding me through the process of revising this book. I am also fortunate to work with the computer science marketing team at Pearson. They do a great job getting my books out to the academic community. I had a great production team for this book, led by Jeff Holcomb, Managing Editor, and Kayla Smith-Tarbox, Production Project Manager. Thanks to you all!

Last, but not least, I want to thank my family for all the patience, love, and support they have shown me throughout this and my many other projects.

About the Author

Tony Gaddis is the principal author of the *Starting Out With* series of textbooks. Tony has nearly 20 years of experience teaching computer science courses at Haywood Community College. He is a highly acclaimed instructor who was previously selected as the North Carolina Community College Teacher of the Year, and has received the Teaching Excellence award from the National Institute for Staff and Organizational Development. The *Starting Out With* series also includes introductory books using C++, Java™, Microsoft® Visual Basic®, Microsoft® C#®, Python, and Programming Logic and Design, all published by Addison-Wesley.

1

Introduction to Alice and Objects

TOPICS

1.1 What Is a Computer Program?
1.2 Algorithms and Programming Languages
1.3 Learning to Program with Alice

1.4 Objects
1.5 Classes and the Alice Galleries
1.6 3D Objects and the Camera

1.1 What Is a Computer Program?

CONCEPT: A computer program is a set of instructions that a computer follows to perform a task.

This book teaches computer programming. The title of this section poses the question "What is a computer program?" Before we can answer that, first we should answer the question "What is a computer?" To learn programming you do not need a deep understanding of how computers work, but you do need to understand in the most basic terms what a computer is. Here's a definition that we can start with:

A computer is a device that follows instructions.

A computer doesn't know how to do anything on its own. It only follows the instructions that are given to it. Having said that, you must realize that a computer cannot follow just any kind of instruction. For example, you can't wake up in the morning and say to your computer "Make an omelet and serve it to me in bed." That's not an instruction that a computer can understand. That's the kind of instruction that a human (like a butler, if you're lucky enough to have one) can understand. Unfortunately, common computers like the ones you and I have on our desktops don't make breakfast. Their purpose is to work with data. They do things like adding and multiplying numbers, displaying data on the screen, storing data so it can be retrieved later, and so forth.

Knowing this, we can expand our definition of what a computer is, as follows:

A computer is a device that follows instructions for manipulating and storing data.

When a computer is designed, it is equipped with a set of operations that it can perform on pieces of data. Most of the operations are very basic in nature. For example, the following are typical operations that a computer can do:

- Add two numbers
- Subtract one number from another number
- Multiply two numbers
- Divide one number by another number
- Move a number from one memory location to another
- Determine whether one number is equal to another number
- And so forth . . .

A computer instruction is merely a command for the computer to perform one of the operations that it knows how to do.

Although an instruction exists for each operation that a computer is able to perform, the individual instructions aren't very useful by themselves. Because the computer's operations are so basic in nature, a meaningful task can only be accomplished if the computer performs many operations. For example, if you want your computer to calculate the amount of interest that you will earn from your savings account this year, it will have to perform a large number of instructions, carried out in the proper sequence. Now we can understand what a computer program is:

A computer program is a set of instructions that the computer follows to perform a task.

So, if we want the computer to perform a meaningful task, such as calculating our savings account interest, we must have a *program*, which is a set of instructions. The instructions in a program must be carefully written so they follow a logical sequence. When a computer is performing the instructions in a program, we say that the computer is *running* or *executing* the program.

1.2 Algorithms and Programming Languages

CONCEPT: **When creating a program, the programmer develops an algorithm, which is a set of steps that must be taken to perform a task. The programmer then translates the algorithm into a programming language.**

Computer programmers do a very important job. They are the people who create computer programs. Their job is important because without programs, computers would do nothing!

When a programmer begins the process of writing a program, one of the first things he or she does is develop an algorithm. An *algorithm* is a set of well-defined logical steps that must be taken in order to perform a task. For example, suppose we are writing a program to calculate an employee's gross pay. Here are the steps that should be taken:

1. Display a message on the screen: "How many hours did you work?"
2. Allow the user to enter the number of hours worked.
3. Once the user enters a number, store it in memory.
4. Display a message on the screen: "How much do you get paid per hour?"
5. Allow the user to enter an hourly pay rate.
6. Once the user enters a number, store it in memory.
7. Multiply the number of hours worked by the hourly pay rate and store the result in memory.
8. Display a message on the screen that shows the amount of money earned. The message must include the result of the calculation performed in Step 7.

Notice that the steps in this algorithm are sequentially ordered. Step 1 should be performed before Step 2, and so forth. It is important that these instructions are performed in their proper sequence.

The steps shown in the pay-calculating algorithm are written in English. Although you and I might easily understand the algorithm, it is not ready to be executed on a computer. The instructions have to be translated into *machine language*, which is the only language that computers understand. In machine language, each instruction is represented by a binary number. A *binary number* is a number that has only 1s and 0s. Here is an example of a binary number:

    1011010000000101

When you or I look at this number, we see only a series of 1s and 0s. To the computer, however, this number is an instruction, which is a command to perform some operation. A computer program that is ready to be executed by the computer is a stream of binary numbers representing instructions.

As you can imagine, the process of translating an algorithm from English statements to machine language instructions is very tedious and difficult. To make the job of programming easier, special programming languages have been invented. *Programming languages* use words instead of numbers to represent instructions. A program can be written in a programming language, which is much easier for people to understand than machine language, and then be translated into machine language. Programmers use special software called *compilers* or *interpreters* to perform this translation.

Over the years, many programming languages have been created. If you are working toward a degree in computer science or a related field, you are likely to study languages such as Java, C++ (pronounced "C plus plus"), Visual Basic, and Python. These are only a few of the languages that are used by professional programmers to create software applications. Each of these languages has its own set of words that the programmer must learn in order to use the language. The words that make up a programming language are known as *keywords*. For example, the word `print` is a keyword in the Python language. It prints a message on the screen. Here is an example of how the `print` keyword might be used to form an instruction in a Python program:

    print "Hello Earthling!"

This causes the message Hello Earthling to be displayed on the computer screen. Compare this instruction to the binary number we saw earlier. You can see from this simple example why programmers prefer to use programming languages instead of machine language. Using words to write a program is much easier than using binary numbers.

In addition to keywords, programming languages have *operators* that perform various operations on data. For example, all programming languages have math operators that perform arithmetic. In Java, as well as most other languages, the + sign is an operator that adds two numbers. The following would add 12 and 75:

```
12 + 75
```

In addition to keywords and operators, each language also has it own *syntax*, which is a set of rules that must be strictly followed when writing a program. The syntax rules dictate how keywords, operators, and various punctuation characters must be used in a program. When you are learning a programming language, you must learn the syntax rules for that particular language.

When you write a program with a traditional programming language, you convert your algorithm into a series of *statements*. A programming statement consists of keywords, operators, punctuation, and other allowable programming elements, arranged in the proper sequence to perform an operation. Programmers call these statements *code*. Typically you type your programming statements into a text editor such as Notepad, which is part of the Windows operating system. There are also specialized text editors that are made specifically for writing programs. For example, Figure 1-1 shows a text editor with part of a Java program typed into it.

Figure 1-1 A text editor

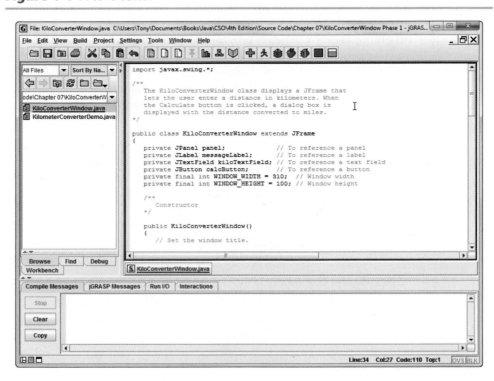

Once you have typed the statements, you save them to a file, and then use a compiler to translate the statements into an executable program. An *executable program* is a file containing machine language instructions that can be directly executed by the computer.

 Checkpoint

1.1 What is a computer?

1.2 What is a program?

1.3 What is an algorithm?

1.4 What is the only language that computers understand?

1.5 Why were programming languages invented?

 Learning to Program with Alice

In this book you will learn to program by using a revolutionary software system named Alice. Alice makes programming fun and exciting because it allows you to create 3D animations and computer games while learning programming concepts. In Alice you create 3D virtual worlds populated with people, animals, fantasy creatures, vehicles, and a variety of other objects. For example, Figure 1-2 shows a scene from a medieval Alice world containing a princess, knights, and other objects.

Figure 1-2 A scene from an Alice world

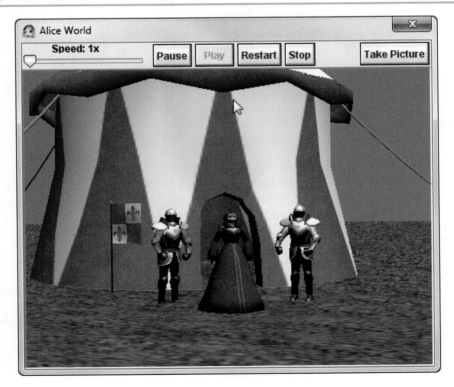

You can program the objects in an Alice world so they perform actions. The objects can even interact with one another. Using Alice, you can create worlds that tell a story (in the same way that a movie tells a story), or become interactive computer games.

Alice is not a system that professional programmers use to develop commercial applications. Alice is designed as a teaching tool to make programming easy to learn. One way that Alice makes programming easy to learn is by eliminating many of the errors that beginning students commonly make. With a traditional programming language, beginners frequently make typing mistakes that result in misspelled keywords, missing punctuation characters, and other such errors. These types of mistakes are known as *syntax errors*. If a program contains even one syntax error, it cannot be translated into an executable program. As a result, students and professional programmers alike spend a lot of time tracking down syntax errors and fixing them. In Alice, however, syntax errors never happen because you do not type programming statements. Instead, you drag and drop *tiles*, which are like graphical building blocks, into an editor. The programming tiles represent fully functional programming statements that you can easily customize. Because you don't have to spend time locating and fixing syntax errors, you can concentrate on planning the actions that you want the objects in your world to perform, and arranging them into the proper sequence.

Perhaps the greatest reason that programming is easy with Alice is that it's fun! Rather than writing programs that perform calculations or analyze data, you will be creating your own 3D virtual worlds, populated with characters and other objects of your choice. You will be able to program the objects in your worlds to perform various actions that you can watch on the screen. The best part of all this is that you will be learning programming concepts while having fun! After finishing this book you will be well prepared to study any traditional programming language, such as C, C++, Java, Python, or Visual Basic.

> **NOTE:** If you're wondering where the name "Alice" came from, the creators of Alice were inspired by Lewis Carroll's books *Alice's Adventures in Wonderland* and *Through the Looking Glass*. They named the software after Alice Liddell, the main character in these books.

Installing and Running Alice

The Student Resource CD that accompanies this book contains a copy of Alice version 2.2. Alice can also be downloaded free of charge from http://www.alice.org. Appendix A gives detailed instructions for installing Alice. Before going any further, make sure that Alice is installed on your system. Once Alice is installed, go through the steps in Tutorial 1-1 to open and play an Alice world.

Tutorial 1-1:
Opening and playing an Alice world

Step 1:   Start Alice on your computer. The Alice splash screen will be displayed for a few seconds. When the software is fully loaded you will see the

Alice environment, as shown in Figure 1-3. By default, the *Welcome to Alice!* dialog box will be displayed, as shown in the figure.

Figure 1-3 The Alice system

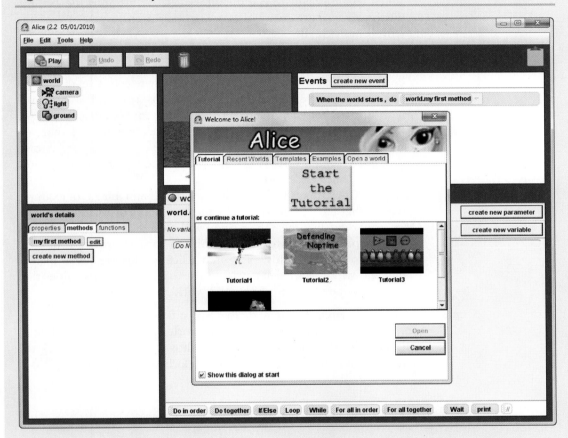

 NOTE: If you don't see the *Welcome to Alice!* dialog box on your system, then Alice has been configured so it will not display the dialog box at startup. This might be the case if you are working in a computer lab shared by other people. You can display the dialog box by clicking *File* on the menu bar, and then clicking the *New World* or *Open World...* menu items.

Notice that at the bottom of the *Welcome to Alice!* dialog box there is a *Show this dialog at start* check box. Make sure that this check box is checked so the dialog box will be displayed each time you start Alice.

Step 2: Near the top of the *Welcome to Alice!* dialog box you see a set of tabs labeled *Tutorial*, *Recent Worlds*, *Templates*, *Examples*, and *Open a world*. The following are brief descriptions of what you see when you click these tabs:

Tutorial: Click this tab and you will see a set of four Alice worlds that work as tutorials. These tutorial worlds guide you through the basic features of Alice. We will not be using the tutorials in this text, but you will find them helpful if you go through them on your own. When you are ready to run the tutorials, click the *Start the Tutorial* button to execute them in order, or select and open any of the worlds individually.

Recent Worlds: Click this tab and you will see thumbnail images of the worlds that were most recently opened on your system. You can open any world shown in this tab quickly by selecting its thumbnail image and then clicking the *Open* button. You will not see any worlds listed here if you haven't yet opened any worlds.

Templates: Click this tab and you will see a set of templates that you can use to begin creating a new world. The templates are named *dirt*, *grass*, *sand*, *snow*, *space*, and *water*. Each template gives you a ground surface and a sky color.

Examples: Click this tab and you will see thumbnail images of example worlds that have been created by the developers of Alice.

Open a world: Click this tab and you will see a dialog box that allows you to open an Alice world. With this tab you can browse your local system for Alice worlds. Note that Alice worlds are saved in files that end with the *.a2w* extension. (The *.a2w* extension signifies that the file contains an Alice version 2 world.)

Step 3: With the *Welcome to Alice!* dialog box still open, click the *Examples* tab. Scroll down in the list of example worlds until you see the thumbnail image for the snowLove world, as shown in Figure 1-4. Click the snowLove thumbnail image and then click the *Open* button.

Figure 1-4 Select the snowLove world from the *Examples* tab

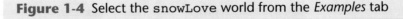

Step 4:   Once the world is loaded, the Alice environment will appear as shown in Figure 1-5. The figure also points out the location of the *Play* button. When you click the *Play* button, the currently loaded world will begin to play. Go ahead and click the *Play* button so you can watch the snowLove world.

Figure 1-5 The snowLove world loaded

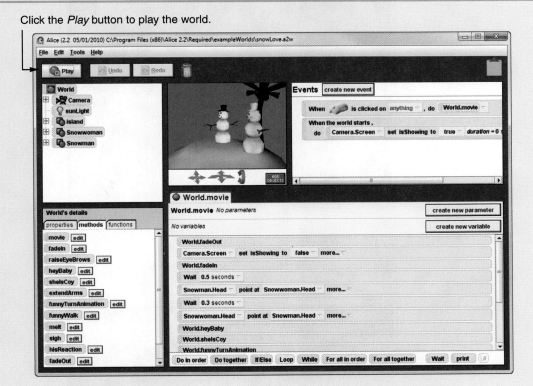

Step 5:   When you click the *Play* button, a separate window titled *World Running...* appears, and the world's animation will play out in that window. Figure 1-6 shows the initial scene of the snowLove world. Click anywhere inside the window to start the animation.

Step 6:   Figure 1-7 shows an image taken from the world as it is playing. The snowLove world tells the sad story of a snowman on an island. The snowman notices a beautiful pink snowwoman. He can hardly believe his eyes, and he approaches her. All of this attention must be too much for the lovely snowwoman because she melts before he reaches her.

Notice the toolbar at the top of the *World Running...* window. The following are brief descriptions of the items that appear on the toolbar:

Speed Slider **control:** This controls the speed at which the world is played. When the slider is set to *1x*, the world plays at normal speed. Moving the slider to the right increases the speed up to 10 times its normal speed.

Figure 1-6 Initial scene of the snowLove world

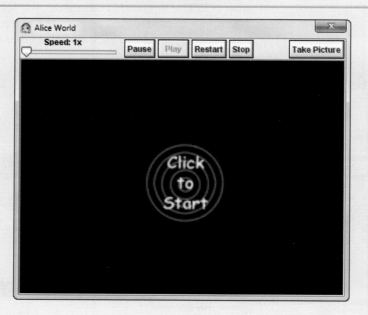

Figure 1-7 The snowLove world playing

Pause **button:** Clicking the *Pause* button causes the world to pause.

Resume **button:** Once a world has been paused with the *Pause* button, you can click the *Resume* button to resume playing.

Restart **button:** Clicking the *Restart* button causes the world to start playing again.

> *Stop* **button:** Clicking the *Stop* button causes the world to stop playing and closes the *World Running...* window.
>
> *Take Picture* **button:** Clicking the *Take Picture* button captures an image from the world and saves it in a file. The dialog box that appears when you click this button reports the name and path of the file containing the image.
>
> Take a moment to experiment with these items.
>
> **Step 7:** When you are finished experimenting with the items on the *World Running...* window's toolbar, click the *Stop* button to close the window.

The Alice Environment

The screen that you work with when using Alice is referred to as the *Alice environment*. The Alice environment is divided into the following areas: the Toolbar, the World View window, the Object Tree, the Details Panel, the Method Editor, and the Events Editor. The locations of these different areas are shown in Figure 1-8.

Brief descriptions of each area in the Alice environment follow:

Toolbar: The toolbar provides a *Play* button, which plays your virtual world; an *Undo* button, which undoes the previous operation; and a *Redo* button, which repeats the operation that was most recently undone. The toolbar also shows a trash can and one or more clipboard icons. These will be covered in in more detail in Chapters 2 and 5.

World View **window:** The World View window shows a view of your virtual world. Each virtual world has a camera, and the World View window acts as the camera's viewfinder. The World View window also provides controls for moving and rotating the camera.

Object Tree: The Object Tree holds a list of all the objects in the world. Each object in the world is represented by a tile, like the one shown in Figure 1-9. A *tile* is simply a small rectangular icon. Tiles are used extensively in the Alice environment, to represent numerous things.

Details Panel: The Details Panel shows detailed information about an object that has been selected in the World View window or in the Object Tree.

Method Editor: The Method Editor is where you create methods (a set of instructions that causes some action to take place) in Alice. As you will see in Chapter 2, you create methods by arranging tiles in the Method Editor.

Events Editor: An event is an action that takes place while the world is playing, such as the clicking of a mouse or the pressing of a key. Alice is able to detect when various events take place. You can use the Events Editor to specify an action that is to take place when a specific event occurs. We will study events in greater detail in Chapter 6.

Figure 1-8 Parts of the Alice environment

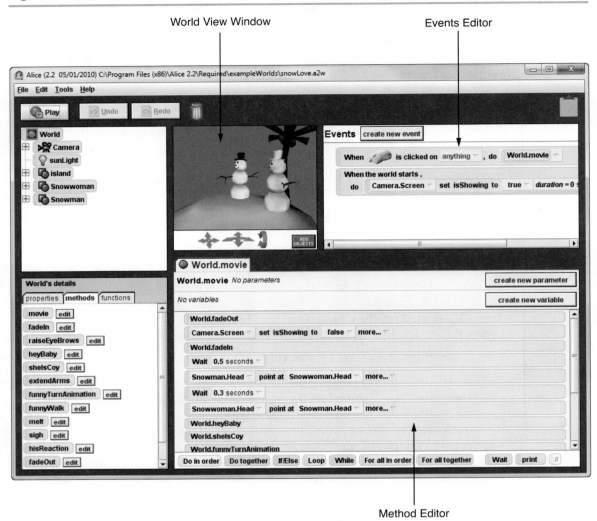

Figure 1-9 A tile

 Checkpoint

1.6   How do you control the speed at which a world is played?

1.7   What part of the Alice environment displays a view of the world, as seen through the camera?

1.8   What part of the Alice environment displays a list of the objects in the world?

1.9   What is a tile? What purpose of tiles did we discuss in this section?

Objects

CONCEPT: Each item that appears in an Alice world is an object. An object has properties, which specify the object's characteristics. Objects also have methods, which are actions that the object is capable of performing. It is common for objects to be made up of other objects. In fact, an Alice world is itself an object, made up of all the objects contained within the world.

The concept of an *object* is probably the most fundamental idea in Alice. Alice worlds are made of objects. In Tutorial 1-1 you played the snowLove world. Think back for a moment about the objects in that world. Recall that there was a snowman, a snow-woman, and an island, as shown in Figure 1-10. Each of these items is a separate object in the snowLove world. The Alice software provides galleries of many different types of objects. Once you have created a world in Alice, you can select the objects that you want to appear in the world from one of the galleries.

Figure 1-10 Three objects in the snowLove world

Properties

Each object in an Alice world has *properties*, which are values that specify the object's characteristics. Once you have placed an object in an Alice world, you can adjust its properties until it has the characteristics you desire. Two common properties that most objects have are color and opacity. If you want an object to be blue, you simply set its color property to *blue*.

The opacity property determines whether you can see through an object. You set this property to some value between 0 and 100 percent. When you set an object's opacity property to 0 percent, the object is completely invisible. When you set the opacity property to 100 percent, the object is completely opaque and you cannot see through it at all. Setting the opacity property to a value between 0 and 100 percent will cause the object to be semitransparent. You can use this property to give objects a ghostly appearance. Figure 1-11 shows a chair object with its color property set to red and its opacity property set to 50 percent. Later in this section you will learn how to set object properties in Alice.

Figure 1-11 A chair with `color` set to red and `opacity` set to 50 percent

Methods

Objects are also capable of performing actions. In Tutorial 1-1, you saw how the snowman turned his head, lifted his eyebrows, and moved toward the snowwoman. You also saw how the snowwoman made various movements, and in the end, melted. Objects are capable of performing actions such as these because they have methods. A *method* is a set of programming statements that an object can execute. Methods commonly result in the object performing some action.

For example, in the `snowLove` world, there is a method that causes the snowman to raise his eyes. There are also methods that cause the snowman to turn and face the snowwoman, move toward her, and react downheartedly when she melts. In addition, there are methods that cause the snowwoman to perform each of her actions. When you create an Alice world, you will spend a big part of your time writing methods. Methods are sets of instructions that you create for the objects in your world to follow. You will learn the basics of writing methods in Chapter 2.

Objects Can Be Made of Other Objects

Objects are commonly made of other objects. For example, in the `snowLove` world the `snowman` object is a combination of three other objects: a bottom section, a middle section, and a head section. Figure 1-12 shows how the snowman is made up of these three objects, which you can think of as the snowman's "parts."

Each of the snowman's sections is a large ball of snow. If you look closely at Figure 1-12, the head section and the middle section appear to include other objects also. The head section contains a hat, eyes, a carrot nose, and a mouth, as shown in Figure 1-13. The middle section has a right arm and a left arm, as shown in Figure 1-14. It is not uncommon for an object, like the snowman, to be made of several layers of sub-objects. In Alice, these inner objects are commonly referred to as *subparts*.

Figure 1-12 The snowman object is made of other objects

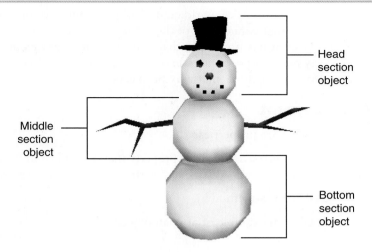

Head
section
object

Middle
section
object

Bottom
section
object

Figure 1-13 The snowman's head section

Hat

Eyes

Mouth

Carrot

Figure 1-14 The snowman's middle section

Right arm

Left arm

Each of the objects that make up the snowman has its own properties and can be manipulated with methods. For example, in the snowLove world, a method is programmed to make the snowman's eyes rise when he turns toward the snowwoman. When you create Alice worlds, you will commonly work with the individual objects that are the parts of a larger object.

NOTE: The island object in the snowLove world is also made of other objects—a ground surface and a palm tree The palm tree object is made up of other objects as well. It is composed of coconuts and leaves.

The World Is an Object

Not only does an Alice world contain objects, but also the world itself is an object. It is an object that contains all of the other objects in the world. Because an Alice world is an object, it has properties that you can adjust. For example, Alice worlds have a property named `atmosphereColor`, which specifies the color of the sky. Alice worlds can also have methods that may be executed.

Checkpoint

1.10 What are properties?

1.11 What is the name of the property that determines an object's color? What is the name of the property that determines whether you can see through an object?

1.12 What is a method?

1.13 Give an example of how an object can be made of other objects.

1.5 Classes and the Alice Galleries

CONCEPT: **Objects are created from classes. A class is a set of specifications that describes a particular type of object. The Alice software provides galleries with collections of classes that can be used to create objects.**

Section 1.4 discussed objects and you learned that each item in an Alice world is an object. When you are creating an Alice world, you use one of Alice's galleries to place objects in the world. A *gallery* is an assortment of different object types that you may place in a world. The galleries are organized into various collections of object types, such as animals, buildings, furniture, people, and so forth.

Alice provides two galleries: a local gallery and a Web gallery. The *local gallery* is stored on your computer, and is installed along with the Alice software. It provides a good sampling of object types, and should be adequate for many of your projects. The *Web gallery* is maintained by the creators of Alice, and may be accessed if your computer is connected to the Internet. It provides a more extensive collection of object types than the local gallery.

Classes

It is important to realize that the Alice galleries do not actually contain objects—they contain classes. A *class* is simply a description of a particular type of object, written in programming statements. Think of a class as a blueprint that objects may be created from. It serves a similar purpose as the blueprint for a house. The blueprint itself is not a house, but rather a detailed description of a house. When we use the blueprint to build an actual house, we could say that we are building an instance of the house that is described by the blueprint. If we want, we can build several identical houses from the same blueprint. Each house is a separate instance of the house that is described by the blueprint. This concept is illustrated in Figure 1-15.

Figure 1-15 A blueprint and houses built from the blueprint

Blueprint that describes a house

Instances of the house described by the blueprint

When you want to add a particular type of object to an Alice world, first you find that object's class in one of the galleries. For example, suppose that you want to add some sort of animal to our world. You would open one of the galleries and look in the *Animals* collection for a suitable class. Figure 1-16 shows a few of the classes in the local gallery's *Animals* collection. You notice that one of these is a `Chicken` class, and decide that you want to add the chicken to the world.

Figure 1-16 Some classes in the local gallery's *Animal* collection

The `Chicken` class that is stored in the gallery is a blueprint that describes all of the characteristics of a `Chicken` object. When you select the `Chicken` class in the gallery, Alice uses its specifications to create a `Chicken` object in the world. If you wish, you can select the `Chicken` class several times, creating several `Chicken` objects. Figure 1-17 shows an Alice world with three `Chicken` objects.

In programming terminology, objects are also called *instances* of a class. Although the local gallery has only one `Chicken` class, the world shown in Figure 1-17 has three instances of the `Chicken` class. Because the three `Chicken` instances are created from the same class, they all have the same properties and methods. Each of the instances is a separate object, however, so we can manipulate them individually. For example,

Figure 1-17 An Alice world with three `Chicken` objects

Figure 1-18 shows the three `Chicken` objects after they have been individually modi-fied. One of the `Chicken` object's `color` properties has been set to red, one of the `Chicken` object's `opacity` properties has been set to 60 percent, and one of the `Chicken` objects has been enlarged.

Figure 1-18 Three `Chicken` objects manipulated individually

Tutorial 1-2 reinforces some of these concepts. In the tutorial you will start a new Alice world and create instances of a class. You will modify the instances by changing some of their properties. You will also learn how to select an object that is contained inside another object and modify its properties.

NOTE: In Tutorial 1-1 you learned how to play an Alice world that performs actions. In this chapter you will learn how to add objects to an Alice world, but we will not discuss adding actions until Chapter 2. Therefore, the worlds that you create in this chapter will not perform any actions if you play them.

VideoNote

Creating a
World and
Adding
Objects

Tutorial 1-2:
Creating a world and adding objects

Step 1: Start Alice on your computer. Once the software is fully loaded you should see the *Welcome to Alice!* dialog box, as shown in Figure 1-19.

Figure 1-19 The *Welcome to Alice!* dialog box

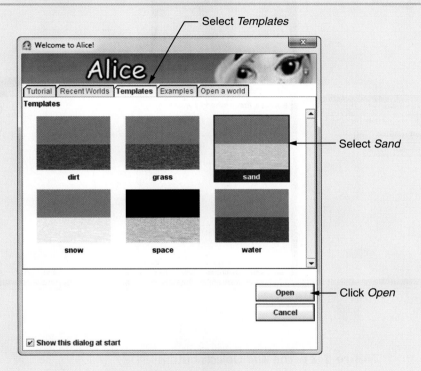

  NOTE: If you do not see the *Welcome to Alice!* dialog box on your system, click *File* on the menu bar, and then click the *New World...* menu item.

Step 2: Make sure that the *Templates* tab is selected, as shown in Figure 1-19. When you select a template from this dialog box, Alice will create a ground surface and set the color of the sky. Select the *sand* template, and then click the *Open* button. The Alice environment should appear, as shown in Figure 1-20. Notice that the World View window shows the world with a sand ground surface and a blue sky.

Step 3: Now we will add an object to the world. As shown in Figure 1-21, you should see the *Add Objects* button just below the World View window. Click the *Add Objects* button now. The Alice environment changes to

Figure 1-20 The Alice environment with a new world created

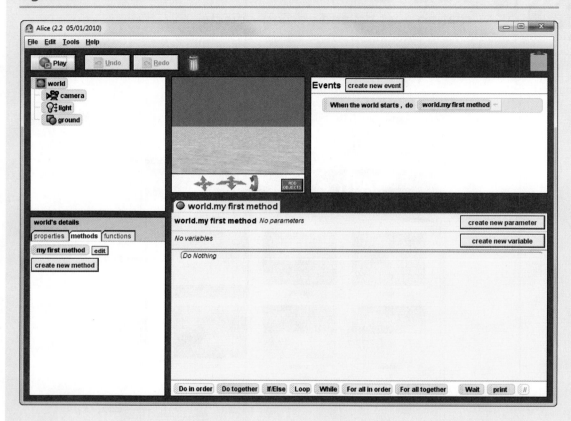

Figure 1-21 The *Add Objects* button

Click the *Add Objects* button
to open the local gallery.

Figure 1-22 Alice in scene editor mode

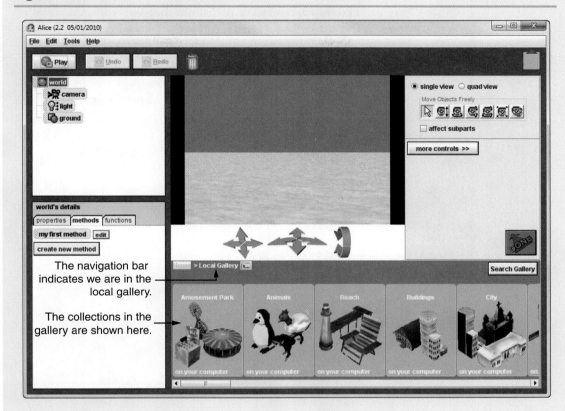

scene editor mode and opens the local gallery, as shown in Figure 1-22. Thumbnail images for the collections in the gallery appear at the bottom of the screen. Just above the thumbnail images is a navigation bar that indicates that you are currently in the local gallery.

Step 4: Scroll the collections until you see the *People* collection thumbnail, as shown in Figure 1-23. Click the thumbnail to open the *People* collection.

Figure 1-23 The *People* collection thumbnail

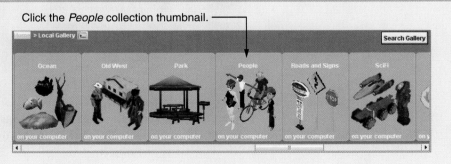

Step 5: You should now see thumbnails for the classes in the *People* collection. There are classes for a variety of people that you can add to your worlds. Scroll the collection until you see the class named Coach, as shown in Figure 1-24. Click the thumbnail for the Coach class.

Step 6: You should now see an information window for the Coach class, as shown in Figure 1-25. This window lists some miscellaneous information about the class. Click the *Add instance to world* button to add an instance of the Coach class to the world.

Congratulations! You have just added your first object to an Alice world. You should see the object in the World View window, as shown

Figure 1-24 The contents of the *People* collection

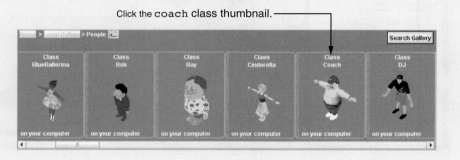

Figure 1-25 Information window for the Coach class

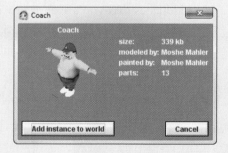

in Figure 1-26. A new tile containing the word coach has also been added to the Object Tree. This tile represents the object that you just added to the world. The word coach, which appears on the tile, is the name that Alice assigned to the object.

Figure 1-26 An object is added to the world

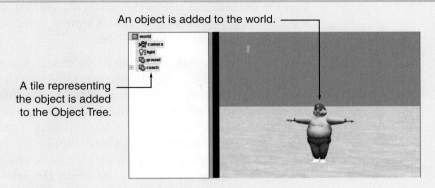

An object is added to the world. ——

A tile representing the object is added to the Object Tree.

Step 7: Often, to work with an object in the Alice environment, first you have to select the object. One way to select an object is to click its tile in the Object Tree. Go ahead and click the coach tile in the Object Tree to select the object. After doing this you should see a yellow box appear around the object in the World View window, as shown in Figure 1-27. This is called a *bounding box*, and it indicates that the object is selected. Also, notice that in the Object Tree the coach tile is highlighted. When you select an object, that object's tile will appear highlighted in the Object Tree.

Figure 1-27 The object is selected

Bounding box ⏋

Step 8: Another way to select an object is to click on the object in the World View window. Try this by clicking anywhere on the ground surface in the World View window. This selects the ground, which is an object in the world. Only one object can be selected at a time, so this also unselects the coach object.

The ground object is so big that you can't really see its bounding box in the World View window, but you can see its tile highlighted in the Object Tree.

Next, click on the coach object in the World View window. This unselects the ground, and selects the coach object. You should see the yellow bounding box once again appear around the coach object, and see its tile highlighted in the Object Tree.

Step 9:   Now we will add another instance of the Coach class to our world, but this time we will use a slightly different technique than we used previously. The thumbnail for the Coach class should still be visible in the gallery. Instead of clicking the thumbnail, as you did before, click and drag the thumbnail into the World View window. As the mouse pointer enters the World View window, you should see an empty, yellow bounding box following the pointer. This is the bounding box for the new object that you are adding to the world. Drag the bounding box to a location near the existing coach object, as shown in Figure 1-28, and release the mouse button. A new instance of the Coach class will be created, as shown in Figure 1-29.

Figure 1-28 The empty bounding box for the new object

Figure 1-29 Two coach objects added to the world

Step 10: Look at the Object Tree and notice that it now contains a tile for the new object. As shown in Figure 1-29, the new tile is labeled `coach2`.

At this point we need to discuss the difference between class names and object names. All classes have a name. In the Alice galleries each of the class thumbnails displays the name of the class it represents. By convention, class names always begin with an uppercase letter. For example, the two objects that you have added to your world are instances of the `Coach` class.

Objects have names too. When you create an object in Alice, the object is automatically given a name, which is displayed in the Object Tree. By convention, object names always begin with a lowercase letter. When you created the first instance of the `Coach` class, Alice automatically named it `coach`. When you created the second instance of the `Coach` class, Alice automatically named it `coach2`. The names `coach` and `coach2` refer to the objects you have in your world, and the name `Coach` refers to the class that these objects were created from.

In case you're wondering, you can change the names that Alice automatically gives your objects. If you don't like names like `coach` and `coach2` you can change them to names you prefer. We will discuss this in greater detail in Chapter 2.

Step 11: Now you will experiment with some of the properties of the two objects you have added to your world. Select the `coach` object either by clicking its tile in the Object Tree or by clicking the object itself in the World View window. After selecting the object, the top of the Details Panel should read *coach's details*.

In the Details Panel, select the *properties* tab to display the `coach` object's properties. Your screen should look similar to the one shown in Figure 1-30.

Figure 1-30 The coach object and *properties* tab selected

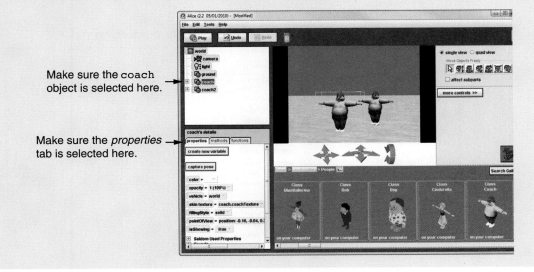

Make sure the coach object is selected here.

Make sure the *properties* tab is selected here.

Step 12: With the *properties* tab selected, the Details Panel displays the `coach` object's properties. Each property is represented by a tile bearing the property's name. Figure 1-31 shows the location of the `color` property.

Next to each property is a drop-down box that you can click to set the property's value. Click the drop-down box next to the `color` property to display the menu shown in Figure 1-32. The menu provides a list of colors that you can choose from. Select *red* from the menu. In the World View window you should see the `coach` object turn red, as shown in Figure 1-33.

Step 13: Now we will change the `coach2` object's `opacity` property. Select the `coach2` object by clicking its tile in the Object Tree or clicking the object itself in the World View window. After selecting the object, the top of the Details Panel should read *coach2's details*.

In the Details Panel, make sure the *properties* tab is still selected.

Figure 1-31 The `color` property's drop-down box

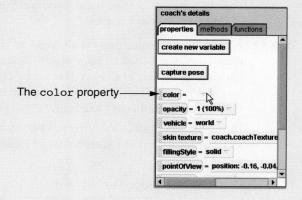

Figure 1-32 Changing the `coach` object's `color` property to red

Figure 1-33 The coach object turned red

Notice that one of the property tiles reads `opacity`. Click the drop-down box next to the `opacity` property to display the menu shown in Figure 1-34. The menu provides a list of percentages that you can choose from. Select 0.5 (50%) from the menu. In the World View window you should see the `coach2` object become semitransparent, as shown in Figure 1-35.

Figure 1-34 Changing the `coach2` object's opacity property to 50 percent

Figure 1-35 The `coach2` object with `opacity` set to 50 percent

Step 14: Earlier in this chapter you learned that an object can contain other objects. So the tiles in the Object Tree are displayed in a hierarchical fashion. (That's why it is called the object *tree* and not the object list.) When a plus sign appears next to an object tile, it means that the object contains other objects. For example, look at the Object Tree and notice that a plus sign appears next to the tiles for the coach and the coach2 objects. This is shown in Figure 1-36.

You can click the plus sign next to an object to expand the tree and see the tiles for the inner objects. The plus sign then turns into a minus sign, which hides the inner objects when clicked. Try expanding the Object Tree by clicking the plus sign next to the coach2 object. As shown in Figure 1-37, the Object Tree reveals that the coach2 object comprises three other objects: rightLeg, leftLeg, and upperBody.

Figure 1-36 The coach and coach2 objects contain other objects

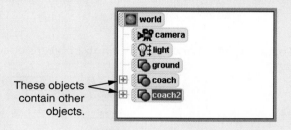

These objects contain other objects.

Figure 1-37 The Object Tree expanded

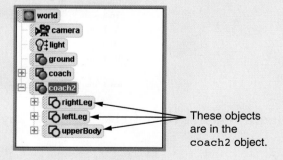

These objects are in the coach2 object.

Step 15: If you want to select one of the inner objects, you can click its tile in the Object Tree. Try this by clicking the tile for the rightLeg object. Notice that a bounding box appears in the World View window around the selected rightLeg object, as shown in Figure 1-38.

Step 16: Notice that the tiles for the rightLeg, leftLeg, and upperBody objects all have a plus sign next to them. This indicates that these

Figure 1-38 The rightLeg object selected

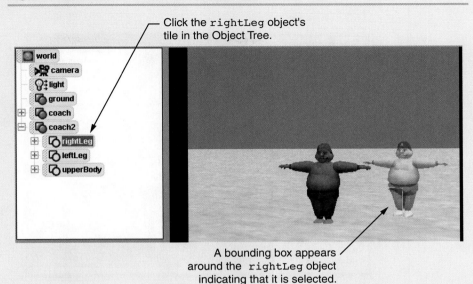

Click the rightLeg object's
tile in the Object Tree.

A bounding box appears
around the rightLeg object
indicating that it is selected.

objects also contain other objects. Continue to click the plus signs to expand the Object Tree and see the other objects that coach2 is made of. Then select one of the inner objects and change its color property. For example, Figure 1-39 shows the head object selected and its color property set to green.

Figure 1-39 The coach2 object with a green head

Step 17: If you wish, expand the coach object in the Object Tree and change some of the properties of its inner objects. When you have finished experimenting, click the *DONE* button shown in Figure 1-40. This exits scene editor mode. Then click the *File* menu and select *Save World* to save your Alice world. You will use this world in Tutorial 1-3.

Figure 1-40 The *DONE* button

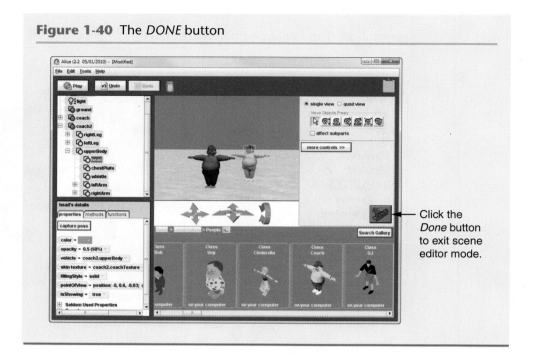

Click the *Done* button to exit scene editor mode.

 NOTE: As you were working through Tutorial 1-2 you probably saw the dialog box in Figure 1-41 appear. This is a reminder that you should frequently save your Alice World. Most of the time you should click the *Save right now* button when this dialog box appears.

Figure 1-41 The Save? reminder

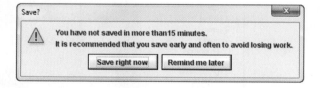

Using the Web Gallery

In Tutorial 1-2 we used the local gallery. If you have an Internet connection, you can also use the Web gallery. On the gallery navigation bar, click *Home* and then click the *Web Gallery* thumbnail. A dialog box will appear reminding you that you are entering an online gallery. Click the *OK* button to load the Web gallery. The amount of time it takes to load the gallery will depend on the speed of your connection. Once the gallery is loaded, you will find that it is organized into collections, like the local gallery.

 **Checkpoint**

1.14 What is a class?

1.15 How are a class and instances of the class similar to a blueprint and houses built from the blueprint?

1.16 What is stored in the Alice galleries: classes or objects?

1.17 When you click the *Add Objects* button, what mode does Alice go into?

1.18 After finding the class you want in one of the Alice galleries, describe two ways to add an instance of the class to the world.

1.19 What are two ways to select an object in the Alice environment?

1.20 What appears around an object in the World View window when you select the object?

1.21 In an Alice world, would the word dog be the name of a class, or the name of an object? How can you tell?

1.22 In what area of the Alice environment do you select an object's properties?

1.6 3D Objects and the Camera

CONCEPT: **Alice worlds and the objects in them are three-dimensional. You view the Alice world through a camera object, which you may move around within the world and point in different directions.**

If you've ever played a simple arcade-style video game, then you are probably familiar with *two-dimensional (2D)* graphics. The objects that appear in 2D graphics have only two dimensions: height and width. Figure 1-42 shows an example of a two-dimensional game character that exists with only height and width. Because the character has no depth, it cannot be viewed from the side.

Figure 1-42 A two-dimensional game character

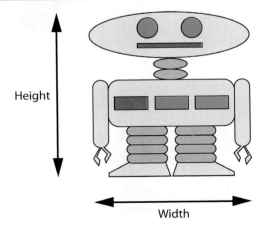

In addition to existing with only a height and a width, two-dimensional objects inhabit a world that has only height and width. This means that two-dimensional objects can only move up, down, left, and right. (Diagonal movement in two-dimensional space is merely the combination of left or right movement with up or down movement.) Figure 1-43 shows an example of a two-dimensional world. The robot character can move around in the world, but its movement is restricted to the dimensions of up, down, left, and right.

Figure 1-43 Movement in 2D space

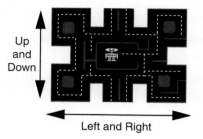

Alice is a *three-dimensional (3D)* system. Objects in Alice have the dimensions of height, width, and depth. Figure 1-44 shows the three dimensions of a coach object. The figure shows that the object has depth because we are viewing it from an angle.

Figure 1-44 A 3D object

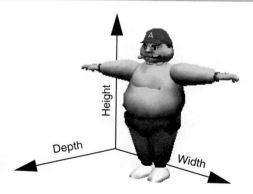

The worlds that you create with Alice also have three dimensions, which means that objects in an Alice world can move up, down, left, right, forward, and backward. This is illustrated in Figure 1-45. Because they can move in six directions, it is commonly said that objects in a 3D world have *six degrees of freedom*.

NOTE: Three-dimensional worlds are commonly called *virtual worlds* because they are virtual representations of the real world.

Figure 1-45 Movement in 3D space

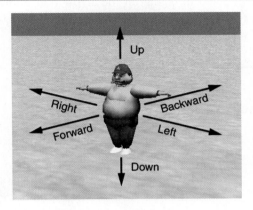

The Camera

When you create an Alice world, a camera is automatically created and placed in the world. The camera's purpose is to display an image of the world in the World View window. You can think of the World View window as the camera's viewfinder. The image that is displayed in the World View window is the view of the world seen through the camera's viewfinder. The camera's position, including the direction it is pointed in, is called the camera's *viewpoint*.

The three camera controls shown in Figure 1-46 appear just below the World View window. You use these controls to move the camera around in the world and point it in different directions. The control on the left moves the camera up, down, left and right. The control in the center moves the camera forward and backward, and rotates the camera toward the left and right. The control on the right tilts the camera up and down.

Figure 1-46 Camera controls

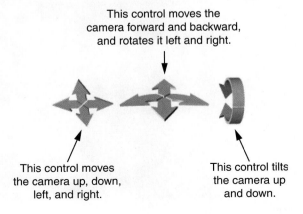

Notice that each of the controls shows a set of arrows. You manipulate these controls by clicking and dragging on the arrow that points in the direction that you want to move, rotate, or tilt the camera. The best way to learn how to use the controls is to actually try them out, as in Tutorial 1-3.

VideoNote
Moving the
Camera in
3D Space

Tutorial 1-3:
Moving the camera in 3D space

Step 1: Start Alice and open the world you created in Tutorial 1-2.

Step 2: You are going to use the center camera control at the bottom of the World View window to move the camera forward, toward the coach object. Click the arrow that points forward and hold down the mouse button. Notice that the arrow highlights, as shown in Figure 1-47. The camera will move forward as long as you hold the mouse button down. Position the camera to get a close-up view of the coach object's face, as shown in Figure 1-48. If necessary, you can also use the left control to move the camera up, down, and left, until you have it in the desired position.

TIP: You can make the camera move faster by dragging the mouse pointer away from the center of the camera control. The farther you drag the pointer away from the center of the camera control, the faster the camera will move.

Figure 1-47 The forward arrow highlighted

Figure 1-48 A close-up of the coach object

Step 3:   Continue to move the camera forward, past the `coach` and `coach2` objects, until you can no longer see them. Then use the left or right rotation arrow in the center control to turn the camera around, which should give you a view of the `coach` and `coach2` objects from behind, similar to the one shown in Figure 1-49.

Step 4:   Use the leftmost camera control to move the camera up, above the objects. Then use the rightmost camera control to tilt the camera down so that you can see the objects below, as shown in Figure 1-50.

Step 5:   Continue to experiment with the camera controls to get other views of the Alice world. When you save the world, the position of the camera will be saved as well. The next time you open the world, the camera will still be in this position.

Figure 1-49 The objects as seen from behind

Figure 1-50 The objects as seen from above

Modifying Objects in 3D

In scene editor mode you can use the mouse to modify the objects in your Alice world. For example, you can use the mouse to move objects, resize objects, rotate and tumble objects, and copy objects. Figure 1-51 shows the location of the *mouse mode buttons*, which determine the action that may be performed with the mouse.

Figure 1-51 Location of the mouse mode buttons

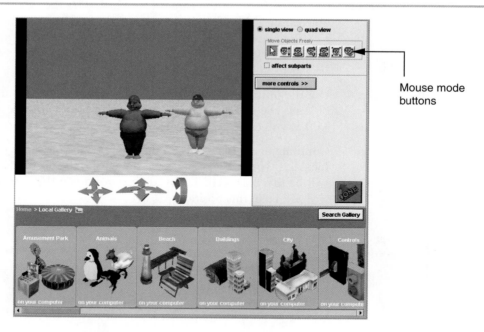

Figure 1-52 shows the purpose of each button. The following are brief descriptions of each one:

- **Move Freely** ▶ When this button is selected the mouse can be used to move an object in the world freely. Here are the actions that you can perform:
  - To move an object horizontally within the world simply click and drag it.
  - To move an object straight up or down, hold down the Shift key while clicking and dragging the object.
  - To rotate an object left or right, hold down the Ctrl key while clicking and dragging the object.
  - To tumble an object (rotate it left, right, forward, backward, or any possible combination of these directions), hold down the Ctrl and Shift keys while clicking and dragging the object.
- **Move Up and Down** ▣ When this button is selected you can move an object straight up or straight down by clicking and dragging the object.
- **Turn Left and Right** ▣ When this button is selected you can rotate an object toward the left or the right by clicking and dragging the object.
- **Turn Forward and Backward** ▣ When this button is selected you can rotate an object forward or backward by clicking and dragging the object.
- **Tumble** ▣ When this button is selected you can tumble an object by clicking and dragging the object. This means you can rotate the object right, left, forward, backward, or in any possible combination of these directions.
- **Resize** ▣ When this button is selected you can make an object larger or smaller by clicking and dragging the object.
- **Copy** ▣ When this button is selected you can make a copy of an object by simply clicking the object.

Figure 1-52 The mouse mode buttons

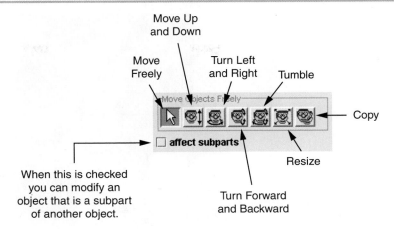

Notice that just below the buttons a check box labeled *affect subparts* appears. By default, this is not checked. When it is not checked, the modifications that you make to an object are applied to the entire object. For example, in the world that you created in the previous tutorials, suppose this check box is not checked and you click the *tumble* button. Then you click and drag the coach object. This action will cause the entire coach object to tumble. However, if you had first checked the *affect subparts* check box, you could have tumbled one of the object's subparts, such as an arm or a leg.

Rotation, Center Points, and Orientation

Three of the mouse mode buttons allow you to rotate objects: Turn Left and Right, Turn Forward and Backward, and Tumble. When you rotate an object, it turns around its *center point*.

You can usually see an object's center point when you select the object. Recall that selecting an object causes a yellow bounding box to be displayed around it in the World View window. In addition to the bounding box, three axes will also be displayed in or near the object. One of the axes will be green, one will be blue, and the other will be magenta (a shade of red). The point where these three axes come together is the location of the object's center point. Figure 1-53 shows an example.

Sometimes when an object is selected you can't see its exact center point because the center point is inside the object. When you need to see inside an object, it is helpful to change the object's fillingStyle property. As shown in Figure 1-54, the fillingStyle property has three settings: solid, wireframe, and points. The default setting is solid, which causes the object to be displayed as a solid. When the fillingStyle property is set to wireframe, the object is displayed as a wire skeleton that you can see through. When the fillingStyle property is set to points, the object is displayed as a set of points. Figure 1-55 shows how an object appears in each of the filling styles.

Figure 1-53 An object's center point

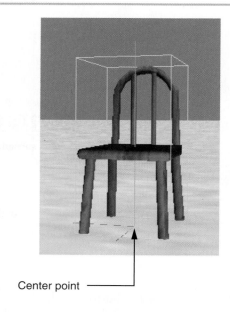

Center point

Figure 1-54 Setting `fillingStyle` to wireframe

fillingStyle
property

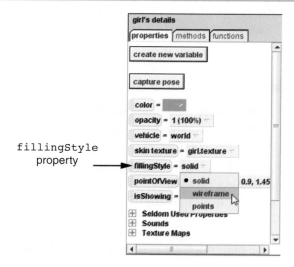

In addition to marking the object's center point, the green, blue, and magenta axes also indicate the object's *orientation*, which is the direction it is facing. In Alice, each object has its own understanding of what is forward and backward, what is right and left, and what is up and down. The green axis points in the object's up direction, the blue axis points in the object's forward direction, and the magenta axis points in the object's right direction. This is shown in Figure 1-56.

Figure 1-55 Solid, wireframe, and points filling styles

fillingStyle property set to solid   fillingStyle property set to wireframe

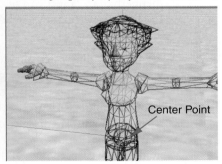

Center Point

fillingStyle property set to points

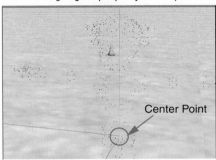

Center Point

Figure 1-56 An object's orientation

NOTE: An object's center point is determined by the person who designed the class. Because the object rotates around its center point, the center point is usually placed in a location that makes sense for that particular type of object. For example, if someone were designing a Tire class, it would make sense that the tire would rotate around its physical center just like a tire in the real world. So the designer would place the center point at the center of the circle making the tire.

Pitch, Roll, and Yaw

3D designers often use the terms pitch, roll, and yaw to describe the rotational movements that an object can perform in three-dimensional space. These terms come from the field of aeronautics, where they are used to describe the rotational movements of aircraft.

Figure 1-57 illustrates pitch, roll and yaw. *Pitch* is the movement that an object makes when it rotates around its right/left axis. This is the motion made by an airplane when its nose pitches up or down. *Roll* is the movement that an object makes when it rotates around its forward/backward axis. This is the motion made by an airplane when it tilts its wings. (This movement is also known as *banking*.) *Yaw* is the movement that an object makes when it rotates around its up/down axis. This is the motion made by an airplane when it turns its nose to the left or right.

It's your turn to practice using the mouse mode buttons. Tutorial 1-4 guides you through the process of copying, rotating, and resizing an object.

Figure 1-57 Pitch, roll, and yaw

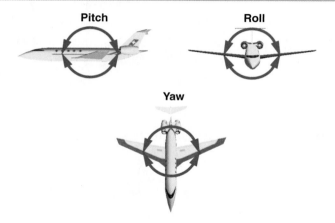

Tutorial 1-4:
Manipulating objects in 3D space

Step 1: Start Alice and create a new world. At the *Welcome to Alice!* dialog box, select the grass template.

Step 2: Click the *Add Objects* button to enter scene editor mode. In the local gallery select the *Furniture* collection, and then add an instance of the Chair class (shown in Figure 1-58) to the world. Notice that a tile for the object is created in the Object Tree, and that Alice automatically names the object chair.

Step 3: Position the camera so its viewpoint gives you a good view of the chair object, as shown in Figure 1-59.

Figure 1-58 The Chair class

Figure 1-59 The chair object

Step 4: Now you will use the mouse to make a copy of the chair object. In the set of mouse mode buttons, click the *Copy* button. Then simply click the chair object in the World View window. A copy of the chair object should appear, similar to that shown in Figure 1-60. Notice that a tile for the new object is created in the Object Tree. The name of the new object is chair2.

Step 5: Now you will move the chair2 object away from the chair object. In the set of mouse mode buttons, click the *Move Freely* button. Then in the World View window click and drag the chair2 object to a position beside the chair object.

Step 6: Next you will increase the size of the chair2 object. In the set of mouse move buttons click the *Resize* button. Then click the chair2 object and drag the mouse in the upward direction. This increases the size of the object. (Dragging the mouse in the downward direction shrinks the object.) Make the chair2 object at least twice as big as the chair object, similar to that shown in Figure 1-61.

Figure 1-60 A copy of the `chair` object

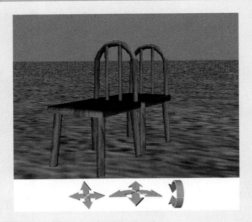

Figure 1-61 The `chair2` object resized

Step 7: Next you will spin the `chair` object so it faces away from the camera. In the set of mouse mode buttons click the *Turn Left and Right* button ⊞. Click and drag the `chair` object in either the left or right directions. This causes the object to spin left or right around its center point. Position the chair object so its back is to the camera, as shown in Figure 1-62.

Step 8: Now you will lay the `chair2` object on its back, on the ground, as shown in Figure 1-63. Although the best approach is to experiment with the mouse mode buttons and come up with your own technique for getting the object into this position, you might want to follow these general steps:

- Click the *Move Up and Down* button ⊞ and then click and drag the `chair2` object up into the air.
- Click the *Tumble* button ⊞ and then click and drag the `chair2` object until it is in approximately the correct position, in the air.

Figure 1-62 The `chair` object facing away from the camera

Figure 1-63 The `chair2` object moved and rotated

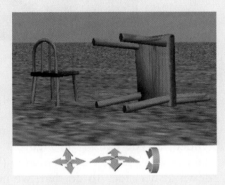

- Click the *Move Up and Down* button ⬆ and then click and drag the `chair2` object down to the ground.

In Tutorial 1-4 you practiced using the different mouse modes to manipulate entire objects. It is also important that you are able to manipulate the subparts of objects. Tutorial 1-5 gives you that practice.

Tutorial 1-5:
Manipulating subpart objects

Step 1: Start Alice and create a new world. At the *Welcome to Alice!* dialog box, select the grass template.

Step 2: Click the *Add Objects* button to enter scene editor mode. In the local gallery select the *People* collection, and then add an instance of the

Girl class to the world. Notice that a tile for the object is created in the Object Tree, and that Alice automatically names the object girl. Move the camera into a position that gives you a view similar to that shown in Figure 1-64.

Figure 1-64 The girl object

Step 3: By default, instances of the Girl class are created with their arms extended, as you can see in Figure 1-64. This is true for many of the People classes. We want to modify this object so her arms are hanging down at her side. To do that, we need to turn her arms downward, with the center of rotation being at the shoulders. This should be possible because the object has subpart objects for the left and right arms, and the center points of the arm objects are located at the shoulders. This is shown in Figure 1-65.

Figure 1-65 Each arm will rotate at the shoulder

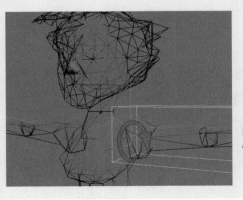

Each arm will rotate
around its center point.

Before we use the mouse mode buttons to turn the `girl` object's arms, however, we need to view her from the proper position in order to get the desired rotation. This is because the camera's viewpoint affects the direction that objects are turned with the mouse mode buttons. If we are viewing the girl from the front, we will twist the arm when we turn it downward. Instead, we should be viewing her from the side, as shown in Figure 1-66.

In the set of mouse mode buttons, click the *Turn Left and Right* button , and then use the mouse to turn the `girl` object sideways, as shown in Figure 1-67.

Figure 1-66 A side view will give the desired rotation

A turn from this viewpoint will twist the arm.

A turn from this viewpoint will rotate the arm down to the girl's side.

Figure 1-67 The `girl` object turned sideways

Step 4: Now you will turn the girl's left arm so it hangs down at her side. In the set of mouse mode buttons, click the *Turn Forward and Backward* button and then check the *affect subparts* check box. Next, click and drag the upper part of the girl's arm so that it is hanging down at her side, as shown in Figure 1-68.

Figure 1-68 The left arm turned

 TIP: You can move the camera closer to get a better look at the part of the girl's arm that you need to click and drag, if necessary. This step might take multiple attempts, especially if you click and drag the wrong part of her arm! Remember, you can always use the *Undo* button if things go terribly wrong!

Step 5: Uncheck the *affect subparts* check box, and then turn the `girl` object around so that you are facing her right arm. Repeat the procedure you performed in Step 4 to make her right arm hang down at her side.

Step 6: Turn the `girl` object around so that you have a front view. The object should appear similar to the one shown in Figure 1-69.

 TIP: Using the mouse mode buttons is just one way to manipulate objects in Alice. In Chapter 2 you will learn another technique for repositioning a character's arms.

Figure 1-69 Both arms hanging at the girl's side

Single View and Quad View Modes

When Alice is in scene editor mode, you can switch the display of the world between *single view mode* and *quad view mode*. So far we have been using single view mode, which is the default display mode. In single view mode you have one view of the world, which is the World View window. In quad view mode you have four views of the world: the World View window, a view from the top, a view from the right, and a view from the front. Figure 1-70 shows an example of these four views, and points out the *quad view* button that you click to switch to quad view mode.

Figure 1-70 Quad view

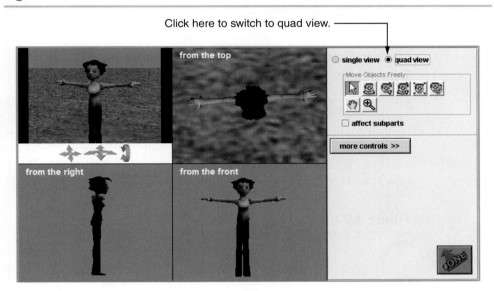

You can use the mouse to modify objects in any of the views. If you look carefully at the mouse mode buttons while in quad view mode, you'll notice that the *Move Up and Down* button 🔘 no longer appears. This is because the right and front viewing windows support up and down movement. If you want to move an object up or down while in quad view mode, simply select the *Move Objects Freely* button and then move the object up or down in either the right view or the front view.

You will also notice that two new buttons appear while in quad view mode: The *Scroll View* button 🔘 and the *Zoom* button 🔍. Often, when you switch to quad view mode the objects in the world will not be fully visible in all of the views. To remedy this, you can use the *Scroll View* button to scroll to the top, right, or front view. To use the button, follow these steps:

1. Select the *Scroll View* button; the mouse pointer changes into a hand tool
2. Move the mouse pointer into the view you wish to scroll
3. Click and drag the view in the direction you wish it to scroll

The *Zoom* button allows you to zoom into or out of the top, right, and front views. To use it, follow these steps:

1. Select the *Zoom* button; the mouse pointer changes into a zoom tool
2. Move the mouse pointer into the desired view and position it over the point that you wish to zoom into or zoom out from
3. Zoom by clicking and dragging—if you want to zoom in, then drag down or to the right; if you want to zoom out, then drag up or to the left

> **TIP:** In Alice, experience is usually the best teacher. This section gives you an idea of how things work in quad view mode, but to really learn quad view mode you should experiment!

Using Coordinates to Determine an Object's Location

Graphical systems commonly use axes to identify locations. Think of an axis as a number line. The midpoint of an axis is position 0. As you move along the axis to the right of 0, all of the points are identified by increasing positive numbers. As you move along the axis to the left of 0, all of the points are identified by decreasing negative numbers. Figure 1-71 shows an example of an axis. The red circle is located at position 3, and the green circle is located at position –2.

Figure 1-71 An axis

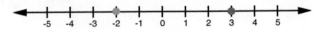

Two-dimensional systems use a set of two axes to identify locations. Figure 1-72 shows an example of such a system. The horizontal axis is known as the *X axis* and the vertical axis is known as the *Y axis*. Notice that the two axes intersect at their 0 positions.

Using these two axes, we can identify positions using a pair of coordinates in the form (X, Y), where X is the position along the X axis and Y is the position along the Y axis. In Figure 1-72 the coordinates of the red circle are (3,1). This is because the circle's position aligns with the 3 on the X axis and the 1 on the Y axis. The figure also shows other colored circles and their coordinates.

Three dimensional systems such as Alice use a set of three axes to identify positions. Figure 1-73 shows such a system. The system consists of an X axis, a Y axis, and a Z axis. The X and Y axes are oriented horizontally and vertically, just as they are in a 2D system. The Z axis is oriented along the third dimension, which is the depth of the world.

Using these three axes, we can identify positions in a 3D world using a set of coordinates in the form (X, Y, Z), where X is the position along the X axis, Y is the position along the Y axis, and Z is the position along the Z axis. Notice that the three axes intersect at their 0 point.

Figure 1-72 X and Y axes

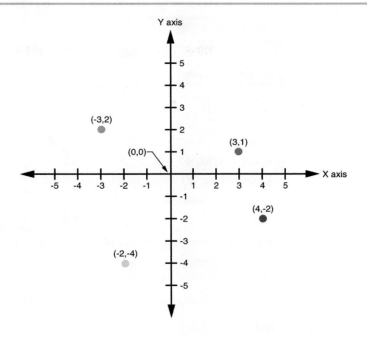

Figure 1-73 X, Y, and Z axes

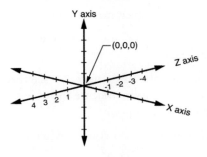

In an Alice world, the point (0,0,0) is at the center of the world, and the axes are measured in meters. When you add an object to the world, you can see the position of the object's center point by looking at the `pointOfView` property. For example, suppose you create a new world, add an instance of the `Hare` class, and then immediately check the object's `pointOfView` property. You should see the value shown in Figure 1-74. This indicates that the object's center point is located at the coordinate (−0.98, 0.6, 0.69) in the Alice world. If you use the mouse to drag the object around in the World View window, and simultaneously watch the `pointOfView` property, you will see the position coordinates change as you move the object around.

Figure 1-74 The `pointOfView` property

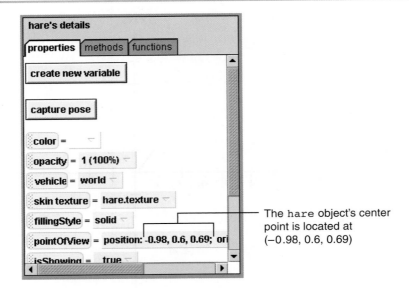

The `hare` object's center point is located at (−0.98, 0.6, 0.69)

Checkpoint

1.23 What dimensions do two-dimensional objects have? What dimensions do three-dimensional objects have?

1.24 In what directions may an object in a two-dimensional world move? In what directions may an object in a three-dimensional world move?

1.25 What are the seven mouse mode buttons?

1.26 Why would you want to know where an object's center point is before you rotate the object?

1.27 When you select an object you see three axes displayed in the vicinity of the object. These axes indicate the object's orientation. In what direction does each of the axes point?

1.28 What four views do you see when in quad view mode?

1.29 Which mouse mode button is not displayed when in quad view mode? Why is the button not displayed?

1.30 In a three-dimensional system, what do the numbers in a coordinate such as (5, 0, 1) indicate?

Review Questions

Multiple Choice

1. This is what a computer device does.

   a. Has its own human-like intelligence
   b. Gives commands to humans
   c. Follows instructions to perform a task
   d. Understands languages such as English

2. This is a set of instructions that the computer follows.

   a. Language
   b. Program
   c. Binary number
   d. Compiler

3. This is a set of well-defined logical steps that must be taken in order to perform a task.

   a. Algorithm
   b. Programming language
   c. Compiler
   d. Execution

4. This is the only language that a computer understands.

   a. Java
   b. Machine language
   c. Keywords
   d. Alice

5. This is a number that consists of only 1s and 0s.

   a. Binary
   b. Decimal
   c. Floating-point
   d. Unary

6. A program written in this is much easier for people to understand than a program written in machine language.

   a. Binary
   b. A programming language
   c. Decimal
   d. Hieroglyphics

7. This translates a program into machine language.

   a. An entry-level programmer
   b. Microprocessor
   c. Disk drive
   d. Compiler

8. These are the words that make up a programming language.

    a. Implied words
    b. External words
    c. Keywords
    d. Synthetic words

9. This is a set of rules that must be strictly followed when writing a program.

    a. Rules of order
    b. Syntax
    c. Procedural rules
    d. Rules of thumb

10. If a program contains even one of these, it cannot be translated into an executable program.

    a. Syntax error
    b. Keyword
    c. Compiler
    d. Binary number

11. This is the part of the Alice environment that holds a list of all the objects in the world.

    a. World View window
    b. Object List window
    c. World Object window
    d. Object Tree

12. Each object in an Alice world has these, which are values that specify the object's characteristics.

    a. Properties
    b. Internal flags
    c. Settings
    d. Methods

13. This is a set of programming statements that an object can execute.

    a. Properties
    b. Methods
    c. Subparts
    d. Orders

14. This is a description of a particular type of object; you can think of it as a blueprint that objects may be created from.

    a. Method
    b. Property
    c. Class
    d. Gallery

15. In programming terminology, this is what objects are also called.

    a. Classes
    b. Instances of a class
    c. Method
    d. Collections

16. This is a yellow box that appears around an object to indicate that it is selected.

    a. Wireframe
    b. Axes
    c. Bounding box
    d. Class

17. This is the part of the Alice environment where an object's properties are displayed.

    a. Details Panel
    b. World View window
    c. Object Tree
    d. Property View window

18. This is how many degrees of freedom objects in a 3D world have.

    a. Three
    b. Four
    c. Six
    d. Twelve

19. This is what an object turns around when you rotate it.

    a. The center of the world
    b. The object's center point
    c. The center of the screen
    d. A randomly selected point

20. When an object is selected you see three axes displayed in or near the object, which indicate the object's orientation. This is the direction in which the blue axis points.

    a. Forward
    b. Up
    c. Right
    d. Left

Short Answer

1. What is a computer?

2. Why were programming languages invented?

3. What is an algorithm?

4. What is the World View window and how does it relate to the camera?

5. Give two examples of a property that we have used in this chapter.

6. What is a method?

7. In Alice, what is a subpart?

8. What is a class?

9. In this chapter, blueprints and houses are used as a metaphor. In the metaphor, does a blueprint represent an object or does it represent a class?

10. Do the Alice galleries contain classes, or actual objects?

Exercises

1. **Snowy World**

   Create a snowy world with a snowman (from the *People* collection) surrounded by a circle of five penguins (from the *Animals* collection). The penguins should all be looking at the snowman.

2. **Table Set for Four**

   Create a world with the table set for four, as shown in Figure 1-75. The table and chairs can be found in the *Furniture* collection. Each setting on the table has a plate and a mug (found in the *Kitchen* collection). On each plate is a cookie (found in the *Kitchen* collection, inside the *Food* folder).

Figure 1-75 Table set for four

3. **Underwater World**

   In the Web gallery's *Environments* collection you will find a class named OceanFloor. An instance of this class can serve as the setting for an underwater world. Use this in a world that has at least three different types of fish (from the *Animals* collection) and a scuba diver (from the *People* collection).

4. **Moon World**

   The *Space* collection provides several space-related classes. Create a Moon world with a moon surface, an astronaut, a lunar lander, and a Hyperion robot.

5. **Talking Coaches**

   Create a world with instances of the Coach class (from the *People* collection). The coaches should be facing each other. The coaches should be in a normal standing position, so move their arms so they are hanging at their sides. Optionally, you can put the coaches inside an instance of the Gym class, found in the *High School* collection.

6. **City Street**

   The *City* collection contains numerous classes for creating a city setting, including buildings, streets, lamps, fire hydrants, and more. Create a city street scene with as much detail as possible. Then add several cars from the *Vehicles* collection. Last, add at least five different people.

7. **Medieval Scene**

   The *Medieval* collection contains several classes from medieval times. Create a world with a castle, a knight, a princess, and a dragon. Add any other items that you wish. The knight should appear to be defending the princess from the menacing dragon.

8. **Farm Scene**

   Create a world and use the *Farm* collection to make a farm scene. Start by creating an instance of the `FarmSky` class. Then place a farmhouse, a barn, a cornfield, a scarecrow, and a fence in the world.

9. **Birthday Party**

   Create a world showing several characters from the *People* collection at a birthday party. The *Holiday* collection holds another collection named *Birthday*, which contains classes for a birthday cake and party items.

10. **High School Cafeteria**

    The local gallery has a *High School* collection, and inside it is another collection named *Students and Teachers*. Use classes from these collections to create a scene in a high school cafeteria.

11. **High School Prom**

    The local gallery has a *High School* collection, and inside it is another collection named *Students and Teachers*, and inside it is another collection named *Prom*. Use classes from these collections to create a scene from a high school prom. Use the `gym` class (in the *High School* collection) as the setting.

2 Programming in Alice

TOPICS

2.1   Writing Methods

2.2   Naming Conventions

2.3   Designing a Program

2.4   Comments

2.5   Tips for Setting Up an Initial Scene

2.6   Executing Instructions Simultaneously

2.7   Exporting Your Code for Printing

2.8   Exporting an Alice World to Video

2.1   Writing Methods

CONCEPT: **A method is a set of instructions that execute when you play an Alice world. You create methods by dragging tiles into the Method Editor. The tiles that you drag into the Method Editor are instructions that cause actions to take place.**

In Chapter 1 you learned the basics of placing objects in an Alice world and then manipulating the way those objects appear. The worlds that you created in Chapter 1 did not perform any actions, however. If you want the objects in an Alice world to perform actions, you have to do a bit of programming. In this chapter you will get your first taste of programming as you learn to add actions to Alice worlds.

Recall from Chapter 1 that a *method* is a set of instructions that causes some action to take place. If you want an action to take place in an Alice world, you have to write a method. Figure 2-1 shows the location of the *Method Editor* in the Alice environment. This is where you write the methods that perform actions in an Alice world.

Notice the *world.my first method* tab at the top of the Method Editor shown in Figure 2-1. All methods have a name; `world.my first method` is the name of the method that is currently open in the editor. When you create a new world, Alice automatically creates an empty method named `world.my first method`.

Figure 2-1 The Method Editor

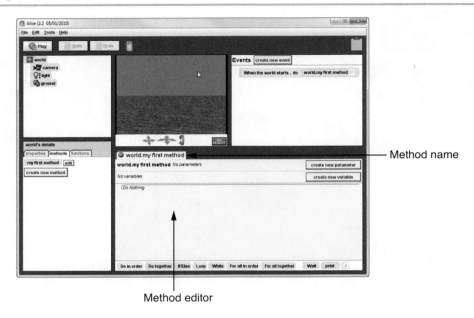

Method name

Method editor

The name `world.my first method` is written in *dot notation*. It's called dot notation because programmers refer to the period as a "dot." The dot separates two pieces of information. On the left side of the dot is the name of the object that the method belongs to. On the right side of the dot is the name of the method. The name `world.my first method` indicates that `my first method` is the name of the method, and `world` is the name of the object that the method belongs to.

Notice an area labeled *Events* at the top right of the screen, as shown in Figure 2-2. You might recall from Chapter 1 that this area of the Alice environment is called the Events Editor. In this area of the screen you see a tile that reads as follows:

```
When the world starts, do world.my first method
```

Figure 2-2 The Event Editor

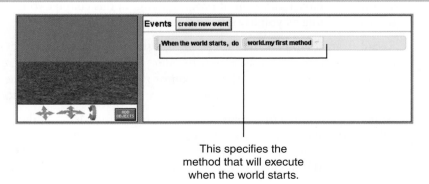

This specifies the
method that will execute
when the world starts.

This tile specifies that the method world.my first method will be automatically executed when you click the *Play* button to play the world. If you want to see an action take place when you play this Alice world, you use the Method Editor to put the desired programming instructions in the method world.my first method.

In Alice, you create methods by dragging tiles into the Method Editor. The tiles that you drag into the Method Editor are instructions that cause actions to take place. Figure 2-3 shows what a method might look like after instruction tiles have been dragged into it. For now, don't worry about what the tiles in the figure do. Just realize that each of the tiles represents an action that will take place when the world is played. As you progress through this chapter you will learn more about instruction tiles and how to arrange them properly in the Method Editor.

 NOTE: The Method Editor is not available when Alice is in scene editor mode.

Figure 2-3 A method that contains instruction tiles

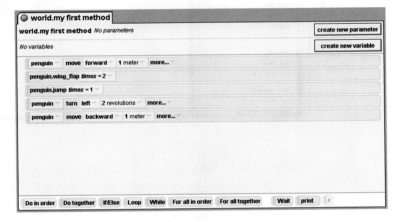

Primitive Methods

Although you have to create your own methods to perform the specific actions that you want to take place, Alice provides numerous methods that have already been created for you. In fact, all objects in Alice have a common set of built-in methods for performing basic actions. These methods, which are known as *primitive methods*, cause objects to move, turn, change size, and perform other fundamental operations. When you are programming in Alice, you will use many of these primitive methods to make the objects in the world do things.

Once you have added an object to a world, you can see a list of all of the methods that the object can perform by doing the following:

1. Select the object
2. In the Details Panel, select the *methods* tab to display a list of tiles that represent the object's methods

For example, Figure 2-4 shows an Alice world with an instance of the `Hare` class (which is in the *Animals* collection). The object, which is named `hare`, is selected. The *methods* tab is selected in the Details Panel, and a list of methods that the `hare` object can perform is displayed.

Figure 2-4 Methods displayed in the Details Panel

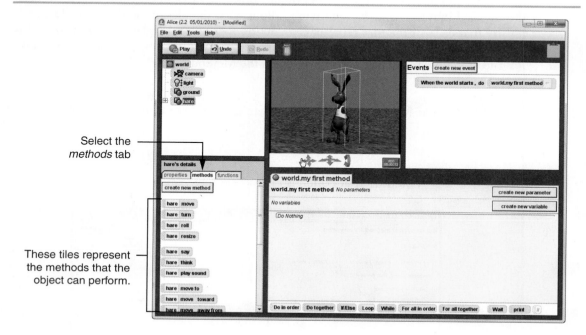

Figure 2-5 gives a closer look at one of the tiles that appears in the Details Panel. Notice that the tile is divided into two sections: the left side of the tile shows the name of the object, and the right side shows the name of the method. The tile that is shown in the figure represents the `hare` object's `move` method. (In dot notation, the method name would be `hare.move`.)

Figure 2-5 Method tile

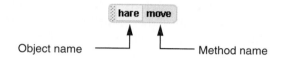

Every object in an Alice world has a `move` method. The `move` method simply causes the object to move in a particular direction for a specified distance. If we are programming in Alice and we want to insert an instruction to execute an object's `move` method, we simply drag the method's tile into the Method Editor, as shown in Figure 2-6.

Figure 2-6 Dragging the `hare.move` method tile into the Method Editor

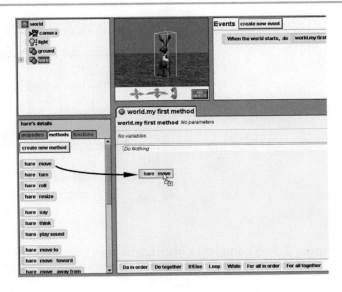

When you drop the tile into the Method Editor, a pop-up menu appears that allows you to select a direction. The allowable directions are up, down, left, right, forward, and backward. After you select a direction, another menu appears that allows you to select an amount, which is the distance that the object moves. In Alice, distances are always measured in meters.

Figure 2-7 shows the pop-up menus. As you can see from the figure, your choices for distance are ½ meter, 1 meter, 5 meters, 10 meters, or other. If you select other, the Custom Number keypad shown in Figure 2-8 appears. You can use the keypad to enter any number you choose.

Once you have selected a direction and an amount, a completed instruction tile, such as the one shown in Figure 2-9, will appear in the Method Editor. When you click the *Play* button, this instruction will cause the `hare.move` method to execute, and as a result, you will see the `hare` object move up a distance of one meter.

You should try these steps for yourself. Tutorial 2-1 leads you through the process of adding two instructions to an Alice world.

Figure 2-7 Specifying a direction and an amount

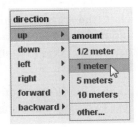

Figure 2-8 Custom Number keypad

Figure 2-9 A completed instruction tile

Tutorial 2-1:
Adding instructions to an Alice world

Step 1: Start Alice and create a new world. At the *Welcome to Alice!* dialog box, select the grass template.

Step 2: Click the *Add Objects* button to enter scene editor mode. In the local gallery select the *Animals* collection, and then add an instance of the Hare class to the world. Notice that in the Object Tree the name of the instance is hare. Click the *Done* button to exit scene editor mode.

Step 3: Select the hare object and click the *methods* tab in the Details Panel.

Step 4: Drag the tile for the hare object's move method and drop it into the Method Editor. On the pop-up menus that appear select *up* for the direction and *1 meter* for the distance. You should see the completed instruction tile shown in Figure 2-9 appear in the Method Editor.

Step 5: Save the world with the file name *HareWorld*.

Step 6: Now click the *Play* button to watch the action produced by this instruction. In the *World Running...* window you should see the hare object move up. As shown in Figure 2-10, the distance that the object moved is one meter.

Step 7: You can click the *Restart* button as many times as you wish to replay the world. When you are finished, click the *Stop* button.

Figure 2-10 The *World Running...* window

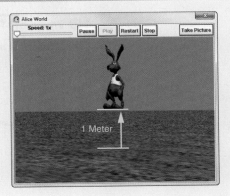

Step 8: If you feel badly about leaving the `hare` hanging in mid-air each time you play the world, you can add another instruction that brings the object back down to the ground. Drag the tile for the `hare` object's `move` method into the Method Editor again, as shown in Figure 2-11, dropping it *below* the existing instruction tile.

Figure 2-11 Drag the `move` method tile into the Method Editor again

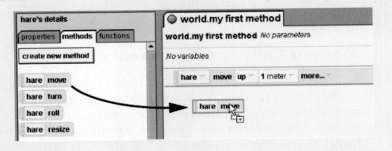

Step 9: At the pop-up menu, select *down* as the direction, and then select *1 meter* as the distance. You should now have two instruction tiles in the Method Editor, as shown in Figure 2-12.

The first instruction, which you created earlier, moves the `hare` object up one meter. The second instruction moves the `hare` object down one meter. This instruction should bring the object back down to the ground. As indicated in Figure 2-12, the instructions will be executed in the order that they appear in the method. The instruction that moves the object up will execute first, and the instruction that moves the object down executes second.

Figure 2-12 Two instructions in the method

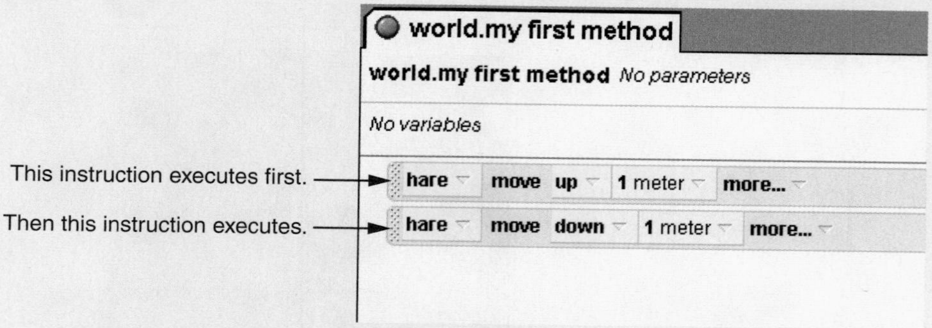

| ● world.my first method |
| world.my first method *No parameters* |
| *No variables* |

This instruction executes first. ⟶ | hare ▽ | **move** up ▽ | 1 meter ▽ | more... ▽ |

Then this instruction executes. ⟶ | hare ▽ | **move** down ▽ | 1 meter ▽ | more... ▽ |

Step 10: Click the *Play* button to watch the actions produced by these instructions. In the *World Running...* window you see the hare object move up, and then move back down to the ground. These two actions together make the hare look like it is doing a slow-motion hop. You can click the *Restart* button as many times as you wish to replay the world. When you are finished, click the *Stop* button.

Step 11: Save the world. We will use it again in the next tutorial.

Method Calls and Arguments

Before going any further, let's discuss some of the terminology that programmers use when referring to methods. When programmers execute a method, they commonly say that they are *calling the method*. In Tutorial 2-1 you created two instructions that execute the hare object's move method. An instruction that executes a method is commonly referred to as a *method call*. Both of the instructions that you created in Tutorial 2-1 (shown in Figure 2-12) are method calls.

As you learned in Tutorial 2-1, each time you call the move method, you have to specify two pieces of information: a direction and an amount. These pieces of information are known as arguments. An *argument* is any piece of information that a method requires in order for it to execute. When you call a method and provide any necessary arguments, it is called *passing the arguments* to the method.

Figure 2-13 shows one of the instructions that you created in Tutorial 2-1. The instruction calls the hare.move method and passes the arguments *up* and *1 meter*.

If you want to change the value of an argument that appears in an instruction tile, you click the argument and a drop-down menu will appear. The menu will show all of the allowable values for the argument. Simply select the new value from the menu.

Figure 2-13 A method call with arguments

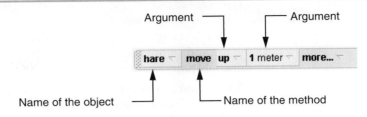

More about the Primitive Methods

The objects that appear in an Alice world have many primitive methods in addition to the move method. Table 2-1 summarizes all of the primitive methods. When you select an object, each of these methods is represented by a tile that appears under the *methods* tab of the Details Panel.

Let's try some of these methods. In Tutorial 2-2 you will continue to modify the Alice world that you created in Tutorial 2-1. In this tutorial you will add a call to the turn method so the hare will spin in mid-air before coming back down to the ground. Because we want the hare to spin in mid-air, the call to the turn method will have to be inserted between the two calls to the move method. You will also add a method call to the say method that causes the hare to say a message in a speech bubble. Finally, you will learn how to rearrange instructions in the Method Editor, and see how rearranging affects the playing of the world.

Table 2-1 Primitive methods (shown in the order that they appear in the Details Panel)

Method Name	Description
move	This method causes the object to move up, down, left, right, forward, or backward. You specify the direction and distance that you want the object to move.
turn	This method causes the object to turn toward the left, right, forward, or backward. You specify the amount you want the object to turn in revolutions.
roll	This method causes the object to roll toward the left or the right. You specify the amount you want the object to roll in revolutions.
resize	This method changes the object's size by a specified amount.
say	This method causes a cartoon-like speech bubble containing a specified message to be displayed, as if the object were saying the message.
think	This method causes a cartoon-like thought bubble containing specified text to be displayed, as if the text were a thought that the object is thinking.
play sound	This method plays a sound. You can specify one of the sounds that Alice provides, or you can import any MP3 or WAV file.

(continued)

Table 2-1 Primitive methods (*continued*)

Method Name	Description
move to	This method causes the object to move to another object. When the method completes, both objects' center points will be in the same location.
move toward	This method causes the object to move in the direction of another object. You specify the distance to move in meters, and the object to move toward.
move away from	This method causes the object to move away from another object. You specify the distance to move in meters.
orient to	This method orients the object in the same direction as another specified object. When this method executes the object will turn so its Up, Right, and Forward axes are aligned with the axes of the specified object.
turn to face	This method causes the object to turn so it is facing another object.
point at	This method is similar to the turn to face method, except the object will be tilted so its forward axis is "aiming" at the specified object's center point.
set point of view to	This method sets the object's point of view to that of another object. It is commonly used with the camera to move it to the location of another object, and give a view from that object's point of view.
set pose	Alice allows you to position an object and its subparts in a certain way and then capture that as a pose. This method causes the object to assume a pose that was previously captured.
stand up	This method makes the object "stand up" by aligning the object's Up axis with the world's Up axis.
move at speed	This causes the object to move in a specified direction (up, down, left, right, forward, or backward) at a specified speed. The speed is measured in meters per second. By default, the object moves for one second, but a different time period can be specified.
turn at speed	This causes the object to turn in a specified direction (left, right, forward, or backward) at a specified speed. The speed is measured in revolutions per second. By default, the object turns for one second, but a different time period can be specified.
roll at speed	This causes the object to turn in a specified direction (left or right) at a specified speed. The speed is measured in revolutions per second. By default, the object rolls for one second, but a different time period can be specified.
constrain to face	This method works like the turn to face method, but the object instantly turns. (The turn to face method causes the object to gradually turn.)
constrain to point at	This method works like the point at method, but the object instantly repositions. (The point at method causes the object to gradually reposition.)

Tutorial 2-2:
Exploring additional primitive methods

Step 1: Open the *HareWorld* world that you created in Tutorial 2-1. Select the hare object, and open the *methods* tab in the Details Panel.

Step 2: Currently we have two calls to the move method in the method world.my first method. The first one makes the hare move up and the second one makes the hare move back down. We are going to add a call to the hare object's turn method, causing it to turn around in mid-air. Because we want the hare to turn around in mid-air, we need to add the method call between the two calls to the move method.

Here's how you do it: drag the tile for the turn method into the Method Editor, but don't drop it yet. Notice that as you hold the tile, a green line appears in the Method Editor. This green line shows where the method will be inserted if you drop it. Drag the tile so the green line appears between the two existing instruction tiles, as shown in Figure 2-14, and drop it.

Figure 2-14 Inserting a method call

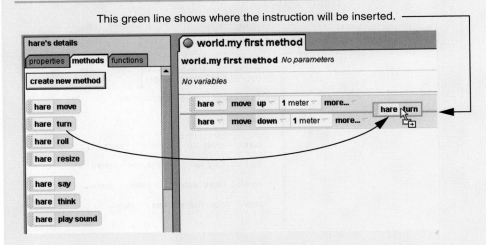

Step 3: A menu appears allowing you to select values for the method's arguments. The turn method requires two arguments: the direction of the turn and the amount of revolutions. For the direction, select *left*, and for the amount select *1 revolution* (all the way around).

You should now have three instruction tiles in the Method Editor, as shown in Figure 2-15. When you play the world, the instructions will be executed in the order that they appear in the method.

Step 4: Click the *Play* button to play the world. You should see the hare move up, spin around, and then move down.

Figure 2-15 Three instruction tiles

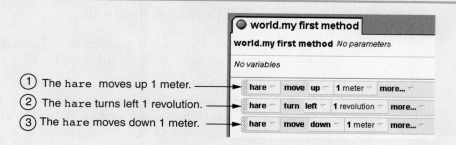

① The hare moves up 1 meter.

② The hare turns left 1 revolution.

③ The hare moves down 1 meter.

Step 5: Let's add one more instruction to our method. We want the hare to say "That was fun!" in a speech bubble after moving back down to the ground. Drag the tile for the hare object's say method into the Method Editor and drop it below the last instruction tile. The say method requires one argument: what you want the object to say. The menu that appears allows you to select *hello, goodbye,* or *other...* Select *other...*

Step 6: The *Enter a string* dialog box appears. A *string* is merely a string of characters. Enter *That was fun!* and click the *OK* button. You should now have four instruction tiles in the Method Editor, as shown in Figure 2-16.

Figure 2-16 Four instruction tiles

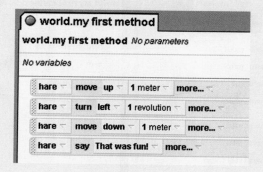

Step 7: Save the world, and then click the *Play* button to play it. You should see the hare move up, spin around, move down, and then say "That was fun!" in a speech bubble, as shown in Figure 2-17.

Step 8: Once you have created an instruction tile in the Method Editor, you can move the tile by dragging it. While you are dragging an instruction tile up or down in the Method Editor, a green line appears showing where the tile will be placed if you drop it.

Let's try it out. Currently, the second instruction tile in the Method Editor calls the hare object's turn method. Drag this tile downward until the green insertion line appears in the position shown in

Figure 2-17 Speech bubble

Figure 2-18, and drop it in that position. After doing this, the tile will be moved to the third position, as shown in Figure 2-19.

Step 9: When you play the world now, the instructions will be executed in the new order in which they appear. Click the *Play* button and watch the world. This time the hare moves up, moves down, turns around, and then says "That was fun!"

Step 10: Save the world.

Figure 2-18 Moving an instruction tile

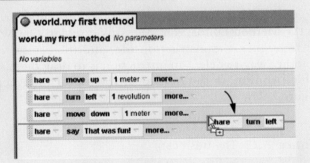

Figure 2-19 The tile moved to the third position

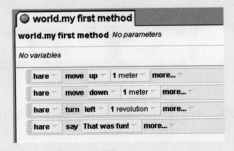

The *more...* Editing Tag

While you were completing Tutorials 2-1 and 2-2 you probably noticed that an area labeled *more...* appeared at the end of the instruction tiles, as shown in Figure 2-20. This is known as an *editing tag*. If you click the *more...* editing tag, a menu appears that allows you to specify additional arguments.

Figure 2-20 The *more...* editing tag

The arguments that are available on the editing tag menu depend on the type of method that is being called. One of the commonly available arguments is *duration*. The duration argument specifies the amount of time that it takes for the method's action to take place on the screen. By default, the duration is one second. So when the hare object moved up one meter, it took the object one second to make the move. If you decrease the duration argument to half a second, then the hare object will move one meter in only half a second—which means the object will move twice as fast.

Deleting and Copying Instructions

If you decide that you do not want to keep an instruction that you have created in the Method Editor, you can easily delete it. One way to delete an instruction is to right-click the instruction tile, and then select *delete* on the pop-up menu. Another way to delete an instruction is to drag the instruction tile to the trash can, which appears in the toolbar at the top of the Alice environment, as shown in Figure 2-21.

Figure 2-21 The trash can

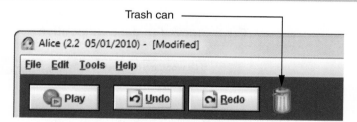

You can also copy an instruction that appears in the Method Editor. You simply right-click the instruction tile that you want to copy, and then select *make copy* on the pop-up menu. A copy of the instruction tile will appear just below the original. Sometimes when you need to create several similar instructions, you will find it more convenient to create the first one and then copy it as many times as needed. Then you can make any necessary changes to the arguments of the copies.

Objects with Custom Methods

In the previous section we discussed the primitive methods of objects in an Alice world. In addition to the primitive methods, objects of some classes have custom methods. A *custom method* is a method that only objects of a specific class have.

Not all classes have custom methods. If a class provides custom methods, you can see a list of those methods in the class's information window. Recall from Chapter 1 that you display a class's information window by going into the gallery and clicking on the class's thumbnail. For example, if you go into the *Animals* collection and click the Frog class's thumbnail, you will see the information window shown in Figure 2-22. The information window shows that the Frog class has three custom methods: foottap, ribbit, and headnod.

Figure 2-22 Information window for the Frog class

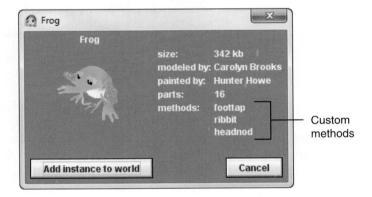

When you add an object to an Alice world and then select that object, tiles representing its custom methods (if it has any) appear above the tiles for the primitive methods in the Details Panel. For example, suppose we add an instance of the Frog class to a world, and then select that object. Figure 2-23 shows how the tiles for the custom methods will appear in the Details Panel.

Usually, it's easy to tell what a custom method does just by looking at the method's name. For example, the foottap method makes the frog tap its foot, the ribbit method makes the frog open its mouth as if it were making a "ribbit" sound, and the headnod method makes the frog nod its head. If a method's purpose is unclear, you can always find out what it does by trying it!

The *Walking People* Collection

You may have noticed that inside the *People* collection there is another collection named *Walking People*. The *Walking People* collection contains many of the same

Figure 2-23 Custom methods

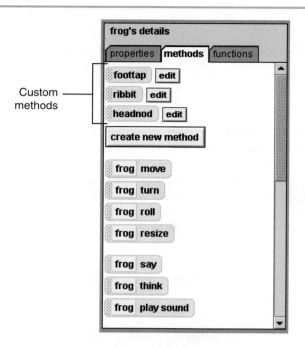

Custom methods

classes as the *People* collection, but the classes in the *Walking People* collection have the ability to walk. Each of the *Walking People* classes has a custom method walk. When you call the walk method, you must specify a distance as an argument. When the method executes, the character will walk the specified distance.

 Checkpoint

2.1 In an Alice world you have an object named hare. The hare object has a method named move. How would you write the method name using dot notation?

2.2 What causes a method to be executed automatically when a world is played?

2.3 What is a primitive method? Which objects have primitive methods?

2.4 How do you see a list of the primitive methods that an object has?

2.5 When specifying a distance for the move method, what happens when you select *other...* from the menu? When would you use this selection?

2.6 A fellow classmate has placed an instruction in the Method Editor. You ask her what the method does, and she says "It calls another method." What does she mean by that?

2.7 What is an argument?

2.8 What is a custom method? Do all classes provide custom methods?

2.9 How can you see a list of the custom methods that a class has?

 ## Naming Conventions

CONCEPT: There are standard conventions that programmers follow when they create names for objects and methods. You should follow these conventions when naming the objects and methods in an Alice world.

Names are used extensively in programming. In the short time that you have been using Alice, you have seen that classes, objects, and methods have names. As you progress in your studies, you will find that other things in a program have names too. Names are also known as *identifiers* because they identify various items in a program.

Each programming language has its own set of rules that must be followed when creating names that are used in a program. In addition to these rules, programmers usually follow a set of conventions, or guidelines, when making up names. In this section we will discuss some of the most commonly used rules and conventions. We will also discuss how to change the names that Alice automatically provides for objects and methods.

Meaningful Names

You've seen that Alice automatically assigns a name to an object when you add the object to the world. Sometimes the default names that Alice gives to objects do not really reflect the purpose of the object. Fortunately, Alice allows you to change the names of objects after you add them to a world. (In a moment you will see how.) When you add an object to a world, you should give it a name that indicates an object's purpose or role. As a result, it will be easier for anyone reading your code to understand what each object is for.

For example, suppose you are creating an Alice world that shows two high school basketball coaches having a conversation. One is the coach of the Cougars and the other is the coach of the Knights. When you add the first instance of the `Coach` class to the world, Alice will automatically name it `coach`. When you add the second instance of the `Coach` class, Alice will automatically name it `coach2`. These names are not ideal because they do not indicate the purpose of the objects. Names such as `cougarsCoach` and `knightsCoach` would be more meaningful for this particular world because they indicate which team each coach belongs to.

The name of a method should also indicate the method's purpose. In the previous tutorials you saw how Alice automatically creates a method for you named `my first method`, which belongs to the `world` object. (In dot notation, it is `world.my first method`.) For most purposes this name is not very descriptive, so you should change it to reflect the purpose that the method actually serves. For example, in the previous tutorials the method animated the `hare` object. A better name for the method might be `hareAnimation`. Shortly you will see how to rename methods in Alice.

Spaces

Most programming languages prohibit spaces from being used in names. Alice, however, allows spaces to appear in names. You've already seen an example of this. When you create a world in Alice, an empty method named `world.my first method` is automatically created. Notice the spaces that appear after `my` and `first`. This name is perfectly legal in Alice, but it would not be allowed in languages such as Java or C++.

Even though Alice allows you to put spaces in names, we will not follow that practice from this point forward in the book. When you begin studying a traditional programming language such as Java or C++, this will make the transition from Alice a little easier.

camelCase Names

Because a name should reflect the purpose of the object or method that it represents, programmers often find themselves creating names that are made of multiple words. For example, suppose you are creating a world that will contain an instance of the `Horse1` class, which is in the *Animals* collection. When you add the instance to the world, Alice automatically names it `horse1`. In the world, the object will represent the horse "Black Beauty," but you can't rename it `black beauty` because you have been discouraged from using spaces in object names. So, you decide to combine the two words into one and rename the object `blackbeauty`.

Unfortunately, a name like `blackbeauty` is not read easily by the human eye because the words are not separated. Since we don't want to get in the habit of using spaces in names, we need to find another way to separate the individual words visually. That's where the *camelCase* naming convention comes to the rescue. You use the camelCase convention to write a multi-word name as follows:

- You begin the name with lowercase letters
- The first character of the second and subsequent words is written in uppercase

For example, in camelCase the name `blackbeauty` is written `blackBeauty`. Notice that the first letter of the second word is uppercase. This visually separates the two words in such a way that the name is more easily read. The following are examples of object names written in camelCase:

```
handsomePrince
travelingSalesman
queenOfEngland
petCockerSpaniel
```

Because camelCase is very popular with programmers, in this book we will use it from this point forward. We will use camelCase for object names and for method names.

 NOTE: This style of naming is called camelCase because the uppercase characters that appear in a name are sometimes reminiscent of a camel's humps.

Class Names and PascalCase

Recall from Chapter 1 that, by convention, class names begin with an uppercase letter. If you look at the class names in the galleries, you will see that this practice is followed in Alice. This practice is also followed in most traditional programming languages. Programmers typically use the *PascalCase* convention when naming classes. PascalCase is exactly like camelCase, except in PascalCase the first letter of the name is written in uppercase. The following are examples of names written in PascalCase:

```
IceSkater
BadGuyRobot
CheshireCat
```

Summary of Our Naming Conventions

The following is a summary of the naming conventions that we will use from this point forward in the book:

- We will give objects and methods meaningful names that reflect their purpose in the world
- We will use only letters and numbers in names because they are the only legal characters allowed by Alice
- We will not use spaces in names
- We will use the camelCase convention for object and method names
- The PascalCase convention is used for class names

Renaming Objects

You can change the name of an object by right-clicking the object's tile in the Object Tree, and then clicking *rename* on the menu that appears. Figure 2-24 shows the menu. After you do this, you will be able to edit the name that appears on the object's tile directly. Figure 2-25 shows the Object Tree of a world that contains two objects that we have named `cougarsCoach` and `knightsCoach`.

Figure 2-24 Renaming an object

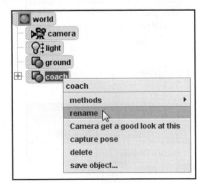

Figure 2-25 Two objects renamed

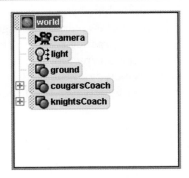

Renaming the `my first method` Method

From this point forward we will rename the method `my first method` so that it has a more meaningful name for each particular world we create. Follow these steps to rename the method:

1. Because the method `my first method` belongs to the `world` object, you must first select the `world` object in the Object Tree.
2. Select the *methods* tab in the Details Panel.
3. Right-click the tile for `my first method` in the Details Panel, and then click *Rename* on the menu that appears. After you do this, you will be able to edit the name that appears on the method's tile directly. (When editing the method name in this step, do *not* type `world.` in front of the method name. That part is understood because you selected the `world` object in Step 1.)

You might find it helpful to refer to Figure 2-26 while performing these steps.

Remember that `world.my first method` is automatically executed when the world is played because of the tile shown in Figure 2-27, which appears in the Events Editor.

Figure 2-26 Renaming a method

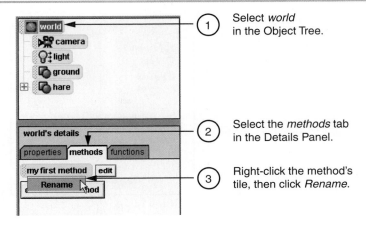

Figure 2-27 Event tile

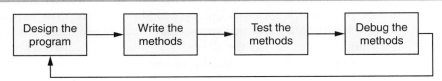

When you rename the method `world.my first method`, the tile in the Events Editor should automatically change to reflect the new name. If for some reason the tile does not change, you will need to click the part of the tile that shows the method name and then select the new name.

Checkpoint

2.10 Why is it important that you give meaningful names to objects?

2.11 In most traditional programming languages, is it acceptable to have spaces in object or method names?

2.12 What is the camelCase naming convention? When is it used?

2.13 What is the PascalCase naming convention? When is it used?

2.3 Designing a Program

CONCEPT: Programmers use a repetitive process known as the Program Development Cycle to plan, develop, and test their programs. You will use a similar process to develop Alice worlds.

Any professional programmer will tell you that writing software requires a good deal of planning. When programmers begin a new project, they never jump right in and start writing methods as the first step. They carefully follow a process that starts with creating a program design. After designing the program, programmers write the methods. Then they test the methods to determine whether any errors exist. If there are errors, they debug the methods. During the debugging process, programmers find and correct faulty code, and sometimes discover that the original design must be changed. This entire process, which is known as the *program development cycle*, is repeated until no errors can be found in the program. Figure 2-28 illustrates the steps in the process.

Figure 2-28 The program development cycle

The program development cycle can also be applied to the development of Alice worlds. Let's take a closer look at each step in the cycle, as we might use it with Alice.

Designing the Program (the Alice World)

The first step is to understand precisely what the Alice world is supposed to do. This is commonly done by reading a *problem statement* that describes the objects that are to appear in the world, and the actions that are to take place. The following is an example of a problem statement for an Alice world:

A hare should show off his acrobatic skill by jumping up and spinning all the way around in mid-air. The hare should come back down to the ground and exclaim "That was fun!"

This could easily be the problem statement for the world we created in Tutorials 2-1 and 2-2. It tells us that we need a hare object, and it gives a general description of the actions that the object should perform.

Once you clearly understand what your Alice world is supposed to do, you can start designing the methods that you will need. This requires that you break down the problem into a series of steps that can be taken. Programmers use two tools to accomplish this: pseudocode and flowcharts. *Pseudocode* is a way of writing the steps of an algorithm in English. The pseudocode steps are not written in a programming language, so they cannot be executed on the computer. They can, however, serve as an outline of the algorithm. Once the algorithm is completely written in pseudocode, you can convert it to programming instructions.

Here is an example of how we might write pseudocode for the method that makes our hare object perform the actions that are described in the previous problem statement:

```
hare moves up in the air
hare turns completely around
hare moves down to the ground
hare says "That was fun!"
```

As you can see, the pseudocode describes each of the individual actions that an algorithm must perform. There are no rules for writing pseudocode; you simply write statements that describe each step of the algorithm, in the correct order. Once the pseudocode algorithm is complete, it can serve as an outline for creating the actual programming instructions.

Flowcharting is another tool that programmers use to design methods. A *flowchart* is a diagram that graphically depicts the steps that take place in an algorithm. Figure 2-29 shows how we might have created a flowchart for the method to animate our hare object.

Notice that there are two types of symbols in the flowchart: ovals and rectangles. The ovals, which appear at the top and bottom of the flowchart, are called *terminal symbols*. The *Start* terminal symbol marks the algorithm's starting point and the *End* terminal symbol marks the algorithm's ending point. Between the terminal symbols are rectangles, which are called *processing symbols*. Each of the processing symbols

Figure 2-29 Flowchart for the method to animate the `hare` object

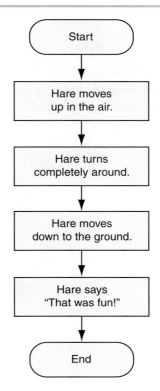

represents a step in the algorithm. The symbols are connected by arrows that represent the "flow" of the algorithm. To step through the symbols in the proper order, you begin at the *Start* terminal and follow the arrows until you reach the *End* terminal.

Like pseudocode, a flowchart serves as an outline that can be used to create actual programming instructions.

 TIP: Most programmers use either pseudocode or flowcharts in their design, but not both.

Writing the Methods

The pseudocode or flowcharts that you create in the design phase will serve as a model for your Alice methods. Once you are satisfied that your model will work correctly, you can begin converting it to actual programming instructions. In Alice, this means that you drag tiles into the Method Editor to assemble a set of instructions. The instructions that you assemble should accurately perform the actions that are set forth in the pseudocode or flowchart. Figure 2-30 shows the flowchart and

Figure 2-30 Flowchart, pseudocode, and actual instructions

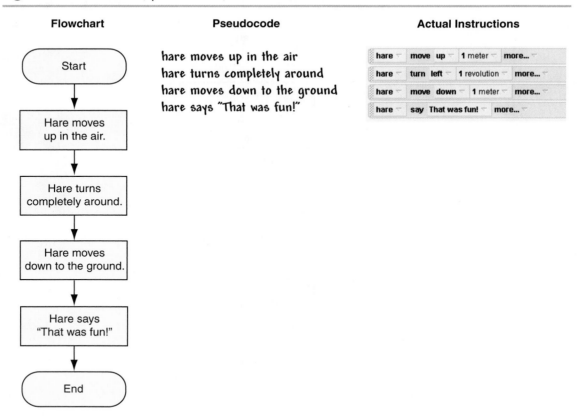

pseudocode that we discussed earlier side by side, along with the actual Alice instruction tiles for the method.

Keep in mind that pseudocode and flowcharts are merely outlines of an algorithm, and when you create them, you will not always provide the same level of detail that is required when creating a method. For example, in both the pseudocode and the flowchart shown in Figure 2-30 the second process is "hare turns completely around." In Alice, there is no primitive method that specifically causes an object to turn completely around. However, there is a primitive method named turn, which causes an object to turn in a specified direction, a specified number of revolutions. We can use that method to make the hare turn completely around. Notice that the instruction tiles shown in Figure 2-30 call the turn method, specifying left as the direction and 1 as the number of revolutions.

TIP: The more you learn about the primitive methods, custom methods, and programming capabilities that are available in Alice, the better you will be at creating pseudocode or flowchart models. As you become more experienced, you will develop an intuition for creating pseudocode or flowchart models that can be easily converted to Alice instructions.

Testing and Debugging

Once you have created a method, the next step is to *test* it. You test a method to make sure it meets the following criteria:

- It does its intended task
- It doesn't have any logical errors, which cause undesired results
- It works efficiently, without performing unnecessary steps

In Alice, you play the world to test your methods. When you play the world, you observe the actions that take place and determine whether they meet the requirements set forth in the problem statement. If they do not, you begin the *debugging* process. In the debugging process you determine how the methods must be corrected or modified in order for the world to meet the specified requirements.

It's common for programs to contain logical errors when they are first written. A *logical error*, also known as a *bug*, is a mistake that does not prevent the program from running, but causes it to produce incorrect results. There are many types of mistakes that can cause logical errors. For example, instructions that are written in an incorrect order can cause a logical error. Suppose a programmer wrote the pseudocode algorithm shown in Figure 2-31, and then created the instruction tiles that are also shown in the figure. The instruction tiles have a logical error. Can you find it?

Figure 2-31 Instructions with a logical error

Pseudocode	Alice Instructions
hare moves up in the air	hare ⌄ move up ⌄ 1 meter ⌄ more... ⌄
hare turns completely around	hare ⌄ move down ⌄ 1 meter ⌄ more... ⌄
hare moves down to the ground	hare ⌄ turn left ⌄ 1 revolution ⌄ more... ⌄
hare says "That was fun!"	hare ⌄ say That was fun! more... ⌄

Do you see the logical error in the instructions?

The instructions tiles shown in the figure are not placed in the correct order. The pseudocode algorithm specifies that the hare should turn completely around after it moves up in the air. The instruction tiles, however, have the hare turning around after it moves down to the ground. As a result, the hare will not perform the actions that are described in the problem statement or the pseudocode algorithm. To fix this error, the tile that calls the `hare` object's `turn` method must be moved to the correct position, which is immediately after the first tile.

Passing incorrect values as arguments to methods will also cause logical errors. For example, look at the pseudocode and the instruction tiles shown in Figure 2-32. Can you find the logical error in the instructions?

The error is in the second instruction tile, which calls the `hare` object's `turn` method. An incorrect value is being passed as an argument for the number of revolutions. The instruction tile passes 0.5 revolutions as the argument, which will cause the `hare` object to turn only halfway around. To fix this error the argument must be changed to 1 revolution.

Figure 2-32 Instructions with another logical error

Pseudocode	Alice Instructions
hare moves up in the air	hare ⌄ move up 1 meter more... ⌄
hare turns completely around	hare ⌄ turn left ⌄ 0.5 revolutions ⌄ more... ⌄
hare moves down to the ground	hare ⌄ move down ⌄ 1 meter ⌄ more... ⌄
hare says "That was fun!"	hare ⌄ say That was fun! more... ⌄

Do you see the logical error in the instructions?

Tutorial 2-3 will show you how to use the program development cycle to create an Alice world. It presents a problem statement, shows an example of pseudocode and a flowchart for the algorithm, and leads you through the process of writing a method and testing the world.

VideoNote

Using the Program Design Cycle

Tutorial 2-3:
Using the program design cycle

The following is a problem statement for an Alice world that you will create in this tutorial:

> *Recreate the opening scene of Lewis Carol's Alice's Adventures in Wonderland, where Alice sees White Rabbit run by her, saying to itself "Oh dear! Oh dear! I shall be late!"*

This problem statement tells you that you will need two objects: one for the Alice character and another for the White Rabbit character. Luckily, the local gallery provides classes for both of these. In the *People* collection you will find a class named `AliceLidell` (in real life, Alice's last name was Lidell), and in the *Animals* collection you will find a class named `WhiteRabbit`.

The problem statement also describes the actions that the objects must perform. If you take a moment to visualize mentally the world as it plays, you might picture the White Rabbit moving to a position in front of Alice Liddell. According to the problem statement, Alice sees the rabbit, so, at this point Alice Lidell looks at the White Rabbit. The White Rabbit then says "Oh dear! Oh dear! I shall be late!" and moves off the screen.

You need to write a method that makes these actions take place, but first, you should develop a model of the method in either pseudocode or a flowchart. An example of the pseudocode follows, and Figure 2-33 shows an example flowchart.

    White Rabbit moves forward to a position in front of Alice
    Alice looks at the White Rabbit
    White Rabbit says "Oh dear! Oh dear! I shall be late!"
    White Rabbit moves forward, off the screen

Figure 2-33 An example flowchart

Step 1: Start Alice and use the grass template to create a new world.

Step 2: Add to the world an instance of the `AliceLidell` class (in the *People* collection), and an instance of the `WhiteRabbit` class (in the *Animals* collection). No other objects are specified in the problem statement, but we can make the world more visually interesting by adding a tree. Add an instance of the `HappyTree` class (in the *Nature* collection). Arrange the objects in a fashion similar to that shown in Figure 2-34.

Step 3: In the Object Tree you should see tiles for the objects that you just added. Notice that the default names of the objects are `aliceLidell`, `whiteRabbit`, and `happyTree`. These names are written in camelCase, and are adequately descriptive, so there is no need to change them.

You do need to change the name of the method `world.my first method`, however. As we discussed earlier in this chapter, the default name is not written in camelCase, and it does not adequately describe the method's purpose. To change the name of the method do the following: (1) select the `world` object in the Object Tree, (2) select the

Figure 2-34 Initial setup

methods tab in the Details Panel, and (3) right-click the method's tile in the Details Panel, and then click *rename* on the pop-up menu. You might find it helpful to refer to Figure 2-35 while performing these steps.

After you do this, you will be able to edit the name my `first method` that appears on the method's tile directly. Change the name to `animation`. After you change the name, you should see the new method name, `world.animation`, appear at the top of the Method Editor, as shown in Figure 2-36.

Figure 2-35 Renaming the method

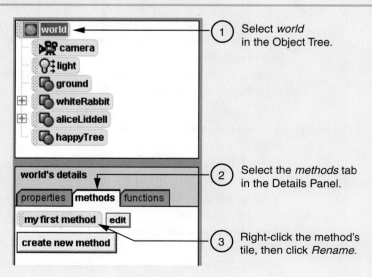

Figure 2-36 The method's new name

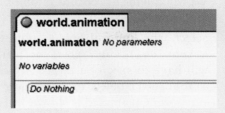

Step 4: When you change the name of the method `world.my first method`, the tile in the Events Editor should automatically change to reflect the new name, as shown in Figure 2-37. Confirm that the tile has changed. If for some reason the tile has not changed, you will need to click the part of the tile that shows the method name and then select `world.animation`.

Figure 2-37 Event tile

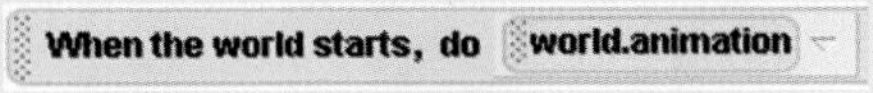

> When the world starts, do   world.animation

Step 5: Now you will begin to convert the algorithm that was shown earlier, in the pseudocode and the flowchart, to instructions in the `world.animation` method. First, the `whiteRabbit` object must move forward to a position in front of the `aliceLidell` object. To accomplish this we will call the `whiteRabbit` object's move method.

Select the `whiteRabbit` object, and then select the *methods* tab in the Details Panel. Drag the tile for the `whiteRabbit.move` method into the Method Editor. For the direction, select *forward*. For the amount, select *other....* The Custom Number keypad will appear. Enter *2* and select *OK*. (Two meters is merely an estimation of the distance that the `whiteRabbit` should move. When you test the method, you can adjust the distance if necessary.) The instruction tile that you just created should look like the one shown in Figure 2-38.

Figure 2-38 The completed instruction

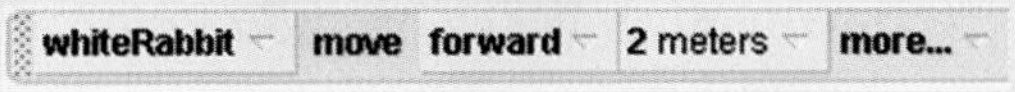

> whiteRabbit   move forward   2 meters   more...

Step 6: Next, the `aliceLidell` object should look at the `whiteRabbit` object. We will call the `aliceLidell` object's `turn to face` method to accomplish this.

Select the `aliceLidell` object and drag the tile for the `aliceLidell.turn to face` method into the Method Editor. You will have to specify a target, which is the object that you want the `aliceLidell` object to face. Select `whiteRabbit`, and then select *the entire* `whiteRabbit`, as shown in Figure 2-39. Figure 2-40 shows the instructions that you should have so far.

Figure 2-39 Selecting `whiteRabbit` as the target

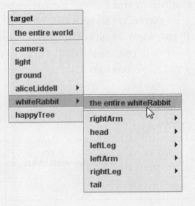

Figure 2-40 The instruction tiles so far

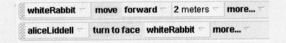

Step 7: The next step in the algorithm is the `whiteRabbit` object saying "Oh dear! Oh dear! I shall be late!" Select the `whiteRabbit` object, and drag the tile for the `whiteRabbit.say` method into the Method Editor. You have to specify what the object is to say. Select *other...* from the menu, and then enter *Oh dear! Oh dear! I shall be late!* into the *Enter a String* dialog box.

Step 8: The last action to take place is the `whiteRabbit` object moving off the screen. Drag the tile for the `whiteRabbit.move` method into the Method Editor. Select *forward* for the direction, and *5 meters* for the distance. (Again, we are estimating the distance. It seems reasonable that a distance of five meters will position the object off the screen, but we can adjust that distance, if necessary, when we test the method.) The instructions in the Method Editor should now appear as shown in Figure 2-41.

Figure 2-41 The completed method

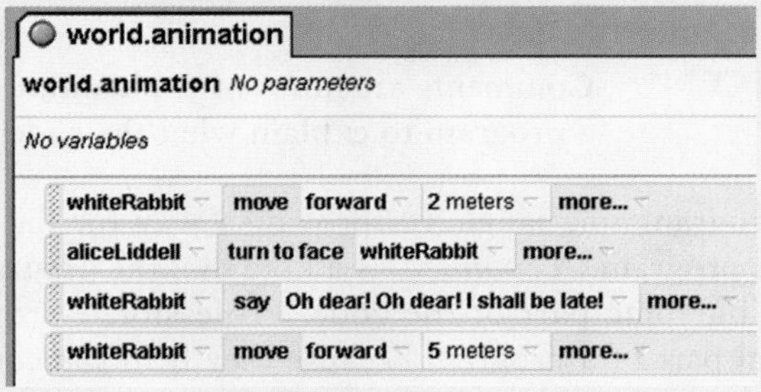

Step 9:   Play the world to test it, and carefully observe the actions that take place. Was the 2 meter distance that you specified for the first instruction suitable? How about the 5 meter distance that you specified for the last instruction? If not, adjust the method arguments and test the world again. Continue adjusting the method arguments and testing the world until you are satisfied with the results.

TIP: The process of repeatedly changing an instruction and testing it until you get the desired result is known as *trial and error*. Although you cannot use this approach to fix every error, it is sometimes effective.

Step 10:   Save the world. We will use this world again in the next tutorial.

Checkpoint

2.14   What are the steps in the program development cycle?

2.15   What are two tools that you can use to break down a problem into a series of steps?

2.16   What is a logical error?

2.17   When testing a method, what are three criteria that you should make sure the method meets?

2.4 Comments

CONCEPT: **Comments are notes of explanation that the programmer inserts into a program to explain what the code does.**

All programming languages provide a way for the programmer to insert comments into a program. A *comment* is a note that the programmer writes into a program, explaining some part of the code. Professional programmers consider comments a crucial part of a program because they help someone reading the program's code to understand the instructions.

Alice provides a special *comment tile* that you can use to insert comments into a method. The tile, which shows two forward slashes (//), appears at the bottom of the Method Editor, as shown in Figure 2-42. When you drag the comment tile into the Method Editor, it creates a default comment, as shown in Figure 2-43. Next you click on part of the comment that reads "No comment," and then you select *other...* from the menu that appears. This gives you an *Enter a String* dialog box. Anything that you type into the dialog box will appear in the tile.

Figure 2-42 The comment tile

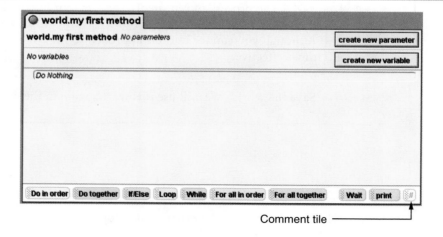

Comment tile ⎯⎯⎯⎯⎯⎯

Figure 2-43 A default comment

// No comment ¬

NOTE: The reason the comment tile shows two forward slashes (//) is that comments begin with two forward slashes in many traditional languages, including Java and C++.

When you play a world, Alice will ignore any comments that appear in the world's methods. Comments do not affect the execution of your world in any way, but they are important because they make your code more understandable. Tutorial 2-4 will give you some practice working with comments. In the tutorial you will insert comments into the world that you created in the previous tutorial.

Tutorial 2-4:
Inserting comments

Step 1: Open the world that you created in Tutorial 2-3.

Step 2: With the `world.animation` method open, drag the comment tile into the Method Editor and drop it at the top of the method, as shown in Figure 2-44.

Figure 2-44 Drag the comment tile to the top of the method

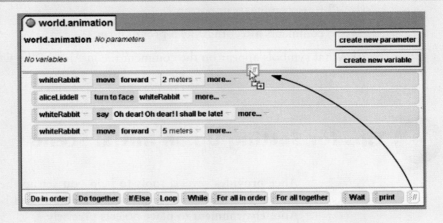

Step 3: The tile that you just placed in the Method Editor currently reads "No Comment." You want the tile to provide an explanation for the instruction that immediately follows it. Change the tile's contents to read *The White Rabbit moves to a position in front of Alice.*

Step 4: Insert additional comments that explain the other instructions in the method. Figure 2-45 shows comment examples, but feel free to word the comments in your own way.

Step 5: Save the world.

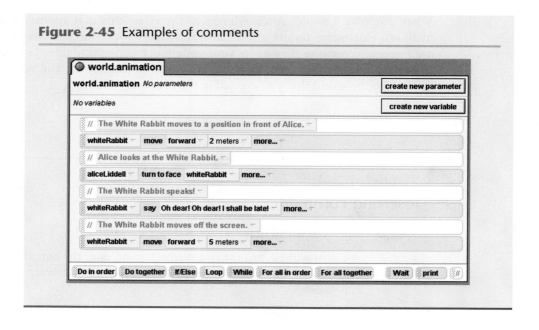

Figure 2-45 Examples of comments

 Checkpoint

2.18 Why are comments important?

2.19 Do comments affect the way a program runs?

2.20 What symbols appear on the comment tile in Alice? Why were these symbols chosen?

 2.5 **Tips for Setting Up an Initial Scene**

CONCEPT: Alice provides several tools to help you set up the initial scene in a world. For example, the primitive methods can be used within the Alice environment to place objects precisely.

So far, we haven't been concerned about precisely placing objects in our Alice worlds, or spacing objects with exact distances between them. Instead, we have used the mouse to move objects into positions that "look" right. Although this approach will work for many of the worlds you will develop, sometimes you will need more precise control over the positioning of objects in the initial scene. In this section we will look at various techniques that you can use in Alice to achieve more exact placement of objects.

Using Primitive Methods to Set Up a Scene

Earlier in this chapter you learned that all of the objects in an Alice world have primitive methods for performing basic actions. You can create instructions that call these methods when the world is played. These instructions create the animation.

You can also call an object's primitive methods from within the Alice environment while you are editing a scene. This causes the method to execute immediately. You can watch the method's action take place in the World View window. This is sometimes helpful for initially positioning objects and the camera.

You call an object's primitive methods in this way by right-clicking either the object in the World View window or the object's tile in the Object Tree. Then you select *methods* from the menu that appears. Another menu appears showing a list of methods that you can immediately execute in the World View window. Figure 2-46 shows an example of these menus.

Figure 2-46 Selecting a primitive method

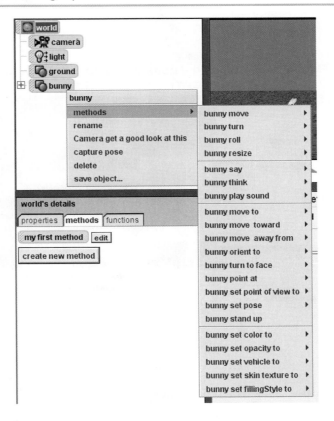

For example, Figure 2-47 shows a world with two instances of the Monkey class, named monkeySee (shown on the left) and monkeyDo (shown on the right). Suppose we want to turn the monkeys so they are facing each other. We can call each object's turn method to turn it so it is facing the other object. Figure 2-48 shows how we would call the monkeySee object's turn method, specifying left as the direction and ¼ revolution as the amount to turn. Then we can call the monkeyDo object's turn method, specifying right as the direction and ¼ revolution as the amount to turn. As a result, the objects will be turned, facing each other, as shown in Figure 2-49.

Figure 2-47 monkeySee and monkeyDo

Figure 2-48 Calling the monkeySee object's turn method

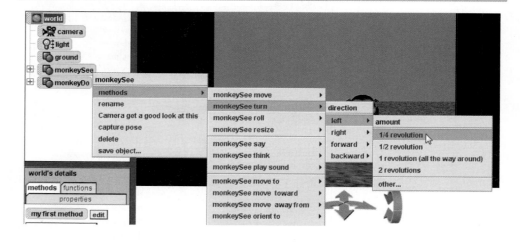

Figure 2-49 The objects facing each other

Using Primitive Methods to Position a Character's Arms

In Tutorial 1-5 in Chapter 1 you used the mouse mode buttons to position a character's arms hanging at her side. You can also use the primitive methods to accomplish this. For example, suppose Figure 2-50 shows a world with an instance of the `Cinderella` class (from the *People* collection). When the instance is created, both of the character's arms are extended. To position her arms so they are hanging at her side, you would perform the following steps:

1. Expand the `cinderella` object in the Object Tree and locate the `leftUpperArm` subpart object.
2. Right-click the `leftUpperArm` tile in the Object Tree, and then select *methods* from the menu that appears. As shown in Figure 2-51, select the `roll` method

Figure 2-50 An instance of the `Cinderella` class

Figure 2-51 Calling the `leftUpperArm` object's `roll` method

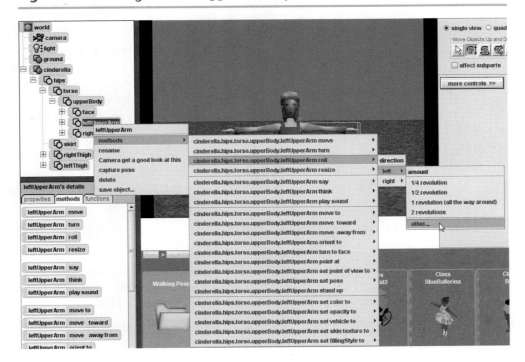

from the next menu that appears. Next, select *left* as the direction and *other...* as the amount. On the Custom Number keypad that appears, enter *0.2* and click the *OK* button. This positions the character's left arm.

3. Right-click the `rightUpperArm` tile in the Object Tree, and then select *methods* from the menu that appears. Select the `roll` method from the next menu that appears. Next, select *right* as the direction and *other...* as the amount. On the Custom Number keypad that appears, enter *0.2* and click the *OK* button. This positions the character's right arm. The character should now appear as shown in Figure 2-52.

In a similar fashion you can use the primitive methods to position the subparts of any object.

Figure 2-52 Both arms positioned

Moving an Object to the Center of the World

Suppose we want to position an object so its center point is at the center of the world, which is (0,0,0). Recall from Table 2-1 that the move to method moves an object to another object. When the method completes, both objects' center points will be in the same location. To move an object to the center of the world, we execute the object's move to method and specify *the entire world* as the method's argument.

For example, Figure 2-53 shows a world with a hare object. In the figure, the hare object's move to method is about to be executed, with the entire world specified as the method's argument. After the method executes, the hare object's center point will be located at the world's center point, which is (0,0,0).

Positioning Objects a Specified Distance Apart

You can use the primitive methods to move objects around so there is a precise distance between their center points. For example, suppose we want to position the teapot and plate objects (from the *Kitchen* collection) shown in Figure 2-54 so that there is exactly ½ meter between their center points. Here are the steps we can take:

- Move the teapot object so its center point is in the same location as the plate object's center point. We can do this by executing the teapot object's move to

Figure 2-53 Executing the move to method

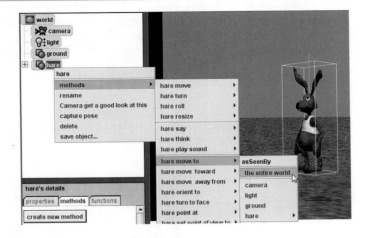

Figure 2-54 teapot and plate objects

method, selecting the plate for the asSeenBy argument. After the method executes, the center points of the teapot and plate objects will be located in the same position, as shown in Figure 2-55. (Alternatively, we can move the plate to the teapot. The idea is to position the objects so their center points are in the same location.)

Figure 2-55 Center points in the same location

- Move the `teapot` object ½ meter in the desired direction. We can do this by executing the `teapot` object's `move` method, specifying a direction, and ½ meter as the amount. Figure 2-56 shows the two objects after we moved the `teapot` object ½ meter to the right. (Alternatively, we could have moved the `plate` ½ meter to the left.)

Figure 2-56 The objects with ½ meter between their center points

Moving the Camera to an Object

When you right-click an object or an object tile in the Object Tree, one of the selections that you can make on the resulting menu is *Camera get a good look at this*, as shown in Figure 2-57. When you select this menu item, the camera will move to a position so the object is in plain view.

Figure 2-57 Moving the camera to an object

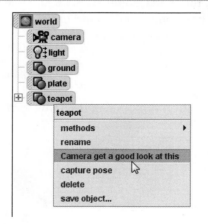

2.6 Executing Instructions Simultaneously

CONCEPT: The **Do together** structure can be used to execute a set of instructions at the same time.

Usually instructions are executed one after the other, in the order that they appear in a method. As a result, the actions that take place in the world happen one after the other. Sometimes, however, you want actions to take place simultaneously. To accomplish this you must be able to execute instructions simultaneously. In Alice this is possible by placing the desired instructions inside a Do together structure, which is simply a group of instructions that Alice executes at the same time instead of one after the other.

To create a Do together structure you drag the Do together tile (shown in Figure 2-58) into the Method Editor. When you drop the tile, a structure is created in which other instructions can be placed. Figure 2-59 shows an example of a Do together

Figure 2-58 The Do together tile

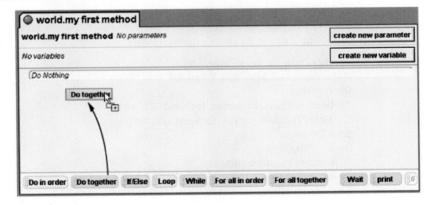

Figure 2-59 A completed Do together structure

structure that contains instructions. In the figure, assume that `monkeySee` and `monkeyDo` are both instances of the `Monkey` class. The `Monkey` class has a method named `monkeyJump`, which causes the object to jump. When the method shown in the figure executes, both the `monkeySee` and `monkeyDo` objects will execute their `monkeyJump` methods at the same time.

Tutorial 2-5 shows you how to create a method containing `Do together` structures.

VideoNote
Creating
Simultaneously
Executed
Instructions

Tutorial 2-5:
Creating simultaneously executed instructions

In this tutorial you will create an Alice world based on the following problem statement:

Two penguins (a brother and a sister) are facing each other, 2 meters apart. The brother penguin says "Hey Sis!" Then the sister penguin says "Hey Brother!" Then the two penguins simultaneously move ¹/₂ meter toward each other, and stop. Then they simultaneously jump into the air.

In the *Animals* collection you will find a `Penguin` class that you can use for this world. You will create two instances of the `Penguin` class, one named `brotherPenguin` and the other named `sisterPenguin`. The following is the pseudocode for the method you will write:

```
brotherPenguin says "Hey Sis!"
sisterPenguin says "Hey Brother!"
Do together
    brotherPenguin moves forward 1/2 meter
    sisterPenguin moves forward 1/2 meter
End Do together
Do together
    brotherPenguin jumps
    sisterPenguin jumps
End Do together
```

This pseudocode uses two `Do together` structures. In the pseudocode the line that reads Do together marks the beginning of the structure, and the line that reads End Do together marks the end of the structure. All of the statements that appear between these lines are inside the structure and are executed simultaneously.

Step 1:   Create a new Alice world, using the *snow* template.

Step 2:   Add an instance of the `Penguin` class to the world. Rename the object `brotherPenguin`.

Step 3:   Add another instance of the `Penguin` class to the world. Rename this object `sisterPenguin`.

Step 4:   Reposition the penguins so they are 2 meters apart (at their center points) and facing each other. Use the techniques that you read about earlier in this chapter, in the sections titled **Using Primitive Methods to Set Up a Scene Section** and **Positioning Objects a Specified Distance Apart** to reposition the objects. Figure 2-60 shows how the objects should appear after being repositioned.

Figure 2-60 The penguins repositioned

Step 5: Change the name of the method `world.my first method` to a more descriptive, camelCase name such as `world.animation`. Make sure the tile in the Event Editor is also updated so the method executes when the world starts.

Step 6: The instructions shown in Figure 2-61 correspond to the first two statements in the pseudocode. Create these instructions in the Method Editor.

Step 7: The next part of the algorithm is a `Do together` structure. Drag the `Do together` tile into the Method Editor and drop it below the existing instructions. The Method Editor should appear as shown in Figure 2-62.

Figure 2-61 The first two instructions

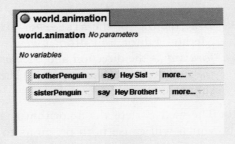

Figure 2-62 The first Do together structure placed

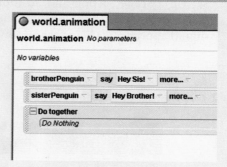

Step 8: This Do together structure should cause the two penguins to move forward $\frac{1}{2}$ meter simultaneously. First, drag the tile for the brotherPenguin object's move method into the Method Editor and drop it onto the Do together tile, as shown in Figure 2-63. Specify *forward* for the direction and $\frac{1}{2}$ *meter* for the amount. This should insert the tile for the method call inside the Do together tile.

Figure 2-63 Dropping a tile onto the Do together tile

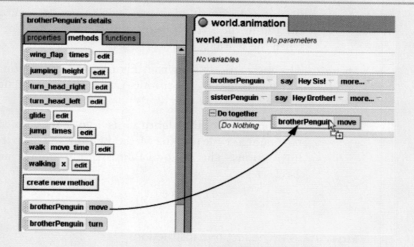

Step 9: Drag the tile for the sisterPenguin object's move method into the Method Editor and drop it *inside* the Do together tile. Specify *forward* as the direction and $\frac{1}{2}$ *meter* as the amount. This completes the first Do together structure. The Method Editor should appear as shown in Figure 2-64.

Step 10: The next part of the algorithm is another Do together structure, which will cause both penguins to jump simultaneously. Drag the

Figure 2-64 The first Do together structure completed

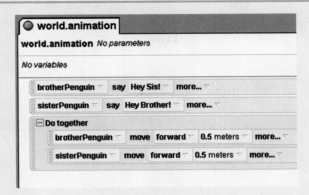

Do together tile into the Method Editor and drop it below the other instructions. Drag the tile for the brotherPenguin object's jump method into the editor and drop it onto the Do together tile that you just placed. Specify *1* for the times argument. Then drag the tile for the sisterPenguin object's jump method into the editor and drop it inside the same Do together tile. Specify *1* for the times argument. The Method Editor should appear as shown in Figure 2-65.

Step 11: Play the world to test it. If the actions are not performed correctly, compare the instructions in your method with the instructions shown in Figure 2-65. Correct any mistakes that you might have made and retest the world.

Figure 2-65 The method completed

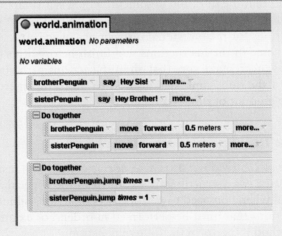

Step 12: Insert comments into the method that explain the different groups of instructions. You can insert your own comments, or insert those shown in Figure 2-66. When you are finished, save the world.

Figure 2-66 Comments inserted

Timing and the `Do together` Structure

Recall that the duration argument, which is available in the *more...* editing tag, specifies the amount of time that an instruction takes to execute. You can specify different durations for the individual instructions inside a `Do together` structure. This means that some of the instructions will finish before others when the structure executes. If you want to make sure that all of the actions performed by a `Do together` structure end at the same time, make sure that all of the instructions in the structure take the same amount of time to execute.

The `Do in order` Structure

Alice also provides a `Do in order` structure. The instructions that you place inside a `Do in order` structure are executed in the order that they appear. This structure is useful when you need to perform sets of actions simultaneously, and each set consists of actions that must be performed in order. For example, suppose you want to create a method to perform the following action:

Two penguins (brother and sister), turn their heads left, and then right, in unison.

The `Penguin` class has custom methods named `turn_head_right` and `turn_head_left`. At first you might think that simply inserting calls to these methods inside a `Do together` structure, as shown in Figure 2-67, will produce the actions you want. However, this method has a logical error. All four of the instructions inside the `Do together` structure will be executed together. (When you play the world, you will not see the penguins moving their heads at all because each penguin is moving its head to the right and to the left at the same time.)

To fix the error, we can insert the `Do in order` structures shown in Figure 2-68 inside the `Do together` structure. The `Do in order` structures will be executed at the same time, but the instructions inside them will take place in the order that they appear. As a result, the penguins will simultaneously move their heads to the right, and then to the left.

Figure 2-67 Method with a logical error

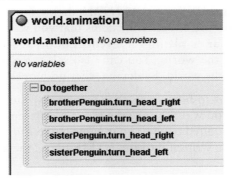

Figure 2-68 The corrected method

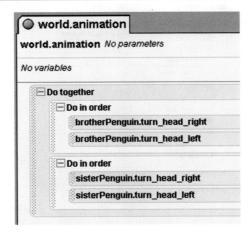

 **Checkpoint**

2.21 How do you cause instructions to execute simultaneously?

2.22 How can you cause some of the instructions in a Do together structure to be executed in order?

 2.7 Exporting Your Code for Printing

CONCEPT: **You can export the code that is part of your world to an HTML file that can be opened in a browser, printed, or submitted to your instructor.**

Alice allows you to export code to an HTML file. Then you can open the HTML file in a browser such as Internet Explorer or Netscape, and print the file or send it to your instructor.

To export a world's code, open the *File* menu and select *Export Code for Printing*. You will see the *Export to HTML* dialog box, as shown in Figure 2-69. The dialog box allows you to select the items that you wish to export. By default, the When the world starts tile (in the Events Editor) is selected, along with any methods that belong to the world. You can also select any custom methods that belong to the objects in the world. By default, they are not selected.

The *Export to* box shows the location on your system where the HTML file will be saved. If you want to save the file in a different location, click the *Browse...* button. You are required to enter your name in the *Author's name* box, which will cause your name to be written into the HTML file as the author of the world. When you click

Figure 2-69 Exported HTML

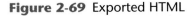

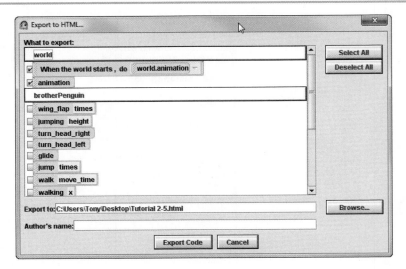

the *Export Code* button, the HTML file will be created. Figure 2-70 shows an example of the resulting HTML file.

Figure 2-70 Tutorial 2-5's code exported to HTML

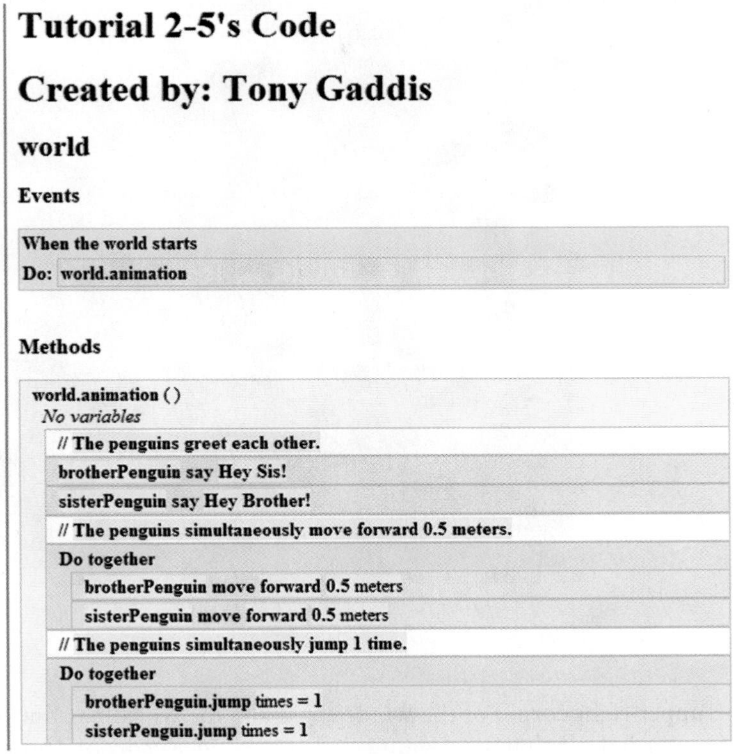

Tutorial 2-5's Code

Created by: Tony Gaddis

world

Events

When the world starts
Do: world.animation

Methods

world.animation ( )
No variables
// **The penguins greet each other.**
brotherPenguin say Hey Sis!
sisterPenguin say Hey Brother!
// **The penguins simultaneously move forward 0.5 meters.**
Do together
brotherPenguin move forward 0.5 meters
sisterPenguin move forward 0.5 meters
// **The penguins simultaneously jump 1 time.**
Do together
brotherPenguin.jump times = 1
sisterPenguin.jump times = 1

2.8 Exporting an Alice World to Video

> **CONCEPT:** An Alice world can be exported as a video, which makes it easy to share your worlds with others on the Internet.

After you've created an Alice world that you're particularly proud of, you'll probably want to show it off to your friends. An easy way to do that is to export the world as a video, and then upload the video to a Web site such as YouTube™, or a social networking site such as Facebook®.

To export an Alice world to video, open the *File* menu and select *Export Video...* You will first be required to save your world. Select a location on your system and click the *Save* button. Next you will see the world displayed in a video capture window, as shown in Figure 2-71. Click the *Record* button to start playing the world and recording it to video. (As the world is being recorded you will see a red dot displayed in the

Figure 2-71 The video capture window

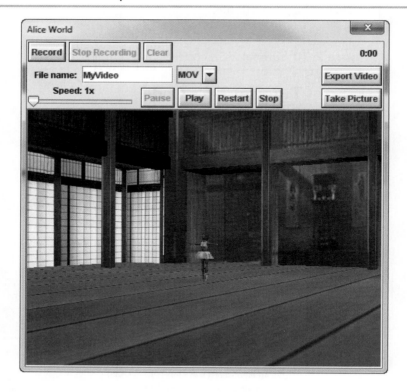

upper-right corner of the window.) When the world has finished playing, or you have recorded all that you want, click the *Stop Recording* button. The *File name* box shows the name that the video will be saved as. The default name is *MyVideo*. Change this to any name that you wish, and then click the *Export Video* button. The video will be created in the same location where you saved the Alice world.

 NOTE: Alice worlds are exported as QuickTime® (.MOV) videos.

Review Questions

Multiple Choice

1. This is what all objects in an Alice world have.
   a. Dummy methods
   b. Custom methods
   c. Primitive methods
   d. Noncallable methods

2. The primitive move method requires two arguments. What are they?

   a. The first argument is direction; the second argument is distance (or amount)

   b. The first argument is distance (or amount); the second argument is direction

   c. The first argument is the object to move; the second argument is the position to move to

   d. The first argument is the position to move to; the second argument is the speed at which to move

3. When programmers execute a method, this is what they commonly say they are doing.

   a. Debugging the method

   b. Tracing the method

   c. Designing the method

   d. Calling the method

4. This is a piece of information that a method requires in order for it to execute.

   a. Argument

   b. Call

   c. Instruction

   d. Property

5. This is a method that only objects of a specific class have.

   a. Primitive

   b. Custom

   c. Argument

   d. Copy

6. This is the naming convention in which monkeySee is written.

   a. PascalCase

   b. CodeCase

   c. camelCase

   d. CodeScript

7. This is the naming convention in which WhiteRabbit is written.

   a. PascalCase

   b. CodeCase

   c. camelCase

   d. CodeScript

8. This is the naming convention in which object names and method names should be written.

   a. PascalCase

   b. CodeCase

   c. camelCase

   d. CodeScript

9. This is the naming convention in which class names are written.

   a. PascalCase

   b. CodeCase

   c. camelCase

   d. CodeScript

10. This is a way of writing out the steps of an algorithm in English.

    a. Instruction diagramming
    b. Pseudocode
    c. Code talk
    d. Code scripting

11. This is a graphical diagram that depicts the steps in a diagram.

    a. Instruction diagramming
    b. Pseudocode
    c. Code chart
    d. Flowchart

12. This is a mistake that does not prevent the program from running, but causes it to produce incorrect results.

    a. Syntax error
    b. Instructional error
    c. Logical error
    d. Pseudocode error

13. This is a note of explanation that is inserted into a program.

    a. Comment
    b. Argument
    c. Codenote
    d. Editing tag

14. This is a structure that causes a group of instructions to be executed simultaneously.

    a. `Do together`
    b. `Do simultaneously`
    c. `Execute together`
    d. `Do in order`

15. This is a structure that causes a group of instructions to be executed in the order that they appear inside the structure.

    a. `Do together`
    b. `Do sequentially`
    c. `Execute in order`
    d. `Do in order`

Short Answer

1. You have a method that is referred to in dot notation as `world.my first method`. What is the name of the object that this method belongs to? What is the method name?

2. What happens when you call a method?

3. What is an argument? What are you doing when you are passing arguments?

4. When you add an object to a world, is it acceptable to give the object a nondescript name such as `object`?

5. What naming convention should you use for object names? For method names?

6. In what naming convention are class names written?

7. Can you think of two reasons for changing the name of the method `world.my first method`?

8. What are two tools that you can use to break down a problem into a series of steps?

9. What is a logical error?

10. Give two examples of the types of mistakes that can cause logical errors.

Exercises

VideoNote
Creating the Scene from *Alice's Adventures in Wonderland*

1. **Scene from *Alice's Adventures in Wonderland***

    In a scene from *Alice's Adventures in Wonderland*, Alice and the Cheshire Cat have the following conversation:

    Alice: "Would you tell me, please, which way I ought to go from here?"

    Cheshire Cat: "That depends a good deal on where you want to get to."

    Alice: "I don't much care where—"

    Cheshire Cat: "Then it doesn't matter which way you go."

    Recreate this scene, using the `say` method to make the objects talk to each other. When you test the world, make sure all of the speech bubbles are displayed long enough to read the dialog. If they are not, change the duration of the method calls so that the speech bubbles will be displayed longer.

2. **Animated Underwater World**

    This exercise assumes that you have completed the Underwater World exercise in Chapter 1 (Exercise 3). Animate the fish and the scuba diver that you placed in the world so that they swim across the screen slowly.

3. **Magic Cookies, Part 1**

    Create a world that has a plate of four cookies. (See the *Kitchen* collection.) The world should also have four empty plates. When the world is played, the cookies should magically levitate one by one, float to one of the empty plates, and then land on the empty plate. When finished, each of the four plates that were initially empty should have a cookie.

4. **Magic Cookies, Part 2**

    Modify the Magic Cookie world you created in Exercise 3 so that the cookies simultaneously float to and land on the empty plates.

5. **Animal and Bicycle**

    Create a world with a road (from the *City* collection) and a kid on a bicycle (use the `BikeKid2` class in the *People* gallery). Resize the road as necessary. The world should also have the animal of your choice from the *Animals* collection. The kid on the bicycle should move along from one end of the road to the other, turn around, and come back to the starting point. As the kid moves, the animal should move along beside him.

6. **Drag Racing**

Create a world with a road (from the *City* collection) and two cars (from the *Vehicles* collection). Resize the road as necessary to match the size of the cars. The cars should be lined up side by side at one end of the road, which is a drag strip. When the world is played, the cars should simultaneously move to the other end of the road and stop. Change the duration of the method call that you use to move one of the cars so it is faster than the other. Position the camera so you can see the cars as they approach the end of the drag strip.

7. **Playing Ball**

Create a world with two people and a ball (see the *Sports* collection for the ball). The two people should be facing each other with 10 meters between them. The ball should be at the feet of one person, who makes a kicking motion. The ball should move to the other person who kicks it back.

8. **Dancing**

Create a world with a room (from the *Environments* collection) and two people. Place the people inside the room, facing each other in a dancing pose. When the world plays, the two people should move together in such a way that they appear to be dancing.

9. **Apollo 15 Experiment**

During the Apollo 15 mission to the moon, astronaut David Scott performed an experiment to prove that Galileo was right when he said that any two objects dropped at the same time would land on the ground at the same time in the absence of air. Scott, standing on the surface of the moon, dropped a hammer and a feather and indeed both objects hit the ground simultaneously. (You can view a video of the experiment at http://www1.jsc.nasa.gov/er/seh/feather.html.)

Create an Alice world that recreates the experiment. You will find classes for the astronaut, lunar lander, and the moon's surface in the *Space* collection. You can find a class for the hammer in the *Objects* collection. Substitute any object of your choice for the feather.

10. **Tables, Chairs, and a Magic Broom**

Use classes from the *Kitchen* collection to create a kitchen with a table, four wooden chairs, and a broom. Initially set up the world as shown in the left image in Figure 2-72. When the world plays, the four chairs should simultaneously reposition as shown in the right image in Figure 2-72. Then the broom should

Figure 2-72 Arrangements of the chairs

sweep all the way around the table. After the broom finishes sweeping, the chairs should simultaneously move to their original positions.

11. **Movie Scene**

Recreate a scene from your favorite movie. Place the necessary characters, background scenery, and props in the world.

12. **Busy Beach**

Use the *Beach* collection to create a beach scene, populated with several people from the *Walking People* collection (in the local gallery, the *Walking People* collection is inside the *People* collection). When the world plays, all of the people should simultaneously walk along the beach.

13. **Exchange Problem Statements**

You and another student should write problem statements and then exchange them. Use your partner's problem statement to create an Alice world. (When writing your problem statement, be careful not to include objects or actions that are too advanced for your partner to complete.)

3 Variables, Functions, Math, and Strings

TOPICS

3.1 Variables

3.2 Using Functions

3.3 Creating Math Expressions

3.4 Working with Strings and Text

3.1 Variables

CONCEPT: A variable is a named storage location in the computer's memory.

Quite often programs need to store data in the computer's memory. For example, you've probably used programs that ask you to enter pieces of information. When you enter those pieces of information, the program stores them in memory. More than likely, you've also used programs that perform mathematical calculations. For example, when you make an online purchase, the Web site calculates the sales tax, shipping cost, and total of the purchase. When the program performs these calculations, it stores their results in the computer's memory. When a program stores information in memory, it does so with variables. A *variable* is a storage location that is represented by a name.

Like traditional programming languages, Alice allows you to use variables to store data. The following categories of variables are available in Alice:

- **Local Variables:** A *local variable* belongs to a specific method. A local variable can be used only by the instructions in the method that the variable belongs to. When a method stops executing, its local variables cease to exist in memory.
- **Parameter Variables:** A *parameter variable* is used to hold an argument that is passed to a method when the method is called.
- **Class-Level Variables:** A *class-level variable* is like a property that belongs to a specific object.
- **World-Level Variables:** A *world-level variable* is like a property that belongs to the world.

In this chapter we will discuss local variables. In Chapter 5, *Methods, Functions, and More about Variables*, we will discuss parameter variables, class-level variables, and world-level variables.

Creating a Local Variable

A local variable belongs to a specific method. Before you can use a local variable in a method, you have to create the variable. In the Method Editor you can create a local variable by clicking the *create new variable* button, as shown in Figure 3-1. This displays the *Create New Local Variable* dialog box, as shown in Figure 3-2. In the *Create New Local Variable* dialog box, you must specify three things: the variable's name, the variable's type, and the variable's initial value. Let's take a closer look at each of these required items.

Figure 3-1 The *create new variable* button

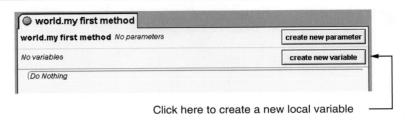

Click here to create a new local variable

Figure 3-2 The *Create New Local Variable* dialog box

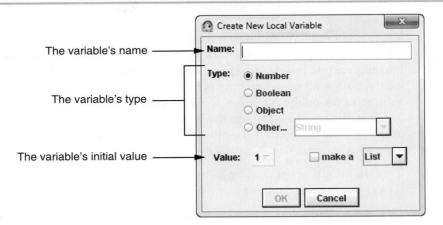

Variable Names

Each variable must have a name. When making up a name for a variable, you should follow these conventions:

- The name must be unique within the method; you cannot have two local variables with the same name in the same method

- The name should be meaningful, and should reflect the variable's purpose
- You should use the camelCase convention

Variable Types

When creating a variable you must specify the type of data that it can hold. The available types that you can select are as follows:

- **Number:** A Number variable can hold any number
- **Boolean:** A Boolean variable can hold either *true* or *false*
- **Object:** An Object variable can hold an object
- **Other:** Alice provides a list of other more specialized types, such as String, Color, Sound, and so forth

When you work with a variable in Alice, you can store only values of the variable's type in the variable.

Initial Value

A variable's initial value is the value that is initially stored in the variable when it is created.

Once you specify a name, type, and initial value in the *Create New Local Variable* dialog box, you click the *OK* button and a tile for the variable is created. Figure 3-3 shows an example of how a variable tile appears in the Method Editor. The section of the Method Editor that contains the variable tile is known as the *variable area*. This area shows tiles for all of the local variables in the method. In the figure, the name of the variable is `distance`. Notice that the tile shows a 123 symbol. This indicates that the variable's type is Number. The tile also shows the variable's initial value. In the figure, the `distance` variable's initial value is 1. If necessary, you can change the initial value by clicking the down arrow that appears next to it.

Programmers use the term *variable declaration* to describe a statement that creates a variable. Variable tiles, such as the one shown in Figure 3-3, can be thought of as variable declarations in Alice. Tutorial 3-1 leads you through the basics of creating and using a variable.

Figure 3-3 A variable tile

Variable area →

VideoNote
Creating
and Using a
Variable

Tutorial 3-1:
Creating and using a variable

Step 1: Create a new Alice world and add an instance of the `Penguin` class (found in the *Animals* collection). To follow the naming convention that we established in Chapter 2, change the name of the method `world.my first method` to `world.animation`.

Step 2: In the Method Editor, click the *create new variable* button. In the *Create New Local Variable* dialog box enter `numberJumps` as the variable's name, select *Number* as the variable's type, and enter *5* as the value. After you click the *OK* button you should see a tile for the variable appear in the Method Editor's variable area, as shown in Figure 3-4.

Figure 3-4 Variable tile

Step 3: Select the `penguin` object and drag the tile for the object's `jump` method into the Method Editor. This method causes the `penguin` object to jump, and it requires an argument specifying the number of times. From the menu that appears, select *expressions*, and then select `numberJumps`, as shown in Figure 3-5. This specifies that you are

Figure 3-5 Specifying `numberJumps` as an argument

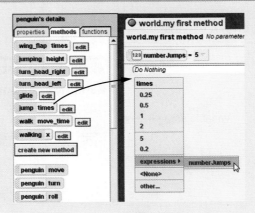

passing the `numberJumps` variable as an argument to the method. The completed instruction tile should appear as shown in Figure 3-6.

Figure 3-6 Completed instruction

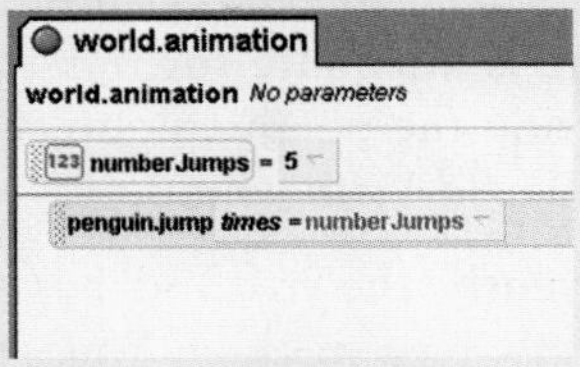

Step 4: Take a moment to think about the instruction that you just created. When you play the world, what do think will happen? Once you have an idea, play the world to see if you are right.

Were you right? The `penguin` should have jumped five times. When the `jump` method is called, the `numberJumps` variable is passed as an argument. When you pass a variable as an argument to a method, the value that is stored in the variable is actually passed. Because the `numberJumps` variable holds the value 5, the `penguin` object jumps five times.

Step 5: Save the world. You will use it again in the next tutorial.

Variable Assignment

When you create a variable, you give it an initial value. While the method is running, the initial value will remain in the variable until a different value is stored in the variable. In an Alice method, you can create *set instructions* that store different values in a variable. A set instruction simply "sets" a variable to a new value. In general programming terminology, an instruction that sets a variable to a value is often called a *variable assignment*.

To create a set instruction for a variable, you drag the variable tile and drop it into the Method Editor at the point where you want the set instruction to occur. A menu then appears, and you select *set value*. Another menu appears that allows you to specify the value you want to store in the variable. As a result, a set instruction is created.

In Tutorial 3-2 you will modify the world that you created in the previous tutorial by adding a set instruction that changes the value of the `numberJumps` variable, and then using the variable as an argument in a subsequent method call.

Tutorial 3-2:
Creating a set instruction for a variable

Step 1: Open the world that you created in Tutorial 3-1.

Step 2: Add another instance of the `Penguin` class (found in the *Animals* collection). Alice will automatically name the object `penguin2`. This name is adequate for our tutorial, so there is no need to change it. Position the `penguin2` object so both penguins are plainly in sight in the *World View* window.

Step 3: Currently the method has one instruction: a call to the `penguin` object's `jump` method. You will create a set instruction after the existing method call, storing the value 2 in the `numberJumps` variable. To do this, drag the tile for the `numberJumps` variable into the Method Editor and drop it below the existing method call tile. The menu shown in Figure 3-7 will appear. Select *set value*, and then select 2 from the next menu that appears. As a result, the instruction tile shown in Figure 3-8 should be created in the Method Editor.

Figure 3-7 Creating a set instruction

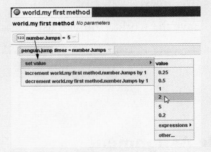

Figure 3-8 The set instruction

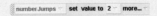

Step 4: Select the `penguin2` object and drag the tile for its `jump` method into the Method Editor, dropping it below the set instruction that you just created. A menu for the argument appears. Select *expressions*, and then select `numberJumps`. This specifies that you are passing the `numberJumps` variable as an argument to the method. The method should now appear as shown in Figure 3-9.

Figure 3-9 The completed method

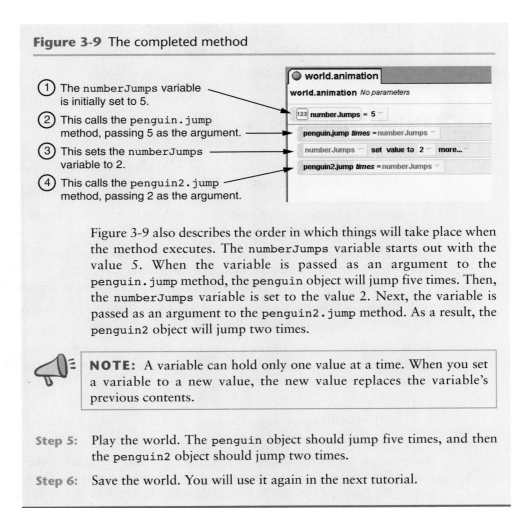

① The numberJumps variable is initially set to 5.

② This calls the penguin.jump method, passing 5 as the argument.

③ This sets the numberJumps variable to 2.

④ This calls the penguin2.jump method, passing 2 as the argument.

Figure 3-9 also describes the order in which things will take place when the method executes. The numberJumps variable starts out with the value 5. When the variable is passed as an argument to the penguin.jump method, the penguin object will jump five times. Then, the numberJumps variable is set to the value 2. Next, the variable is passed as an argument to the penguin2.jump method. As a result, the penguin2 object will jump two times.

NOTE: A variable can hold only one value at a time. When you set a variable to a new value, the new value replaces the variable's previous contents.

Step 5: Play the world. The penguin object should jump five times, and then the penguin2 object should jump two times.

Step 6: Save the world. You will use it again in the next tutorial.

Changing Properties with Set Instructions

In the first part of this section you learned how to create set instructions to change the values of variables. You can also create set instructions to change the values of properties. Follow these steps to create a set instruction for a property:

- Select the object with the property
- Drag the property's tile from the Details Panel into the Method Editor
- When you drop the tile, a menu will appear allowing you to select a value for the property

✔ Checkpoint

3.1 What is a variable?

3.2 What three things must you specify when creating a new variable?

3.3 In what part of the Method Editor do variable tiles appear?

3.4 What do the characters 123 appearing on a variable tile tell you?

3.5 How do you create a set instruction for a variable?

3.2 Using Functions

CONCEPT: A function is a special type of method that returns a value back to the instruction that called the function.

A *function* is a special type of method. Everything that you've learned about methods so far also applies to functions:

- A function is a set of instructions that cause some action to take place
- To execute a function you create an instruction that calls it
- Some functions require additional pieces of data known as arguments

The difference between a function and a method is that a function returns a value back to the instruction that called it, and a method does not.

In Alice, the `world` object has a set of primitive functions, and each object in an Alice world also has its own set of primitive functions. You can see a list of an object's functions by doing the following steps:

1. Select the object
2. In the Details Panel, select the *functions* tab to display a list of tiles representing the object's functions

For example, to see the `world` object's functions, you would select the `world` object's tile in the Object Tree and then select the *functions* tab in the Details Panel. As a result, the Details Panel will appear as shown in Figure 3-10. If you scroll down in the Details Panel, you will see that the list of functions is extensive. Also notice that the list is categorized. The categories are Boolean logic, math, random, string, ask user, mouse, time, advanced math, and other.

Figure 3-10 Functions displayed in the details panel

Using a Function to Ask the User for Input

The world object has three primitive functions that can be used to ask the user to input a value. If you select the world object and then scroll down in its list of functions until you see the *ask user* category, you will see the functions shown in Figure 3-11. Table 3-1 shows a summary of each of these functions.

Figure 3-11 The ask user functions

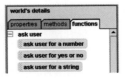

Table 3-1 The ask user functions

Function	Description
ask user for a number	When this function is called, it displays a dialog box in which the user must enter a number. The function returns the number that was entered. (An error will occur if the user enters non-numeric data, such as alphabetic characters.)
ask user for yes or no	When this function is called, it displays a dialog box with a *Yes* button and a *No* button. If the user clicks the *Yes* button, the function returns the Boolean value *true*. If the user clicks the *No* button, the function returns the Boolean value *false*. (We will discuss this function in greater detail in Chapter 4.)
ask user for a string	When this function is called, it displays a dialog box in which the user can enter a string. (A string is merely a series of characters. We will explore strings in greater detail later in this chapter.) The function returns the string that was entered.

Each of the functions described in Table 3-1 displays a message in a dialog box. When you call any of these functions you specify the message that you want to be displayed as an argument to the function.

In Alice, functions are not called the same way that methods are called. Because functions return a value, a function call must be placed in an instruction that does something with the value that is returned. For example, suppose we want to display a dialog box asking the user to enter a distance, and we want to store the value that is entered in a variable named distance. To accomplish this, we would write a set instruction that calls the `ask user for a number` function and stores the value that is returned in the `distance` variable. Figure 3-12 shows an example of such an instruction.

Figure 3-12 A set instruction with a function call

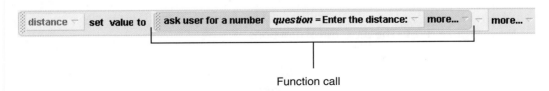

Function call

Compare this instruction with the set instruction shown in Figure 3-13, which sets the `distance` variable to the value 1. Notice that the instruction in Figure 3-12 does not set the `distance` variable to a specific value. Instead, it calls the `ask user for a number` function. As a result, the function will execute, and the value that is returned will be stored in the `distance` variable.

Figure 3-13 A set instruction with a specified value

In Tutorial 3-3 you will continue to modify the world from the previous tutorial. In this tutorial you will call the `ask user for a number` function to get the user to enter the number of times each penguin should jump.

VideoNote

Calling an ask user Function

Tutorial 3-3:
Calling an `ask user` function

Step 1: Open the world that you modified in Tutorial 3-2.

Step 2: Drag the tile for the `numberJumps` variable and drop it in the Method Editor above the call to the `penguin.jump` method, as shown in Figure 3-14. Select *set value* from the menu that appears, and then select *1* from the next menu that appears. As a result, a set instruction should be created, as shown in Figure 3-15.

Actually, it does not matter which value you select. When creating a set instruction, you have to select a value from the pop-up menu to store in the variable. In Step 2 you selected 1 as a temporary *placeholder* because you cannot select the `ask user for a number` function. In the next step you will replace the placeholder value with a function call.

Figure 3-14 Creating a set instruction

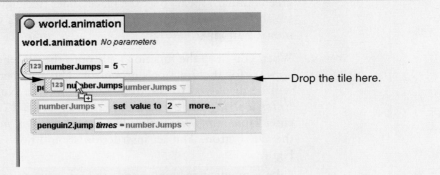

Figure 3-15 The set instruction

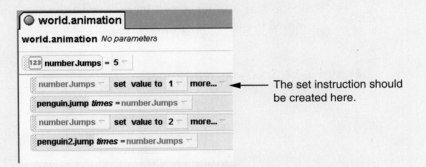

Step 3: Select the world object in the Object Tree, and then select the *functions* tab in the Details Panel. Scroll down until you find the ask user for a number function. As shown in Figure 3-16, drag the function's tile over the placeholder value that you specified for the set instruction in

Figure 3-16 Dropping the function's tile on the placeholder value

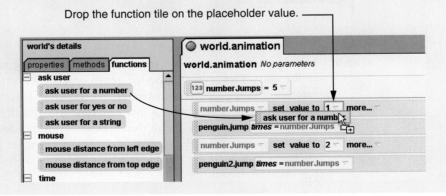

Step 2. Notice that as you drag the tile over the placeholder value, a green outline appears over the placeholder (see Figure 3-16). When you see the green outline appear, drop the function's tile by releasing the mouse button.

Step 4: When you drop the function's tile onto the placeholder value, a menu appears for the function's argument. The argument is a message that will be displayed to the user. Select *other....* Next you will see the *Enter a string* dialog box shown in Figure 3-17. In the dialog box enter *How many times should the first penguin jump?* and then click the *OK* button. The set instruction should now appear as shown in Figure 3-18.

Take a moment to think about the set instruction that you just completed, and what it will do when you play the world. The `ask user for a number` function will be called, which will display a dialog box with the message *How many times should the first penguin jump?* The value that is entered will be returned from the function and will be stored in the `numJumps` variable.

Figure 3-17 Specifying a message

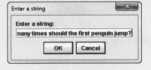

Figure 3-18 The completed set instruction

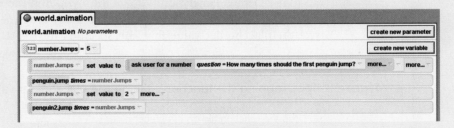

Step 5: In the previous tutorial you inserted a set instruction just before the call to the `penguin2.jump` method. The set instruction currently stored the number 2 in the `numJumps` variable. As shown in Figure 3-19, drag the tile for the `ask user for a number` function and drop it onto the 2. Select *other...* from the menu that appears. In the *Enter a string* dialog box enter *How many times should the second penguin jump?* and then click the *OK* button. The method should now appear as shown in Figure 3-20.

Figure 3-19 Modify the second set instruction

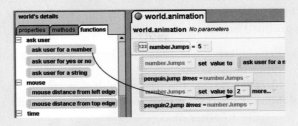

Figure 3-20 The completed method

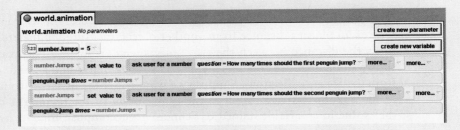

Step 6: Think about the completed method. When you play the world, what do you think will happen? Once you have an idea, play the world to see if you are right.

First, you should see a dialog box like the one shown in Figure 3-21. Enter a number and click the *OK* button. You should see the `penguin` object jump the number of times that you entered. Next you should see a similar dialog box asking *How many times should the second penguin jump?* Enter a number and click the *OK* button. You should then see the `penguin2` object jump the number of times that you entered.

Figure 3-21 The first dialog box

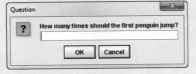

 TIP: When you are entering a value into the dialog box that is displayed by the `ask user for a number` function, you must enter a number. If you enter non-numeric characters an error will occur.

Step 7: Save the world.

Primitive Object Functions

Each object in an Alice world has a set of primitive functions. If you select an object and then select the *functions* tab in the Details Panel you will see that the functions are grouped into the following categories:

- **Proximity:** These functions return values indicating the object's proximity to other objects
- **Size:** These functions return values pertaining to the size of the object
- **Spatial relation:** These functions return values indicating the object's position relative to other objects
- **Point of view:** These functions return values pertaining to the object's point of view
- **Other:** These functions return miscellaneous values

One of the proximity functions is named `distance to`. The `distance to` function returns an object's distance from another object, measured in meters. (Precisely, it returns the distance between the two objects' center points.) For example, the world shown in Figure 3-22 contains a `baseballGlove` object and a `baseball` object (both from the *Sports* collection). Suppose we want to get the distance from the center point of the `baseballGlove` object to the center point of the `baseball` object, and store that value in a variable named `distance`. To accomplish this, we would write a set instruction that calls the `baseballGlove.distance to` function, passing the `baseball` object as an argument, and stores the value that is returned in the `distance` variable. Figure 3-23 shows an example of such an instruction.

Figure 3-22 `baseballGlove` and `baseball` objects

Figure 3-23 Set instruction

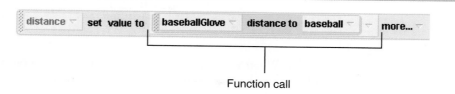

Function call

In Tutorial 3-4, you will get to practice using the `distance to` function. You will build an Alice world where a penguin will always be able to find a hole in the ice and jump into it, regardless of where you place the hole!

Tutorial 3-4:
Using a proximity function

In this tutorial we will create a world for the following problem statement:

> A *penguin turns to face a hole in the ice, regardless of where the hole is located. The penguin should then walk to the center of the hole and jump into it, disappearing below the surface of the ice.*

The following pseudocode outlines the algorithm:

> penguin turns to face the hole
> penguin walks the distance to the center of the hole
> penguin falls down into the hole

Step 1: Start a new Alice world using the *snow* template. Insert an instance of the `Penguin` class (from the *Animals* collection), and an instance of the `Circle` class (from the *Shapes* collection). Select the `circle` object, then select the *properties* tab in the Details Panel, and then change the color property to *black*.

Figure 3-24 shows an example of how the world might look, although you may place the `penguin` and `circle` objects anywhere you wish. The black circle represents a hole in the ice.

Figure 3-24 A penguin and a hole in the ice

Step 2: First you want the penguin to turn to face the hole in the ice. Select the `penguin` object and drag the tile for its `turn to face` method into the Method Editor. When you drop the tile into the editor a menu will appear for the method's argument, which is the object that you want the `penguin` to turn toward. Select `circle` from the menu. As a result, the instruction tile shown in Figure 3-25 should appear in the Method Editor.

Figure 3-25 Completed instruction tile

> penguin turn to face circle more...

Step 3: Next you want the `penguin` object to walk to the hole in the ice. The `Penguin` class has a custom method named `walking` that causes the object to walk a certain distance. (The tile for the method reads `walking x`. The `x` represents an argument that you have to specify, which is the distance that you want the object to walk.) Drag the tile for the `walking` method into the Method Editor and drop it below the instruction tile that you just created in Step 2.

As an argument you specify the distance that the object is to walk. Simply select *1* as the argument. This value will be a placeholder that we will replace with a function call. Your method should now contain the instructions shown in Figure 3-26.

Figure 3-26 Two instruction tiles

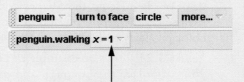

The argument you specified here is a placeholder.
You will replace this value with a function call.

Step 4: The instruction that you created in Step 3 will cause the `penguin` object to walk a distance of 1 meter. We don't really want the penguin to walk 1 meter. Instead we want the `penguin` object to walk the distance from itself to the center of the `circle` object. To accomplish this we will replace the argument, 1, with a call to the `penguin.distance to` function.

With the `penguin` object still selected, click the *functions* tab in the Details Panel. Drag the tile for the `distance to` function from the *proximity* category into the Method Editor and drop it onto the argument for the `penguin.walking` method, as shown in Figure 3-27.

Figure 3-27 Drag the `distance to` function onto the placeholder argument

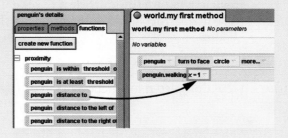

A menu will appear allowing you to select an argument for the distance to function. Select circle. The instructions in your method should appear as shown in Figure 3-28.

Figure 3-28 The instructions so far

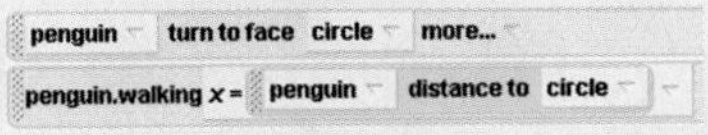

Before going any further, let's take a closer look at the instruction you just created. The instruction calls the penguin.walking method. This method requires an argument—the distance you want the object to walk. Instead of giving a specific number for the argument, you have called the penguin.distance to function to get the distance from the penguin to the circle. The function's return value will be passed as an argument to the penguin.walking method. As a result, the penguin will walk the distance from its starting position to the center of the circle.

Step 5: The last action to perform is to make the penguin fall into the hole. You can accomplish that by moving the penguin down until it disappears underneath the ground. Drag the tile for the penguin object's move method into the Method Editor and drop it below the instructions you have already placed there. For the direction, select *down*, and for the amount select *5 meters*. The instructions in the method should now appear as shown in Figure 3-29.

Figure 3-29 The completed method

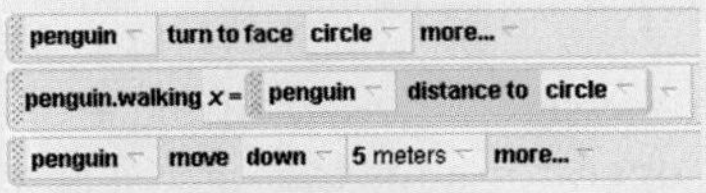

Step 6: Play the world to test it. You should see the penguin object turn to face the circle, walk to its center, and then fall below the ground surface. After the penguin falls through the hole click the *Stop* button to close the *World Running...* window.

Step 7: Modify the world by moving the circle, or the penguin, or both. Then play the world again. Notice that regardless of where you move the objects to, the penguin always finds the hole, walks to it, and falls through it.

Step 8: Save the world.

Checkpoint

3.6 What makes a function different from a method?

3.7 How do you see a list of the functions that an object has?

3.8 What are the three primitive world functions that ask the user to input a value?

3.9 What does the primitive `distance to` function do?

 3.3 Creating Math Expressions

CONCEPT: Alice provides operators that you can use to create math expressions.

Most real-world algorithms require calculations to be performed. A programmer's tools for performing calculations are *math operators*. Most programming languages provide the operators shown in Table 3-2.

Table 3-2 Math operators

Operator	Description
+	Addition
−	Subtraction
*	Multiplication
/	Division

Programmers use the operators shown in Table 3-2 to create math expressions. A *math expression* performs a calculation and returns a value. The following is an example of a simple math expression:

```
12 + 2
```

The values on the right and left of the + operator are called *operands*. These are values that the + operator adds together. The value that is returned from this expression is 14.

Variables may also be used in a math expression. For example, suppose we have two variables named `payRate` and `hoursWorked`. The following math expression uses the * operator to multiply the value in the `payRate` variable by the value in the `hoursWorked` variable:

```
payRate * hoursWorked
```

Alice also provides the math operators shown in Table 3-2. In Alice, you use the menu system to build math expressions. For example, look at the Alice method shown in Figure 3-30. The method has two variables: `diameter` and `radius`. Both of these variables are of the Number type. The set instruction shown in the method calls the `ask user for a number` function, asking the user to enter the diameter of a circle. The value that is entered is stored in the `diameter` variable.

Figure 3-30 A method

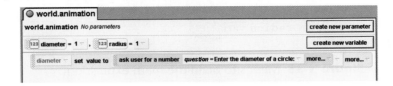

Suppose that after the user enters the diameter of a circle we want to calculate the radius of the circle. The formula for the calculation is as follows:

$$radius = diameter / 2$$

To calculate the radius, we divide the diameter by 2 and store the result in the `radius` variable. To do this, we create a set instruction by dragging the tile for the `radius` variable into the Method Editor. A menu appears, and we select *set value*, and then we select *expressions*. When we select expressions, another menu appears listing all of the variables in the method. From that menu we select `diameter`. The series of menu selections is shown in Figure 3-31.

Figure 3-31 Menus for the set instruction

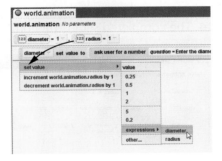

As a result, the set instruction shown in Figure 3-32 is created. We aren't finished yet, however. We want to set the `radius` variable to the value of `diameter / 2`, so we need to keep building the math expression. To do this, we click the down arrow that is next to the word `diameter` in the set instruction, as shown in Figure 3-32.

Figure 3-32 The set instruction

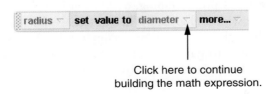

Click here to continue
building the math expression.

From the menu that appears, we select *math*, then we select *diameter /*, and then we select *2*. These menu selections are shown in Figure 3-33. As a result, the set instruction will appear as shown in Figure 3-34. Now the set instruction stores the correct value in the `radius` variable.

Figure 3-33 Menus to build the math expression

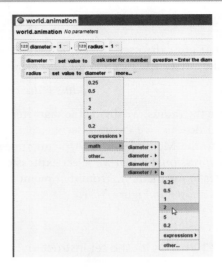

Figure 3-34 The completed set instruction

Tutorial 3-5 gives you more extensive practice building math expressions. In the tutorial you will create a math expression to calculate the distance that an object should move.

VideoNote

Using Math to Avoid Collisions

Tutorial 3-5:
Using math to avoid collisions

In graphics programming, a *collision* is when two graphical objects come into contact with each other. When objects collide, nothing prevents them from passing through each other, or occupying the same space. It is unrealistic, however, for objects to pass through each other. Usually you want to prevent collisions from taking place. In this tutorial you will create an Alice world in which one object moves to another object, but does not collide with it. Here is the problem statement:

> *A snowman and a snowWoman are standing, facing in the same direction. The snowman turns to face the snowWoman, and then the snowWoman turns to face the snowman. The snowman moves to the snowWoman, and stops just in front of her. He engages her in a conversation.*

The following pseudocode is our first attempt to develop an algorithm for this problem:

First Version of Pseudocode

```
snowman turns to face snowWoman
snowWoman turns to face snowman
snowman moves forward the distance between himself and the snowWoman
snowman says "Come here often?"
snowWoman says "No, it's my first time."
```

Although this algorithm outlines the general steps that we want to perform, it leaves out an important detail: how do we prevent the snowman from colliding with the snowWoman? In the pseudocode's third line we can use the snowman's `distance to` function to get the distance from the snowman to the snowWoman. Perhaps we could create the instruction shown in Figure 3-35. What do you think this instruction will do?

Figure 3-35 Possible instruction

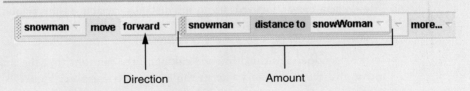

The instruction in Figure 3-35 moves the snowman object forward. The amount of the move is the value returned from the `distance to` function. However, the `distance to` function returns the distance between the two objects' center points. This instruction will cause the snowman object to collide with the snowWoman object. In fact, the two objects' center points will be in the same location after this instruction executes.

If we want the snowman to move to the snowWoman without colliding, then we must calculate the correct amount of the move. Figure 3-36 shows two key distances that we can use in our calculation: the distance between the centers of the two objects and the depth of the snowWoman object. If we subtract the snowWoman object's depth from the distance between the center points, we should have a reasonably accurate distance. We can use the snowWoman's depth function to get the object's depth. (In the list of primitive functions you will find the depth function in the size category.)

Figure 3-36 Key distances

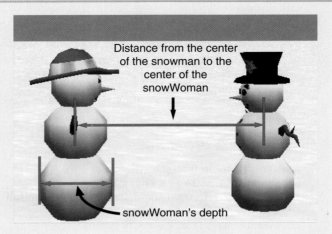

Distance from the center of the snowman to the center of the snowWoman

snowWoman's depth

The following pseudocode represents our second attempt to develop the algorithm. In this pseudocode we use a variable named `distance`.

Second Version of Pseudocode

```
snowman turns to face snowWoman
snowWoman turns to face snowman
set the distance variable to the distance from the snowman to the snowWoman
    minus the snowWoman's depth
snowman moves forward, using the distance variable as the amount
snowman says "Come here often?"
snowWoman says "No, it's my first time."
```

In the pseudocode's third line we calculate the amount that the `snowman` should move and we store the value in the `distance` variable. Figure 3-37 shows the actual Alice instruction for this step.

Figure 3-37 Set instruction for the `distance` variable

Now that we know how to approach the problem, let's start building the world. The following steps will guide you through the process.

Step 1: Start a new Alice world using the *snow* template. Add an instance of the `Snowman` class and an instance of the `SnowWoman` class (both from the *People* collection) to the world. Position the objects as shown in Figure 3-38.

Figure 3-38 Initial setup

Step 2: Rename the method `my first method` to `animation` (or any other camelCase name that you prefer). Create a variable named `distance`. The variable's type should be Number. You can select *1* as the variable's value.

Step 3: Create the instructions and comments shown in Figure 3-39.

Figure 3-39 Initial instructions

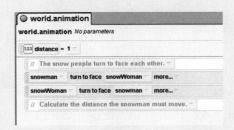

Step 4: Now you will begin to create the set instruction that you saw in Figure 3-37. Drag the tile for the `distance` variable into the Method Editor and drop it below the last instruction. Select *set value* from the menu that appears, and then select *1*. This will be a placeholder.

Step 5: Next you will replace the placeholder value with a call to the `snowman.distance to` function. Select the `snowman` object, and then drag the tile for the `distance to` function and drop it on top of the 1 placeholder in the set instruction. When you drop the tile a menu will appear for the function's argument. Select `snowWoman`, and then select the entire `snowWoman`. The set instruction should now appear as shown in Figure 3-40.

Figure 3-40 The set instruction, part 2

Step 6: Next you will begin the math expression. Click the down-arrow shown in Figure 3-41. As shown in the figure, select *math* from the menu, then select *snowman distance to snowWoman −*, and then select *1*. The value 1 is a placeholder. When you complete this the instruction should appear as shown in Figure 3-42.

Figure 3-41 Next step in the math expression

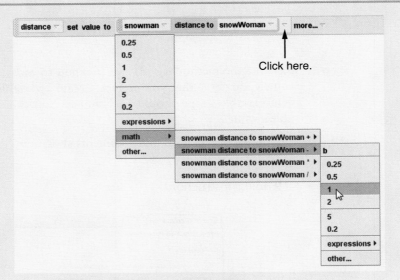

Figure 3-42 The set instruction, part 3

Step 7: Now you will complete the math expression. Select the snowWoman object, and then locate the tile for the snowWoman's depth function. (You will find the depth function in the *size* category of functions.) Drag the tile for the depth function into the Method Editor and drop it on top of the 1 placeholder that you created in Step 6. The instruction should now appear as shown in Figure 3-43. After this instruction executes, the distance variable will hold the distance that you want the snowman object to move.

Figure 3-43 The completed instruction

Step 8: Below the instruction that you just created add a comment that reads:

`// Move the snowman to the snowWoman.`

Then, drag the tile for the `snowman.move` method into the Method Editor and drop it below the comment that you just created. As shown in Figure 3-44, specify *forward* as the direction and select the `distance` variable as the amount. This should create the instruction shown in Figure 3-45.

Figure 3-44 Calling the `snowman.move` method

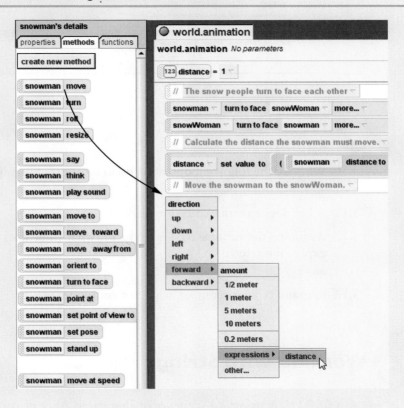

Figure 3-45 The completed call to the `snowman.move` method

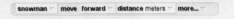

Step 9: Complete the method by creating the last three tiles shown in Figure 3-46.

Step 10: Save the world and play it. You should see the snowman walk very close to the snowWoman, but not collide with her.

Figure 3-46 The completed method

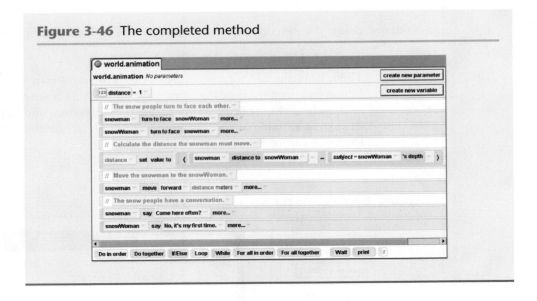

 Checkpoint

3.10 What do the following operators do in most programming languages?

+ - * /

3.11 What does a math expression do?

3.12 Assuming the variable days is set to *14*, what value does the following expression return?

days / 2

3.13 In graphics programming, what is a collision?

 3.4 Working with Strings and Text

CONCEPT: A string is a sequence of characters. Alice provides numerous features for working with strings and text.

A *string* is a sequence of characters. In a computer program, strings are used to represent things such as names, addresses, warning messages, and so forth. In this section you will learn a variety of techniques for working with strings in Alice.

Asking the User to Enter a String

In Section 3.2 we mentioned the world object's ask user for a string function. When this function is called, it displays a dialog box in which the user can enter a string. The function returns the string that was entered. For example, Figure 3-47

Figure 3-47 *RepeatingNerd* world

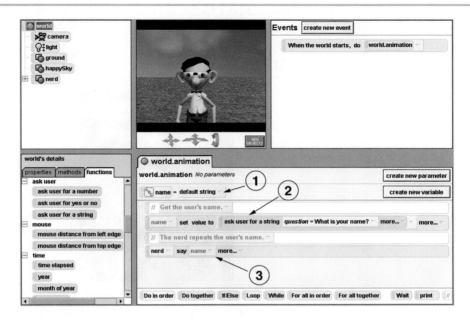

shows the *RepeatingNerd* world, which is one of the example worlds on the Student CD. The figure points out three of the tiles in the method:

① This tile creates the `name` variable. The variable's type is String and its initial value is default string.

② This tile is a set instruction. It calls the `ask user for a string` function, which asks the user "What is your name?" The user's input is stored in the `name` variable.

③ This tile calls the `nerd` object's `say` method, passing the `name` variable as the argument. When this instruction executes, the `nerd` object will say the contents of the `name` variable.

In a nutshell, when you play this world a dialog box appears asking you *What is your name?* You enter your name and click the *OK* button. The `Nerd` object then says your name in a speech bubble.

Joining Strings

Sometimes it is necessary to join two strings into one string. For example, if we join the strings "Good" and "Morning" we get the string "Good Morning". This type of operation is commonly called *string concatenation*. In Alice you join two strings with the world object's `a joined with b` function, where `a` and `b` are strings that you pass as arguments. The function does not change the strings `a` or `b`, but it returns a string that is the combination of `a` and `b`. (The `a joined with b` function is in the `world` object's *string* category of functions.)

To demonstrate, look at the *GreetingNerd* world, which is one of the example worlds on the Student CD. This world is a modified version of the *RepeatingNerd* world shown previously. In the *GreetingNerd* world, you enter your name in a dialog box, and then the nerd object says "Hello" followed by your name. For example, Figure 3-48 shows how the nerd responds if you enter *Christopher* in the dialog box.

Figure 3-48 Playing the *GreetingNerd* world

Figure 3-49 shows the method in the world. Notice that in the last tile, the string "Hello" is joined with the name variable, and the result is passed as an argument to the nerd object's say method.

Figure 3-49 Method in the *GreetingNerd* world

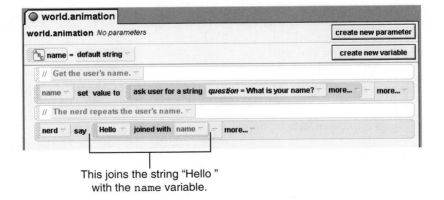

This joins the string "Hello " with the name variable.

Converting a Non-String to a String

Sometimes it is necessary to convert a non-string object to a string. For example, suppose you want to display the contents of a Number variable in a speech bubble or a thought bubble. The primitive methods say and think accept only string arguments, however, so you cannot directly pass a Number variable to either of these methods. Instead, you must use the world object's what as a string function to convert the variable to a string. (You can find the function in the string category.) You pass the variable as the *what* argument and the function returns a string containing its value. In Tutorial 3-6 you will use this function as you modify an example world on the Student CD.

Tutorial 3-6:
Converting a Number variable to a string

In this tutorial you will complete the `AccountantBob` world, which is on the Student CD. Here is the problem statement for the world:

A dialog box should appear asking the user to enter his or her annual salary. The amount of taxes, which is 25 percent of the salary, is then calculated. The accountant, Bob, tells the user the amount of the taxes.

The following pseudocode outlines the algorithm:

Ask the user "What is your annual salary?" and store the input in the salary variable.
Set the taxes variable to salary multiplied by 0.25.
Bob says the amount in the taxes variable.

Step 1: Copy the `AccountantBob` world from the Student CD and open it. (It is in the file *AccountantBob.a2w*.) As shown in Figure 3-50, the `salary` and `taxes` variables have already been created, as well as instructions for the first two steps in the pseudocode algorithm.

Figure 3-50 `AccountantBob` world

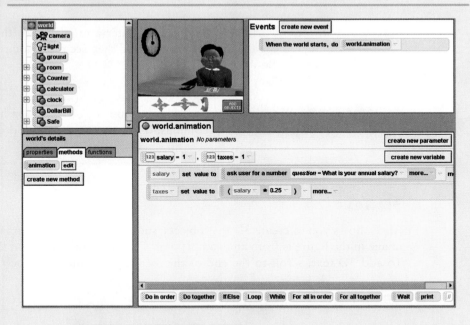

Step 2: You will complete the method by creating the instruction for the last step in the algorithm. Select the `bob` object and drag the tile for the `say` method into the Method Editor. Drop the tile below the last instruction in the editor. When you drop the tile a menu appears allowing you to specify the argument. You only want to create a placeholder, so select *hello* from the menu.

Step 3: Now you will replace the hello argument with a call to the `what as a string` function, and you will pass the `taxes` variable to the function. Select the `world` object in the Object Tree, and in the Details Panel, scroll down to the *string* category of functions. Drag the tile for the `what as a string` function into the Method Editor. Drop the tile on top of the *hello* argument in the last instruction that you created.

A menu appears for the *what* argument. Select *expressions*, and then select *taxes*. The method should now appear as shown in Figure 3-51. Take a moment to think about the instruction that you created. The instruction calls the `bob` object's `say` method. The argument that is passed to the `say` method is the `taxes` variable converted to a string.

Figure 3-51 The completed method

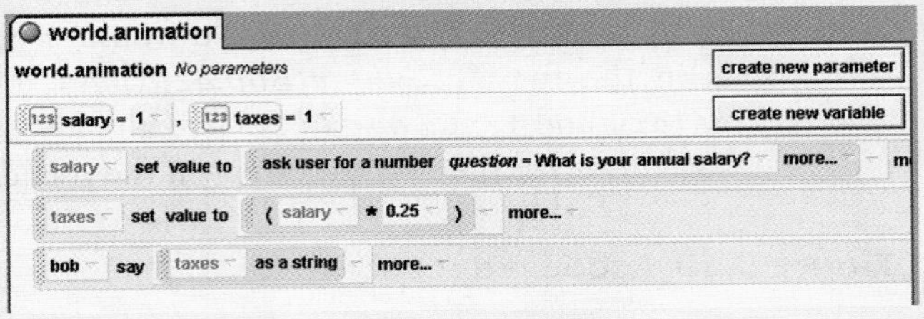

world.animation
world.animation *No parameters* — create new parameter
`123` salary = 1 , `123` taxes = 1 — create new variable
salary ▾ set value to — ask user for a number *question* = What is your annual salary? — more... ▾ — m
taxes ▾ set value to — (salary ▾ * 0.25 ▾) ▾ — more...
bob ▾ say — taxes ▾ as a string ▾ — more...

Step 4: Save the world and then play it. Enter a number into the dialog box and click the *OK* button. You should then see the amount of taxes displayed in Bob's speech bubble.

 TIP: When entering a dollar amount into the dialog box, do not enter a dollar sign or commas. If you do, an error will occur.

3D Text

Alice allows you to create 3D text objects, such as the one shown in Figure 3-52. The image in the figure is from an example world named *Hollywood*, on the Student CD. To add 3D text, scroll to the end of the local gallery and click the *Create 3D Text*

Figure 3-52 3D text

thumbnail, shown in Figure 3-53. This brings up the *Add 3D Text* dialog box shown in Figure 3-54. In the dialog box you enter the text that you want to appear in 3D and select the desired font.

When you create a 3D text object, a tile for the object will appear in the Object Tree. The name of the object will be the same as the object's text. For example, the 3D text object shown in Figure 3-52 appears as an object named HOLLYWOOD in the Object Tree. This is shown in Figure 3-55.

Figure 3-53 Create 3D text thumbnail

Figure 3-54 *Add 3D Text* dialog box

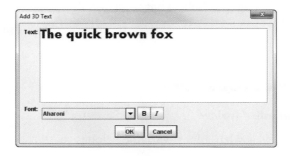

Figure 3-55 The 3D text object in the Object Tree

A 3D text object has four unique properties as follows:

- `text`: This property contains the text that is displayed in the object. If you change this property, the text that is displayed by the object will change accordingly. The name of the object will not change, however.
- `font`: This property specifies the text object's font.
- `extrusion`: This property specifies the depth of the 3D text object. The larger the value specified here, the thicker the text appears.
- `curvature`: This property controls the smoothness of curved characters. Higher values cause the characters to appear smoother, and lower values cause the characters to appear less smooth.

 ## Checkpoint

3.14 What is a string?

3.15 What world function do you use to get a string from the user?

3.16 What is string concatenation?

3.17 If you want to display the contents of a Number variable in a speech or thought bubble, what must you do?

Review Questions

Multiple Choice

1. This is what a local variable belongs to.

   a. An object
   b. A method
   c. A class
   d. A property

2. What is meant when the characters 123 appear on a variable tile?

   a. The variable holds the value 123
   b. The variable's name is 123
   c. The variable is the third in the method
   d. The variable's type is Number

3. This type of instruction changes the contents of a variable.

   a. Primitive method call
   b. Write instruction
   c. Copy instruction
   d. Set instruction

4. This is what an instruction that sets a variable to a value is often called.

   a. A variable assignment
   b. A variable modification
   c. A variable duplication
   d. A variable mutation

5. This is the difference between a method and a function.

   a. You cannot pass an argument to a function
   b. You must pass an argument to a function
   c. A function returns a value back to the instruction that called the function
   d. Functions are not called, but methods are

6. This `world` function allows the user to enter a number, and returns that number.

   a. `get number`
   b. `ask user for a number`
   c. `input number`
   d. `enter a number`

7. This primitive function returns the distance from one object's center point to another object's center point.

   a. `distance to center`
   b. `distance from`
   c. `distance to`
   d. `distance between`

8. This symbol is used as the multiplication operator in most programming languages.

   a. `x`
   b. `&`
   c. `*`
   d. `.`

9. This `world` function allows the user to enter a string, and returns that string.

   a. `get string`
   b. `ask user for a string`
   c. `input string`
   d. `enter a string`

10. This is what joining two strings is also known as.

   a. String concatenation
   b. String splicing
   c. String grafting
   d. String building

11. What `world` function do you use to join two strings?

   a. The `a concatenated with b` function
   b. The `a appended to b` function
   c. The `a plus b` function
   d. The `a joined with b` function

12. What `world` function do you use to convert a non-string object to a string?

   a. The `what as a string` function
   b. The `convert what to a string` function
   c. The `object to string` function
   d. The `what becomes a string` function

Short Answer

1. What is a variable?

2. How do you write an instruction to change the value of a property?

3. In Alice, are functions called in the same way as methods, or is there a difference? Explain.

4. What is a string?

5. Assume that an Alice world has an object named hampster. When the method shown in Figure 3-56 executes, what will the hampster object say?

6. Assume again that an Alice world has an object named hampster. When the method shown in Figure 3-57 executes, what will the hampster object say?

Figure 3-56 Method

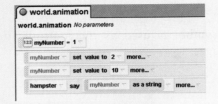

Figure 3-57 Method

VideoNote
Creating the
Miles Per
Gallon World

Exercises

1. **Miles per Gallon**

Create a world in which the user is asked for the number of gallons of fuel his or her car can hold, and the number of miles that he or she can drive on a full tank. Use variables to hold these values. You should also have a variable to hold the car's miles-per-gallon (MPG). Calculate the MPG with the following formula:

MPG = miles / gallons

The world should have a person (from the *People* collection), and a car (from the *Vehicles* collection). In the initial setup the car should be positioned off-camera. After the data is entered, the person should approach the camera and the car should drive into view and stop in front of the camera. The person should then say a message indicating the car's MPG, as calculated from the data entered by the user. Then, the car should drive away, to a position off camera. Figure 3-58 shows an example of the world.

Figure 3-58 MPG world

2. **Penguin on a Table**

   Create a world with a penguin and a table. The penguin should be facing the table, standing next to it. The penguin should simultaneously flap its wings (use the `wing_flap` method) and move up in the air a distance that is exactly one meter higher than the height of the table. (You can call the table's `height` function to get its height.) The penguin should then move forward to approximately the center of the table, and then move down to the surface of the table.

3. **Fahrenheit to Celsius**

   The following formula is used to convert a Fahrenheit temperature to a Celsius temperature:

   $$C = (5 / 9) * (F - 32)$$

   In the formula, C is the Celsius temperature and F is the Fahrenheit temperature. Create a world in which the user is asked to enter a Fahrenheit temperature. Use a math expression to convert the temperature to Celsius, and store the converted temperature in a variable. Use a character from the *People* collection to say the Celsius temperature. Figure 3-59 shows an example of the world.

Figure 3-59 *Fahrenheit to Celsius* world

4. **Blimps**

   Create a world with two blimps (from the *Vehicles* collection). When you play the world, the blimps should simultaneously turn to face each other, and then simultaneously move toward each other. The blimps should stop close to each other, but should not collide. The world should be programmed so that regardless of where you position the blimps, the blimps will perform the same way.

5. **Chicken Clock**

   Farmer MacDonald has a chicken on his farm that can tell the time. The chicken is trained to flap its wings a number of times to indicate the current hour. For example, if it is three o'clock, the chicken will flap its wings three times. Create a world in which Farmer MacDonald's chicken will tell you the current hour by flapping its wings.

   Currently there are two `Chicken` classes in the Web gallery's *Animals* collection. For this world, create an instance of the `Chicken` class that is shown in Figure 3-60. This class has a custom method named `flap`, which causes the chicken to flap its wings. The method accepts two arguments: *times* and *speed*. The *times* argument specifies the number of times the chicken should flap its wings and the *speed* argument specifies the speed of the flapping (the higher the value, the faster the flapping).

Figure 3-60 `Chicken` class

   The `world` object has a category of functions named time. One of the functions in the time category is `hour of AM or PM`. This function uses the computer's internal clock to get the current time, and it returns the hour. Use this function to get the current hour and pass that value as the *times* argument to the chicken's `flap` method. As a result, the number of times the chicken flaps its wings will indicate the current hour.

6. **Chicken Clock with 3D Text**

   Modify the *Chicken Clock* world that you created in Exercise 5 by adding a 3D text object that reads *hour*. This should create an object in your world that is named `hour`. Feel free to change the color and extrusion properties to get the look that you want.

   Next, create a set instruction that stores the current hour in the 3D text object's `text` property. (Because the current hour is a number, you will need to use the world's `what as a string` function to convert it to a string.) When you play the world the 3D text object should display the current hour.

7. **Kick Ball**

   Create a world with your choice of ball from the *Sports* collection and your choice of person from the *People* collection. Position the ball in front of one of the person's feet. When you play the world, it should ask the user how far the person should kick the ball. Then the `person` object should move one of its legs in a kicking motion, and appear to kick the ball. The ball should move the distance specified by the user.

8. **Spaceship Repair**

   Create a space world with an astronaut and two spaceships (from the Web gallery's *Space* collection). One of the spaceships is stranded with engine trouble, and the astronaut has arrived in the other spaceship to perform a repair. The astronaut should initially be positioned just outside one of the spaceships, about to perform a spacewalk to the other ship. When the world is played, the astronaut should float to the stranded spaceship, appear to work for a few moments, and then float back to the rescue ship. The repaired ship should then fly away, off the screen.

4 Decision and Repetition Structures

TOPICS

4.1   Boolean Values

4.2   The If/Else Decision Structure

4.3   Relational Comparisons and Logical Operators

4.4   The Loop Instruction

4.5   The While Instruction

4.1 Boolean Values

CONCEPT: Algorithms and programs commonly use Boolean values, which are either *true* or *false*.

Computer programs work with many kinds of data. You've already seen Alice worlds that work with values such as 1, 2, and 0.25. These values are numbers. You've also seen Alice worlds that work with values such as "Hello" and "Enter the distance." These are strings.

Programs can also work with the values *true* and *false*. These two values, *true* and *false*, are known as *Boolean values*, in honor of the English mathematician George Boole. In the 1800s Boole invented a system of mathematics in which the abstract concepts of true and false can be used in computations. Today, computer programming languages allow you to store the values *true* and *false* in memory, and use those values in algorithms. In this chapter we will look at many examples of operations involving Boolean values, such as the following:

- Creating Boolean variables, which can store either the value *true* or the value *false*
- Using Boolean functions that return either *true* or *false*
- Testing a Boolean value and performing one set of instructions if it is *true*, or another set of instructions if it is *false*
- Repeating a set of instructions as long as a Boolean value is *true*

151

Boolean Variables

A Boolean variable can hold only one of two possible values: *true* or *false*. Figure 4-1 shows a Boolean variable being created in the *Create New Local Variable* dialog box. The name of the variable is `wantCookie`, the type Boolean is selected, and the value is initially set to *true*. Figure 4-2 shows the tile that is created for the variable. The T/F symbol that appears in the tile indicates the Boolean type.

Figure 4-1 Creating a Boolean variable

Figure 4-2 Boolean variable tile

Boolean Functions

A Boolean function is a function that returns either *true* or *false*. There are numerous primitive functions in Alice that return Boolean values. One example is the `world` object's `ask user for yes or no` function, which we briefly mentioned in Chapter 3. When this function is called, it displays a dialog box with a question that you specify as an argument, a *Yes* button and a *No* button. If the user clicks the *Yes* button, the function returns the Boolean value *true*. If the user clicks the *No* button, the function returns the Boolean value *false*.

Figure 4-3 shows an example of how to call the `ask user for yes or no` function in a set instruction. When this instruction executes, the dialog box in Figure 4-4 will

Figure 4-3 Calling a Boolean function

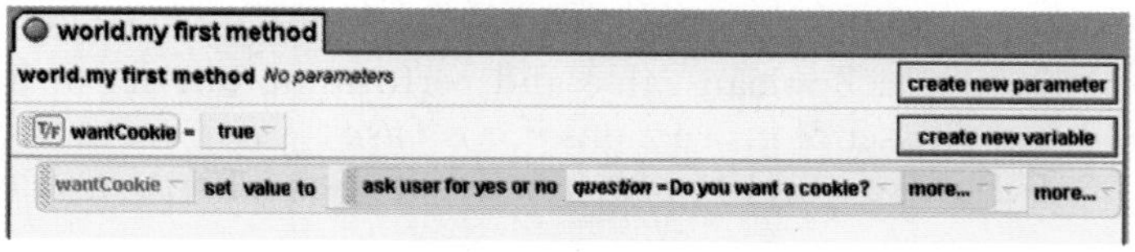

Figure 4-4 Dialog box

be displayed. If the user clicks the *Yes* button, the `wantCookie` variable will be set to *true*. If the user clicks the *No* button, the `wantCookie` variable will be set to *false*.

 Checkpoint

4.1 What values can you store in a Boolean variable?

4.2 What value does the `world` object's `ask user for yes or no` function return if the user clicks the *Yes* button? What if the user clicks the *No* button?

 4.2 The `If`/`Else` Decision Structure

CONCEPT: The `If`/`Else` decision structure executes one set of instructions if a Boolean condition is true, or a different set of instructions if the condition is false.

In all the methods that you have written so far, the instructions are executed one after the other, in the order they appear. You might think of sequentially executed instructions as the steps you take as you walk down a road. To complete the journey, you must start at the beginning and take each step, one after the other, until you reach your destination. This is illustrated in Figure 4-5.

The method that is shown in Figure 4-5 is from Tutorial 3-4 in Chapter 3. Recall that the world in that tutorial has a penguin and a hole in the ice. The code causes the penguin to turn facing the hole, then move to the hole, and then fall down into the hole.

Figure 4-5 A sequence structure

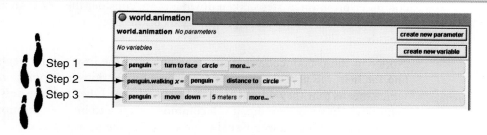

This type of code is called a *sequence structure* because the instructions are executed in sequence, without branching off in another direction. Programs often need more than one path of execution, however. For example, many algorithms require a program to execute a particular set of instructions only under certain circumstances. This can be accomplished with a *decision structure*.

The decision structure that you use in Alice is the `If/Else` instruction. The `If/Else` instruction tests a *condition*, which is anything that gives a Boolean value. If the value is *true*, then one set of instructions is executed. If the value is *false*, then a different set of instructions is executed. For example, suppose you want to modify the world from Tutorial 3-4 so the penguin falls into the hole only if the hole is wider than the penguin. Otherwise, you want the penguin to say "Drats!" because it doesn't fit into the hole. This will require an `If/Else` instruction. Here is the pseudocode for an instruction that works in this instance:

If the hole is wider than the penguin
    penguin falls down into the hole
Else
    penguin says "Drats!"
End If

This instruction determines whether the condition **the hole is wider than the penguin** is true or false. If the condition is true, the code that appears between the `If` line and `Else` is executed—**penguin falls down into the hole**. If the condition is false, the code that appears between `Else` and `End If` is executed—**penguin says "Drats!"**. The `End If` statement marks the end of the instruction. This is illustrated in Figure 4-6.

Figure 4-6 Annotated pseudocode

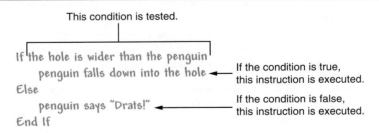

When this `If/Else` instruction executes, either the penguin falls down into the hole or it says "Drats!" depending on the outcome of the condition. Under no circumstance will both of these actions be performed. If you think of the instructions in a computer program as steps taken down a road, consider the `If/Else` instruction as a fork in the road. It causes the program execution to follow one of two paths, skipping the other path.

Notice in the pseudocode that we have indented the instructions **penguin falls down into the hole** and **penguin says "Drats!"**. These instructions are *conditionally executed*, which means that they do not always execute. Instead they execute only under certain conditions. In programming, it is a common practice to indent conditionally executed instructions. This creates a visual cue that makes them easy to spot.

Figure 4-7 shows a flowchart for the If/Else instruction. The diamond symbol represents a true or false condition. If the condition is true, the program branches to the right. If the condition is false, the program branches to the left.

Figure 4-8 shows the location of the If/Else instruction tile at the bottom of the Method Editor. When you drag the tile and drop it into the Method Editor, a menu appears allowing you to select either *true* or *false* as the value of the condition. The value that you select from the menu is used as a placeholder that you will replace later. An empty If/Else instruction will then be created. Figure 4-9 shows an example.

Figure 4-7 Flowchart for a decision structure

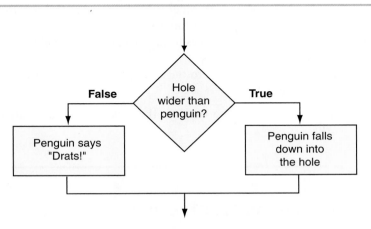

Figure 4-8 Location of the If/Else instruction tile

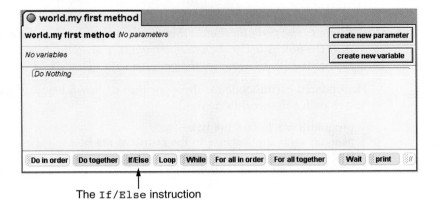

Figure 4-9 An empty If/Else instruction

Notice that there are two empty "slots" in the instruction. We refer to these as the `If` part and the `Else` part.

> **TIP:** Notice that the `If/Else` instruction tile is a green-blue color. This color helps you to distinguish the `If/Else` instruction from the other tiles that surround it in a method.

Once you have created an empty `If/Else` instruction, you complete it by doing the following:

- Replacing the placeholder value for the condition with either a Boolean variable or a call to a Boolean function
- Adding instruction tiles to the `If` part, which will be executed when the condition is true
- Adding instructions to the `Else` part, which will be executed when the condition is false

Tutorial 4-1 leads you through the process of adding an `If/Else` instruction to a world.

VideoNote
Creating an
`If/Else`
Instruction

Tutorial 4-1:
Creating an `If/Else` instruction

In this tutorial you will modify the world that you created in Tutorial 3-4 in Chapter 3. After completing this tutorial, the penguin will fall into the hole only if the hole is wider than the penguin. Here is the updated problem statement:

> *A penguin turns to face a hole in the ice, regardless of where the hole is located. The penguin should then walk to the center of the hole and jump into it. If the hole is wider than the penguin, the penguin disappears below the surface of the ice. Otherwise, the penguin says "Drats!"*

The updated pseudocode for the algorithm is shown below. Figure 4-10 shows a flowchart for the world's method.

```
penguin turns to face the hole
penguin walks the distance to the center of the hole
If the circle is wider than the penguin
    penguin falls down into the hole
Else
    penguin says "Drats!"
End If
```

Step 1:   Open the world that you completed for Tutorial 3-4 in Chapter 3. If you don't have the world, you can open the *PenguinIce* world on the Student CD.

Step 2:   Drag the `If/Else` tile into the method and drop it below the last instruction. A menu appears allowing you to select either *true* or *false*

Figure 4-10 Flowchart

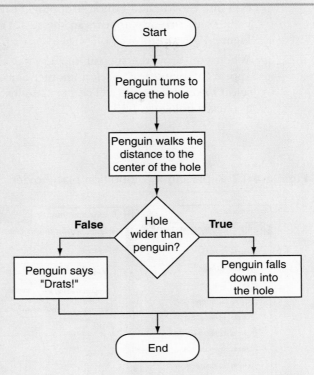

as a placeholder value for the condition. Select *true*. An empty If/Else instruction should be created, as shown in Figure 4-11.

Step 3: All objects in an Alice world have a Boolean function named is wider than, which determines whether the object is wider than another object. We will use the circle object's is wider than method to determine whether it is wider than the penguin object.

Figure 4-11 The If/Else instruction added

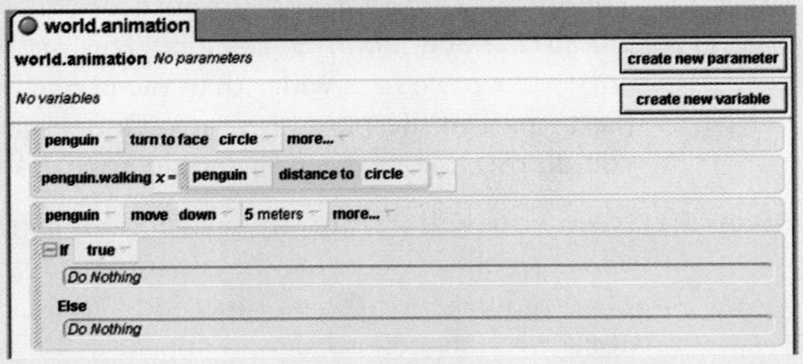

Select the `circle` object and drag the tile for its `is wider than` function into the Method Editor, dropping it on top of the *true* placeholder value that currently appears in the `If/Else` instruction, as shown in Figure 4-12.

When you drop the tile for the `is wider than` function, a menu appears allowing you to select another object. Select `penguin`, and then select *the entire* `penguin`. The `If/Else` instruction should now appear as shown in Figure 4-13.

Figure 4-12 Replacing the condition placeholder

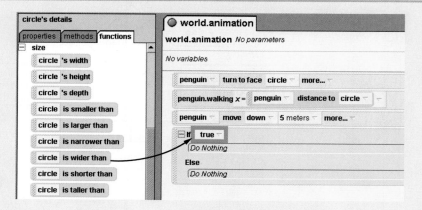

Figure 4-13 The condition replaced

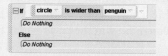

Step 4: The instruction that appears just above the `If/Else` instruction is `penguin.move down 5 meters`. This instruction should be executed only if the `circle` is wider than the `penguin`. Move this instruction to the `If` part of the `If/Else` instruction, as shown in Figure 4-14. Once you do this, the instruction should appear as shown in Figure 4-15.

Step 5: Now you will create an instruction in the `Else` part. Select the `penguin` object and drag the tile for its `say` method into the `Else` part. The argument for the `say` method should be `Drats!` Once you have done this, the method should appear as shown in Figure 4-16.

Step 6: Save the world and then play it. You should see the penguin go to the hole in the ice and then fall into it. Close the *World Running...* window. In the *World View* window make the circle very small so the penguin will not fall into it. Play the world again. If you made the circle small enough, you should see the penguin walk to it, but then say "Drats!" instead of falling into it.

Figure 4-14 Moving the instruction to the `If` part

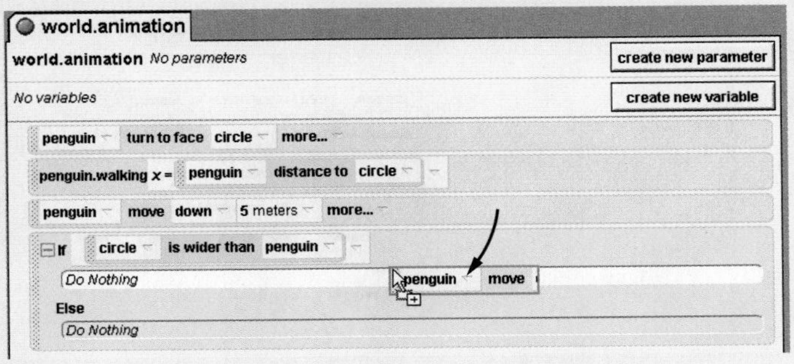

Figure 4-15 The instruction moved to the `If` part

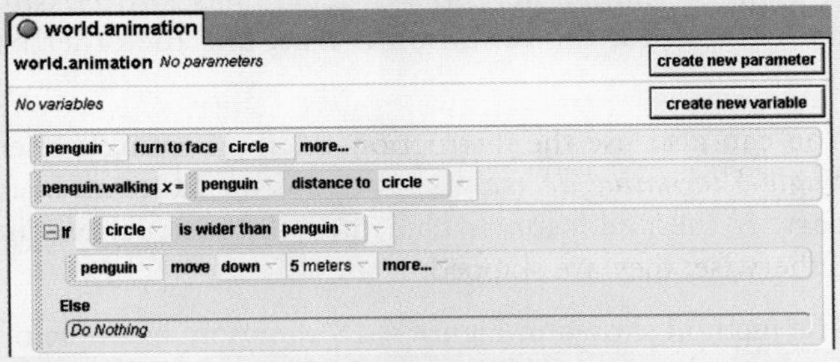

Figure 4-16 The completed method

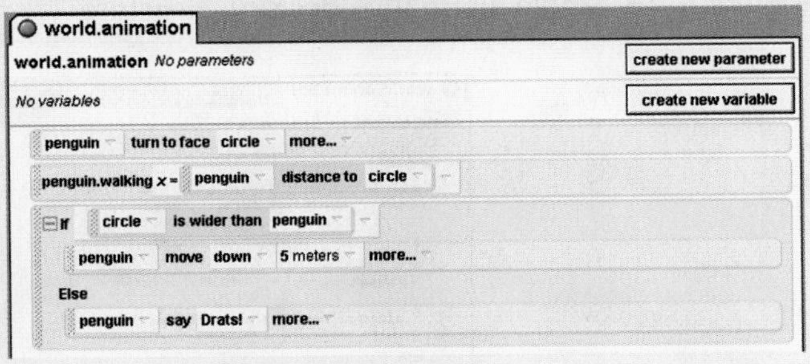

Having Multiple Conditionally Executed Instructions

The method that you wrote in Tutorial 4-1 had an `If/Else` instruction with only one instruction in its `If` part, and only one instruction in its `Else` part. If necessary, you can have multiple instructions in the `If` and `Else` parts. Figure 4-17 shows an example. The `If/Else` instruction in the figure has two instructions in its `If` part. If the condition is true, the two instructions in the `If` part will be executed in the order that they appear.

Figure 4-17 Multiple instructions in the `If` part

Creating a Single-Alternative Decision Structure

The `If/Else` instruction is an example of a dual-alternative decision structure. A *dual-alternative decision structure* has two possible paths of execution—one path is taken if the condition is true, and the other path is taken if the condition is false.

You can also use the instruction to create a single-alternative decision structure. A *single-alternative decision structure* is an `If/Else` instruction with an empty `Else` part. If the condition is true then the instructions in the `If` part are executed. Otherwise, they are skipped.

The method shown in Figure 4-18 shows an example of a single-alternative decision structure that we could have used in Tutorial 4-1. In this method, the penguin turns to face the circle. If the circle is wider than the penguin, it walks to it and jumps in.

Figure 4-18 Single-alternative decision structure

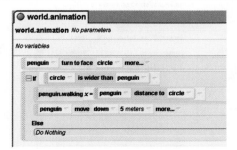

Otherwise, the penguin does nothing. We would write pseudocode for the method as follows:

```
penguin turns to face the hole
If the circle is wider than the penguin
    penguin walks the distance to the center of the hole
    penguin falls down into the hole
End If
```

Notice that the word "Else" is omitted from the pseudocode, since it is not being used. Figure 4-19 shows a flowchart for the method.

 NOTE: Most traditional programming languages allow you to write a simple If statement, with no Else, as well as an If/Else statement.

Figure 4-19 Flowchart with a single-alternative decision structure

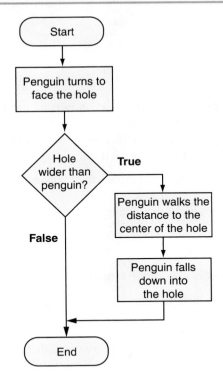

Nested `If/Else` Instructions

In some situations an algorithm will require that you place an `If/Else` instruction inside another `If/Else` instruction. For example, look at the method shown in Figure 4-20. This method has an `If/Else` instruction, and inside that instruction's `If` part another `If/Else` instruction appears. We say that the inner `If/Else` instruction is *nested*. In this example, the only way that the nested `If/Else` instruction will execute is for the condition of the outer `If/Else` instruction to be true. The inner `If/Else` instruction is conditionally executed.

Figure 4-20 Nested `If/Else` instructions

The first `If/Else` instruction shown in the figure calls the `penguin` object's `is within` function to determine whether the `penguin` is within 2 meters of the `circle`. If the function returns *true* then the second `If/Else` instruction is executed. Figure 4-21 shows a flowchart for the method.

You can also nest an `If/Else` instruction inside the `Else` part of another `If/Else` instruction. In such a statement, the nested `If/Else` statement will execute only when the condition of the outer `If/Else` instruction is false.

Checkpoint

4.3 What is a sequence structure?

4.4 What is a decision structure?

4.5 Describe how the `If/Else` instruction works.

4.6 What is the difference between a dual-alternative decision structure and a single-alternative decision structure?

4.7 How do you create a single-alternative decision structure in Alice?

4.8 What is a nested `If/Else` instruction?

Figure 4-21 Flowchart with a nested decision structure

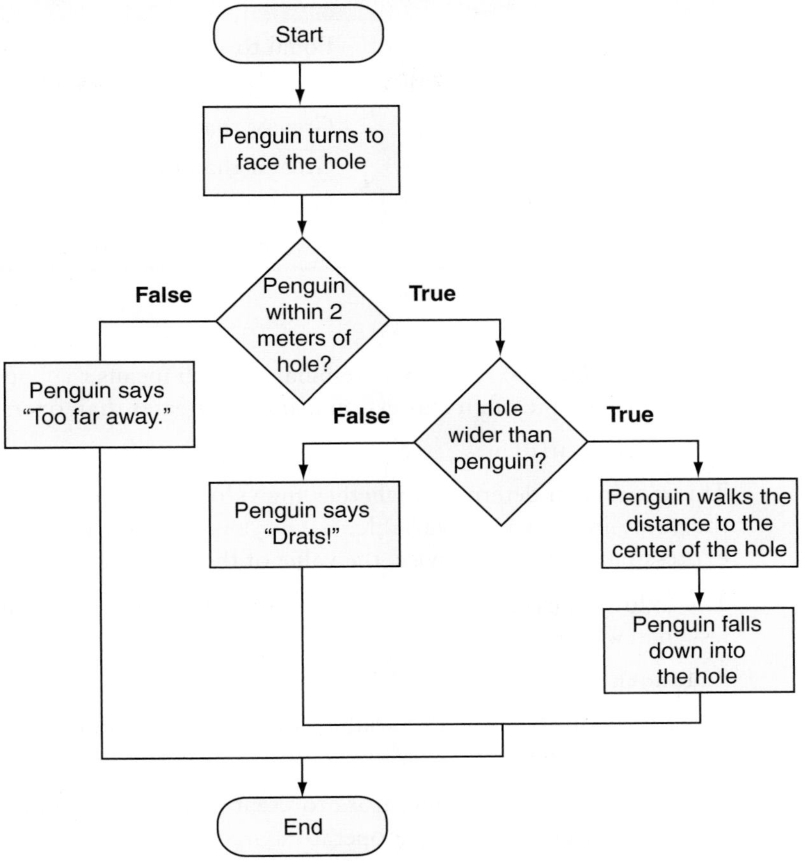

4.3 Relational Comparisons and Logical Operators

CONCEPT: You use relational operators to compare values and determine whether relationships such as greater than, less than, or equal to exist. You use logical operators to connect two or more relational comparisons, or to reverse the logic of a condition.

Programmers commonly need to compare two values to determine how they relate to each other. For example, you might need to determine whether one value is greater than another value. You use *relational operators* to determine whether a specific relationship exists between two values. For example, the greater than operator (>) determines whether one value is greater than another. The equal to operator (==) determines whether two values are equal. Table 4-1 shows the relational operators that are provided in Alice. These same operators are also supported by many traditional programming languages.

Table 4-1 Relational operators

Operator	Meaning
==	Equal to
!=	Not equal to
>	Greater than
>=	Greater than or equal to
<	Less than
<=	Less than or equal to

All of the relational operators are binary, which means they operate on two pieces of data. An example of an expression using the greater than operator follows:

```
length > width
```

This expression determines whether the value in the `length` variable is greater than the value in the `width` variable. If `length` is greater than `width`, the value of the expression is *true*. Otherwise, the value of the expression is *false*.

The following expression uses the less than operator to determine whether `length` is less than `width`:

```
length < width
```

If the value in the `length` variable is less than the value in the `width` variable, the expression is *true*. Otherwise, it is *false*.

You can use relational operators to create conditions in an `If/Else` instruction. As shown in Figure 4-22 the operators are found in the `world` object's list of functions, under the math category. Notice that each operator has two operands, *a* and *b*. When you create a condition using one of the operators you specify values for *a* and *b*.

Figure 4-22 Relational operators

Here are the steps you follow to use one of the relational operators in an If/Else instruction's condition:

- Drag the desired operator's tile and drop it onto the If/Else instruction's condition.
- A menu appears allowing you to select a value for operand *a*. Select a placeholder value (which you will replace later) or a variable from the expressions submenu.
- A menu appears allowing you to select a value for operand *b*. Select a placeholder value (which you will replace later) or a variable from the expressions submenu.
- Replace any placeholder values that you created for the operands. You may replace them with anything that gives a numeric value, such as a Number variable or a function that returns a number.

Tutorial 4-2 leads you through the process of creating an If/Else instruction that uses a relational operator to compare two values.

VideoNote

Using a Relational Operator

Tutorial 4-2:
Using a relational operator

Here is the problem statement for this tutorial:

A big fish is in the water with two gumdrops. One of the gumdrops is red and the other is yellow. The big fish doesn't realize it, but these are magic gumdrops. If it eats the red gumdrop, the big fish will become twice its size. If it eats the yellow gumdrop, the big fish will shrink to half its size. The big fish swims to the gumdrop that is closest to it and eats it. The gumdrop has its magical effect on the big fish. The big fish turns to look at the camera.

To determine which gumdrop is closest to the big fish we will use the less than operator (<) to compare the distance to the red gumdrop with the distance to the yellow gumdrop. Here is the pseudocode for the algorithm:

```
If bigfish's distance to red gumdrop is less than bigfish's distance to yellow
gumdrop
    bigfish turns to face the red gumdrop
    bigfish moves to the red gumdrop
    bigfish eats the red gumdrop
Else
    bigfish turns to face the yellow gumdrop
    bigfish moves to the yellow gumdrop
    bigfish eats the yellow gumdrop
End If
bigfish turns to face the camera
```

Step 1: A world for this tutorial has been partially created for you. Copy the *GumdropBigfish* world from the Student CD to your hard drive and open it. The world already has a bigfish object, a redGumdrop object, and a yellowGumdrop object.

Step 2:   In the Method Editor create a comment that reads *Determine which gumdrop is closest*, and then create an empty `If/Else` instruction, as shown in Figure 4-23.

Figure 4-23 Empty `If/Else` instruction

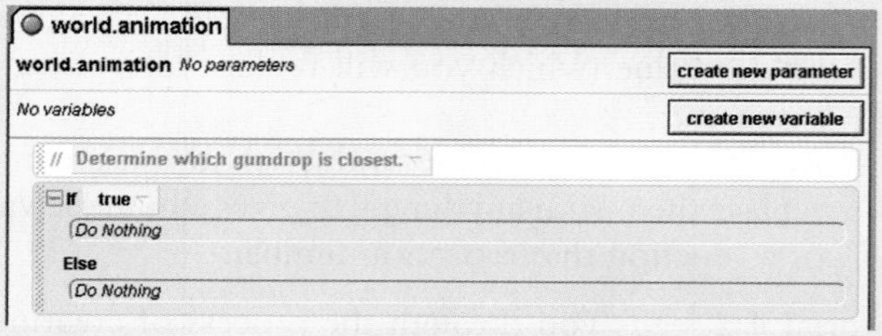

Step 3:   According to the pseudocode algorithm, the condition in the `If/Else` instruction should determine whether the `bigfish`'s distance to the red gumdrop is less than the `bigfish`'s distance to the yellow gumdrop. To make this determination we will use the less than operator (<). Select the `world` object in the Object Tree, and in the list of functions locate the tile for *a* < *b*. (You will find it under the *math* category.) Drag the tile and drop it on top of the placeholder that you created for the condition in the `If/Else` statement.

When you drop the *a* < *b* tile, a menu will appear for the *a* operand. You only need to select a placeholder, so select *1*. Next a menu for the *b* operand will appear. Again, you only need to select a placeholder, so select *2*. The method should now appear as shown in Figure 4-24.

Figure 4-24 Relational operator placed

Step 4:   Now you will replace the placeholder that you selected for the *a* operand. Select the `bigfish` object. Drag the tile for the `bigfish` object's `distance to` function and drop it on top of the *1* that you previously selected as the placeholder for the *a* operand. Select `redGumdrop` from the menu that appears. The `If/Else` instruction should now appear, as shown in Figure 4-25.

Figure 4-25 The *a* operand replaced

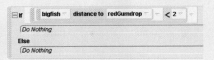

Step 5: Now you will replace the placeholder that you selected for the *b* operand. Drag the tile for the `bigfish` object's `distance to` function and drop it on top of the *2* that you previously selected as the place-holder for the *b* operand. Select `yellowGumdrop` from the menu that appears. The `If/Else` instruction should now appear as shown in Figure 4-26.

Take a moment to think about the condition that you just created. The `If/Else` instruction will determine whether the `bigfish` object's dis-tance to the `redGumdrop` is less than the `bigfish` object's distance to the `yellowGumdrop`. If this is true, then the `If` part of the instruction will be executed. If it is false, the `Else` part will be executed. In the next step you will create the instructions for these two parts of the `If/Else` instruction.

Figure 4-26 The *b* operand replaced

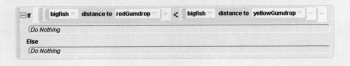

Step 6: Figure 4-27 shows the completed method. Add the additional instruc-tions shown in the figure. The figure points out the following three items:

(1) This tile is a set instruction that sets the `redGumdrop` object's `isShowing` property to *false*. When you set an object's `isShowing` property to *false*, the object becomes invisible. To create this instruction, simply select the `redGumdrop` object, then select the *properties* tab in the Details Panel, then drag the tile for the `isShowing` property into the Method Editor. When you drop the tile, select *false* from the menu that appears.

(2) This tile is a set instruction that sets the `yellowGumdrop` object's `isShowing` property to *false*. Select the `yellowGumdrop` object and follow the same procedure as outlined in item 1.

(3) Note that these tiles are not inside the `If/Else` instruction, but are placed below it.

Figure 4-27 The completed method

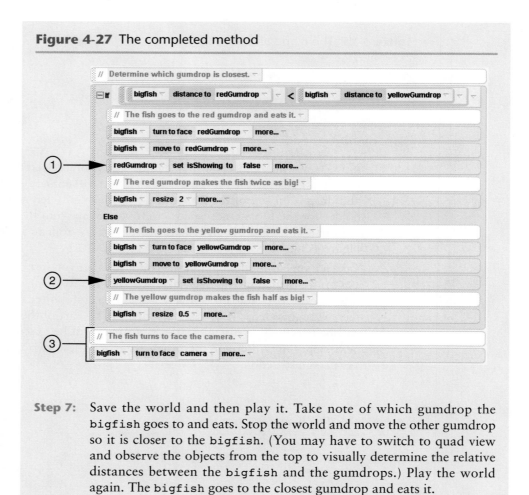

Step 7: Save the world and then play it. Take note of which gumdrop the `bigfish` goes to and eats. Stop the world and move the other gumdrop so it is closer to the `bigfish`. (You may have to switch to quad view and observe the objects from the top to visually determine the relative distances between the `bigfish` and the gumdrops.) Play the world again. The `bigfish` goes to the closest gumdrop and eats it.

Testing the Value of an Object's Property

In some situations you might want to test the value of an object's property. For example, you might want to determine whether an object's `color` property is set to a specific color, or whether an object's `opacity` property is less than a certain value. Here are the steps that you follow to test the value of an object's property in an `If/Else` instruction's condition:

- Create an empty `If/Else` instruction.
- Select the object whose property you want to test, and then click the properties tab in the Details panel.
- Drag the desired property's tile and drop it onto the `If/Else` instruction's condition.
- A menu appears showing all of the comparisons that may be performed with the property. For example, the `color` property can be compared with only the `==` and `!=` operators, but the `opacity` property can be compared with any of the relational operators. Select the desired operator.

- Another menu appears allowing you to select the value that you want to compare the property *to*. For example, with the `color` property you will get a list of all the colors that you can compare the property to. With the `opacity` property you can select (or enter) a number to compare the property to.

Tutorial 4-3 leads you through the process of creating an `If/Else` instruction that tests an object's `color` property.

VideoNote
Testing an
Object's
Color
Property

Tutorial 4-3:
Testing an object's color property

Here is the problem statement for this tutorial:

One morning, Gilbert the frog is sitting quietly in a garden minding his own business. He doesn't realize it, but this same garden is popular with the local ladybugs. He suddenly hears someone behind him say, "Excuse me." Gilbert turns around to see a ladybug. As it turns out, Gilbert is terrified of red ladybugs. If the ladybug he sees is red, Gilbert responds with an "EEK!" and tells the ladybug to go away. If the ladybug is any other color, however, Gilbert responds with a polite "Good morning."

Here is the pseudocode for the algorithm:

```
The ladybug says "Excuse me."
The frog turns to face the ladybug.
If the ladybug's color is red
    The frog says "EEK! Go away!"
Else
    The frog says "Good morning."
End If
```

Step 1:   A world for this tutorial has been partially created for you. Copy the *Gilbert* world from the Student CD to your hard drive and open it. Figure 4-28 shows the opening scene. The world already has a `frog` object and a `ladybug` object.

Figure 4-28 The *Gilbert* world

Step 2: First, the ladybug will say "Excuse me" and Gilbert will turn to face the ladybug. In the method editor, create the comments and instructions shown in Figure 4-29.

Figure 4-29 Starting sequence of instructions

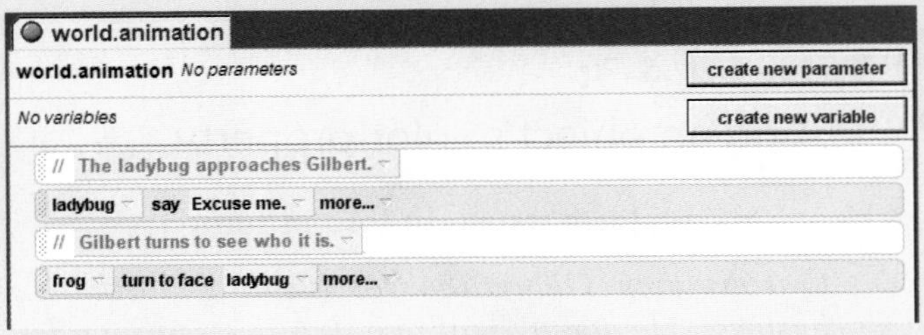

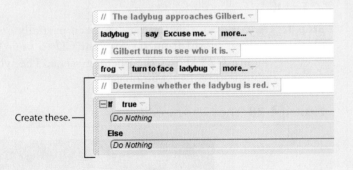

Step 3: According to the pseudocode algorithm, the condition in the If/Else instruction should determine whether the ladybug's color is red. To make this determination we will compare the ladybug object's color property to the color red to see if they are equal. Create the comment and empty If/Else instruction shown in Figure 4-30.

Figure 4-30 Comment and empty If/Else instruction added

Create these.

// The ladybug approaches Gilbert.
ladybug say Excuse me. more...
// Gilbert turns to see who it is.
frog turn to face ladybug more...
// Determine whether the ladybug is red.
If true
  (Do Nothing
Else
  (Do Nothing

Step 4: Now you will replace the *true* placeholder that appears in the If/Else statement. Select the ladybug object, and in the Details panel, click the *properties* tab. Drag the tile for the ladybug object's color property and drop it on top of the *true* placeholder that appears in the If/Else statement. Select ladybug.color == from the menu that appears, and then select *red* from the next menu. The If/Else instruction should now appear as shown in Figure 4-31.

Figure 4-31 The *true* placeholder replaced

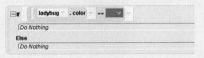

Take a moment to think about the condition that you just created. The If/Else instruction will determine whether the `ladybug` object's `color` property is equal to red. If this is true, then the `If` part of the instruction will be executed. If it is false, the `Else` part will be executed. In the next step you will create the instructions for these two parts of the If/Else instruction.

Step 5:   Figure 4-32 shows the completed method. Add the additional instructions shown in the figure to the If/Else statement.

Figure 4-32 The completed method

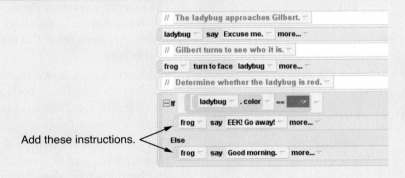

Add these instructions.

Step 6:   Save the world and then play it. Notice that Gilbert isn't afraid of the ladybug because it isn't red. He responds to the ladybug by saying "Good morning." Stop the world and change the `ladybug` object's `color` property to red. Play the world again. This time Gilbert says "EEK! Go away!" to the ladybug.

Logical Operators

The problems we have looked at so far test a single Boolean condition to determine whether it is true or false. Some problems, however, require more complex tests involving multiple conditions. For example you might need to test two conditions to determine whether they are both true. Or you might need to test two conditions to determine whether either is true, or both are true. To perform such tests you use *logical operators*.

As shown in Figure 4-33, the logical operators are found in the `world` object's function list, under the *Boolean logic* category. Table 4-2 describes each of the operators.

Figure 4-33 Logical operators in Alice

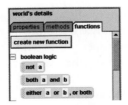

Table 4-2 Logical operators

Logical Operator	Effect
not *a*	This operator reverses the truth of its operand *a*, which is a Boolean condition. If *a* is true, the operator returns *false*. If *a* is false, the operator returns *true*.
both *a* and *b*	This operator takes two Boolean conditions as its operands *a* and *b*. If both *a* and *b* are true, then the operator returns *true*. Otherwise, the operator returns *false*.
either *a* or *b*, or both	This operator takes two Boolean conditions as its operands *a* and *b*. If either *a* or *b* are true, or if both are true, then the operator returns *true*. Otherwise the operator returns *false*.

For example, look at the method shown in Figure 4-34. The `If/Else` instruction tests the following Boolean condition:

```
both penguin.is within 2 meters of circle and
circle.is wider than penguin
```

This is a complex condition that is constructed with the both *a* and *b* logical operator. The *a* operand is `penguin.is within 2 meters of circle`, and the *b* operand is `circle.is wider than penguin`. In order for this complex condition to be true, both *a* and *b* must be true. In this method, it means that the `penguin` must be within 2 meters of the `circle` *and* the `circle` must be wider than the `penguin`. If both are true, then the instructions in the `If` part will be executed. Otherwise, the instruction in the `Else` part will be executed.

Figure 4-34 A method with a logical operator

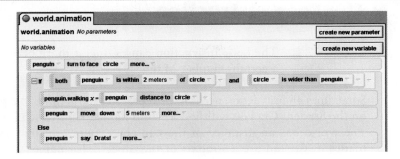

The not *a* operator reverses the truth of its operand *a*. For example, look at the method shown in Figure 4-35. The If/Else instruction tests the following Boolean condition:

not circle.is narrower than penguin

You can think of the If/Else instruction as saying "If the circle is *not* narrower than the penguin..." The not *a* operator reverses the outcome of the circle.is narrower than penguin function.

Figure 4-35 Method using the logical not *a* operator

 **Checkpoint**

4.9 Give the meaning of each of the following relational operators:

==   !=   >   >=   <   <=

4.10 Where are the relational operators located in the Alice environment?

4.11 When creating complex conditions using logical operators, what is the difference between the both *a* and *b* operator and the either *a* or *b*, or both operator?

4.12 What does the logical not *a* operator do?

4.4 The Loop Instruction

CONCEPT: The Loop instruction causes one or more other instructions to repeat a certain number of times.

Sometimes an instruction needs to be repeated several times in a program. For example, on the Student CD you will find a world named *Fan*, which is shown in Figure 4-36. The world has an instance of the Fan class (found in the *Objects* collection). The blades of the fan are a subpart of the object, also named Fan. If we use the roll method to rotate the Fan we will see the blades turn realistically.

Figure 4-36 A method with a series of identical instructions

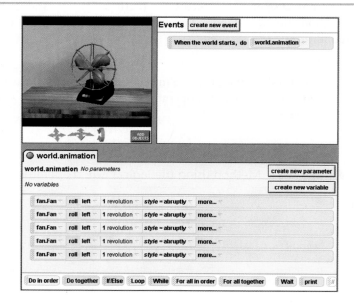

The method shown in the figure has five instructions that are identical. Each rolls the Fan left one revolution. When we play this world we will see the blades of the fan spin five times. Note that we have used the *more...* editing tag to change the method's style to *abruptly*. By default the style is set to *gently*, which will cause the blades to start slowly and stop slowly. To give the appearance of continuous motion, we have changed the style to *abruptly*, which causes the rotation to start and stop quickly.

Because programmers commonly need to repeat instructions, all programming languages provide repetition structures. A *repetition structure*, which is more commonly called a *loop*, causes one or more instructions to be repeated.

One of Alice's repetition structures is the Loop instruction, which is found at the bottom of the Method Editor (next to the If/Else instruction). When you drag the Loop tile into the Method Editor and drop it, a menu appears allowing you to select the number of times the loop should repeat. This creates an empty Loop instruction. Figure 4-37 shows an example of an empty Loop that will repeat five times.

Figure 4-37 An empty Loop instruction

Insert the instructions that are to be repeated here.

Notice that the Loop instruction shown in Figure 4-37 has an empty slot where other instructions may be inserted. Any instructions that are inserted in the Loop will be repeated the specified number of times. For example, Figure 4-38 shows how we could have used a Loop instruction in the *Fan* world, instead of creating five copies of the same instruction. When this method runs, the instruction that is inside the Loop will be repeated five times. (To see this method run, look at the *FanLoop* world on the Student CD.)

Figure 4-38 The Loop instruction

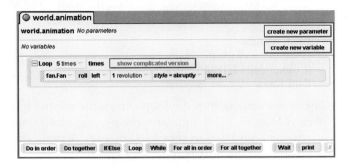

Take a moment to go through the steps in Tutorial 4-4, where you will create a Loop instruction that animates a clock.

Tutorial 4-4:
Using the Loop instruction

Here is the problem statement for the world you will create in this tutorial:

Create an Alice world with a clock that has a minute hand and an hour hand. The clock should simulate the movements that a clock makes when keeping time. The minute hand should make one revolution around the face of the clock, and then the hour hand should advance to the next hour. (The movements do not have to occur in real time. For convenience, the movements can occur at a faster rate of speed.) The clock should make these movements for a total of 12 simulated hours.

A world named *ClockLoop* has been partially created for you to use in this tutorial, and is on the Student CD. The world has the clock object shown in

Figure 4-39. The `clock` object has two subparts: `minute` (the minute hand), and `hour` (the hour hand).

Figure 4-39 The `clock` object

When we play the world, we want to see a simulation of the movements that a clock makes when keeping time. The minute hand should make one revolution around the face of the clock, and then the hour hand should advance to the next hour. Here is the pseudocode for the algorithm:

```
Loop 12 times
    minute rolls left 1 revolution.
    hour rolls left 1/12 revolution.
End Loop
```

The first instruction in the loop causes the minute hand to rotate left one complete revolution. This simulates the passing of 60 minutes. The next instruction causes the hour hand to rotate $1/12$ of a revolution. This will cause the hour hand to advance to the next hour position on the clock.

Step 1: Copy the *ClockLoop* world from the Student CD to your hard drive and open it.

Step 2: Drag the `Loop` tile and drop it into the Method Editor. A menu appears for you to select the number of times that the loop should repeat. Select *other...* and then enter *12* on the *Custom Number* keypad. An empty `Loop` instruction like the one shown in Figure 4-40 should appear.

Figure 4-40 The empty `Loop` instruction

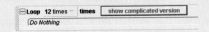

Step 3: In the Object Tree, expand the `clock` object so you can see the tiles for its two subparts, `minute` and `hour`.

Step 4: Drag the tile for the `minute` object's `roll` method and drop it inside the `Loop` instruction. Select *left* for the direction and select *1 revolution (all the way around)* for the amount. The instruction tile should be created inside the `Loop`.

Step 5: Drag the tile for the `hour` object's `roll` method and drop it inside the `Loop` instruction, below the instruction that you created in Step 4. Select *left* for the direction. For the amount, select *other...* and then in the Custom Number keypad enter *1/12*. When you click the *OK* button the instruction tile will be created. (Note that the amount has been converted to 0.08.) The `Loop` instruction should now appear as shown in Figure 4-41.

Figure 4-41 The completed method

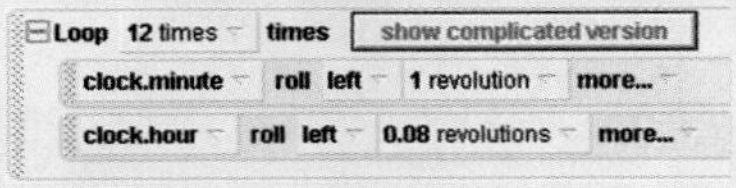

Step 6: Save the world and then play it. You should see the clock make the simulated movements of a real clock's hands, but in faster time. It might take a while for the entire loop to complete all 12 iterations, so you can stop the simulation at any time by clicking the *Stop* button.

Computing the Number of Times to Repeat

In the examples you have seen so far, a specific number of repetitions was chosen when the `Loop` was created. For example, in Tutorial 4-4 you specified that the `Loop` should repeat 12 times. You can also use a variable or a function call to specify the number of repetitions. This is useful for situations where you need to calculate the number of times while the world is playing.

For example, look at the *SoccerGoal* world on the Student CD. When this world is played, the soccer ball turns to face the soccer goal, and then moves to the center of the goal. It will perform these actions regardless of where the goal is located.

Figure 4-42 shows the method that executes when the world is played. Notice that the `Loop` instruction uses the `soccerBall.distance to` function to get the distance from the soccer ball to the soccer goal. The function's return value is used as the number of times to repeat the loop. This means that if the goal is three meters away from the soccer ball, the loop will repeat three times. Likewise, if the goal is 20 meters away from the soccer ball, the loop will repeat 20 times. The instruction inside the loop moves the soccer ball forward one meter, each time the loop repeats.

The `Loop` instruction can use only integers, or whole numbers, as the number of times to repeat. If you provide a fractional number as the number of times to repeat, the fractional part of the number will be discarded. For example, suppose that in the *SoccerGoal* world the `soccerBall.distance to` function returns 4.8. Because the `Loop` instruction cannot repeat 4.8 times, the .8 part of the number is dropped. The `Loop` instruction will then repeat four times. As a result, the ball will move a total of 4 meters, not 4.8 meters.

NOTE: Discarding the fractional part of a number is called *truncating* the number.

Figure 4-42 The *SoccerGoal* world

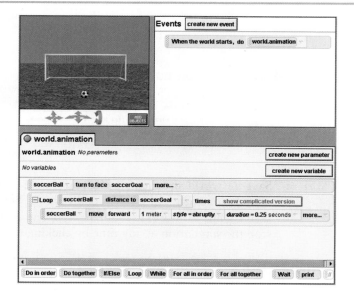

Infinite Loops

When selecting the number of times that you want a Loop instruction to repeat, one of the available menu selections is *infinity times*. If you select *infinity times*, the loop will repeat without ending, until the world is stopped by the user. Such a loop is known as an *infinite loop*.

In most situations, you do not want a loop to repeat an infinite number of times. However, there are some circumstances where this might be desired. If you wish a particular action to take place continuously while the world is running, an infinite loop that runs simultaneously with other actions in a Do Together structure might be the best solution. The Helicopter class (in the *Vehicles* collection) is an example of an object that uses infinite loops. The class has a custom method named heli blade, which uses infinite loops to make the helicopter's blades spin continuously.

The Complicated Version of the Loop Instruction

By now you have probably noticed that the Loop instruction has a button that reads *show complicated version*. The chances are good that you've clicked the button out of curiosity. When you click this button, it reveals the "inner workings" of the Loop instruction. For example, Figure 4-43 shows the complicated version of the Loop instruction in Tutorial 4-4. Recall that this loop repeats 12 times.

Figure 4-43 Complicated version of a Loop instruction

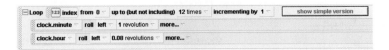

Internally, the Loop instruction creates a variable named index. The index variable is used to count the number of times that the loop repeats. In fact, programmers refer to this type of variable as a *counter variable*. Notice that the first line of the loop shown in Figure 4-43 begins as follows:

```
Loop index from 0
```

This means that the index variable starts with the value 0. The next part reads as follows:

```
up to (but not including) 12 times
```

This means that the index variable will be used to count up to (but not including) 12. The next part reads as follows:

```
incrementing by 1
```

This means that after each repetition of the loop, the index variable will be incremented by 1 (meaning that 1 will be added to the index variable).

By putting all of these pieces together, can you see how the loop uses the index variable to control the number of times it repeats? In a nutshell, the index variable starts with the value 0. After each repetition of the loop, one is added to the index variable. The loop continues to repeat as long as the index variable contains a value that is up to, but not including, 12. As a result, the loop will repeat 12 times.

TIP: To understand how the counter variable is used, imagine that someone tells you to recite out loud the numbers from 0 up to, but not including, 12. You would recite the following numbers: 0, 1, 2, 3, 4, 5, 6, 7, 8, 9, 10, 11. Although you stopped counting at eleven, you recited a total of twelve numbers out loud. This is because you started counting at zero.

Flowcharting a Loop Instruction

A loop that uses a counter variable to control the number of times it repeats is commonly referred to as a *count-controlled loop*. When flowcharting a count-controlled loop, normally you show the actions that take place involving the counter variable. For example, Figure 4-44 shows a flowchart for the Loop instruction that is shown in Figure 4-43. Notice that the flowchart shows when the index variable is initially set to 0, when it is tested to determine whether it has reached its ending value, and when it is incremented.

Figure 4-44 Flowchart of a Loop instruction

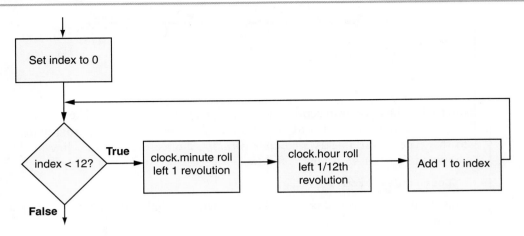

 Checkpoint

4.13 What type of structure is the Loop instruction?

4.14 In the Method Editor, how do you see the code that works with a Loop instruction's counter variable?

4.15 What is an infinite loop?

4.16 What is the name of the Loop instruction's counter variable?

 4.5 **The While Instruction**

CONCEPT: The While instruction is a loop that repeats as long as a Boolean condition is true.

The second repetition structure that Alice provides is the While instruction. When creating a While instruction, you do not specify the number of times that it should repeat. Instead, you provide a Boolean condition. The While instruction repeats as long as the Boolean condition is true. Because this type of loop is controlled by a condition, it is commonly called a *conditional loop*.

For example, look at the *Tennis* world on the Student CD. This world contains a tennis racket and a tennis ball positioned as shown in Figure 4-45. When this world is played, the racket rotates forward until it strikes the ball, launching it off screen.

Figure 4-46 shows the method that runs when the world is played. The first instruction in the method is a While instruction, shown in the green-blue colored tile. The Boolean condition in the While instruction is as follows:

```
tennisRacket.distance behind tennisBall > 0
```

This condition calls the `tennisRacket` object's `distance behind` function to determine how far the `tennisRacket` object is behind the `tennisBall` object. As long as this distance is greater than 0, the `While` loop will repeat. The instruction inside the `While` loop rotates the `tennisRacket` object forward 0.06 revolutions. (This is $^1/_{16}$ of a revolution.) Figure 4-47 shows a flowchart for the method.

Figure 4-45 *Tennis* world

Figure 4-46 Method with a `While` loop

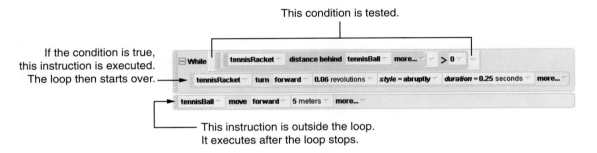

This instruction is outside the loop.
It executes after the loop stops.

Figure 4-47 Flowchart for the `While` instruction

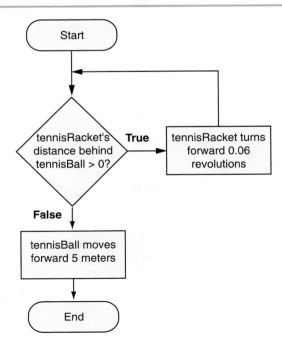

The `While` Instruction Is a Pretest Loop

Notice from the flowchart in Figure 4-47 that the loop's condition is tested before each repetition of the loop. This is a characteristic of the `While` instruction. It first tests its condition. If the condition is true, it performs a repetition and then starts over. If the condition is false, the loop terminates.

A loop that tests its condition before it performs a repetition is called a *pretest loop*. Because it tests its condition before repeating, it is possible that a pretest loop will never repeat. This will happen if the loop's condition is false to start with.

Creating a `While` Instruction

The tile for the `While` instruction is found at the bottom of the Method Editor (next to the `Loop` instruction). When you drag the `While` tile into the Method Editor and drop it, a menu appears allowing you to select either *true* or *false* as a placeholder for the condition. After selecting a placeholder, an empty `While` instruction is created. Figure 4-48 shows an example of an empty `While` instruction.

Figure 4-48 Empty `While` instruction

```
☐ While   true
  Do Nothing
```

Once you have created an empty `While` instruction, you complete it by doing the following:

- Replacing the placeholder value for the condition with a Boolean condition
- Inserting instructions that are to be repeated into the loop

In Tutorial 4-5 you will go through the process of adding a `While` loop to a world.

VideoNote
Using a While Instruction to Make an Object Vanish

Tutorial 4-5:
Using a `While` instruction to make an object vanish

Here is the problem statement for this tutorial:

Marcello the Magician is practicing a magic trick in which he makes a cookie slowly vanish into thin air. He holds the cookie in his hand, says the magic word "Abracadabra," and the cookie vanishes.

Recall from Chapter 1 that an object's `opacity` property determines whether you can see through an object. The `opacity` property holds a value between

0 and 100 percent. When the `opacity` property is set to 0, the object is completely visible, and when the `opacity` property is set to 100, the object is completely opaque.

To make the cookie vanish, you will repeatedly decrease its `opacity` property by 1. This will give the illusion that the cookie is vanishing into thin air, rather than abruptly disappearing. You will create a `While` instruction that repeats while the cookie object's `opacity` property is greater than 0. During each repetition, the `opacity` property will be decreased by 1. Here is the pseudocode for the algorithm:

> The magician says "Abracadabra!"
> While the cookie's opacity is greater than 0
>   Decrease the cookie's opacity by 1
> End While

Step 1: A world for this tutorial has been partially created for you. Copy the *Vanishing Cookie* world from the Student CD to your hard drive and open it. Figure 4-49 shows the opening scene. The world already has a `magician` object and a `cookie` object.

Figure 4-49 The *Vanishing Cookie* world

Step 2: First, the magician will say "Abracadabra!" In the method editor, create the comment and instruction shown in Figure 4-50.

Figure 4-50 Starting sequence of instructions

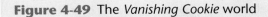

Step 3: According to the pseudocode algorithm, the While instruction will repeat while the cookie object's opacity property is greater than 0. Create the comment and empty While instruction shown in Figure 4-51.

Figure 4-51 Comment and empty While instruction added

Create these ——
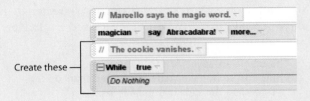

Step 4: Now you will replace the *true* placeholder that appears in the While instruction. Select the cookie object, and in the Details panel, click the *properties* tab. Drag the tile for the cookie object's opacity property and drop it on top of the *true* placeholder that appears in the While instruction.

Select cookie.opacity > from the menu that appears, and on the next menu select *0*. (If you do not see 0 on the second menu, select *other...* and then enter *0* on the *Custom Number* keypad.) The While instruction should now appear as shown in Figure 4-52.

Figure 4-52 The *true* placeholder replaced

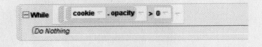

Step 5: Now you will create a Set instruction, inside the While instruction, that decreases the cookie object's opacity property by 1. Several steps are involved in building this instruction; Figure 4-53 shows what it will look like after you have completed it.

Figure 4-53 A preview of the completed Set instruction

Drag the cookie object's opacity property tile from the Details panel and drop it inside the While instruction. On the menu that appears, select the value *1 (100%)* to serve as a placeholder. At this point the instruction appears as shown in Figure 4-54.

Figure 4-54 The Set instruction inserted with a placeholder

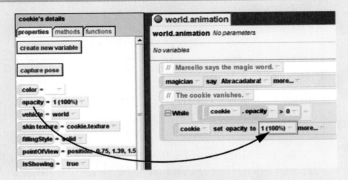

Step 6:   Now you will replace the *1 (100%)* placeholder that appears in the Set instruction. Drag the cookie object's opacity property tile from the Details panel and drop it onto the *1 (100%)* placeholder, as shown in Figure 4-55.

Figure 4-55 Replacing the *1 (100%)* placeholder

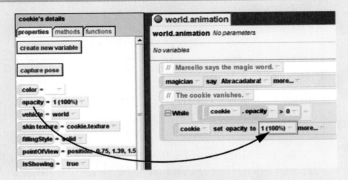

Step 7:   The instruction should now appear as shown in Figure 4-56. Click the down-arrow that is indicated in the figure.

Figure 4-56 The *1 (100%)* placeholder replaced

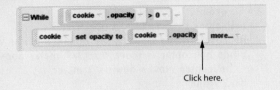

Click here.

Step 8:   When you click the down-arrow indicated in Figure 4-56, a menu appears. Select *math*. A second menu appears. Select *cookie.opacity -*. A third menu appears. Select 1. (If you do not see 1 on the third menu, select *other...* and then enter *1* on the *Custom Number* keypad.) The instruction should now appear as shown in Figure 4-57.

Figure 4-57 The completed `While` instruction

| While | cookie . opacity > 0 |
| cookie set opacity to (cookie . opacity - 1) more... |

Step 9: Save the world and then play it. You should see the magician say "Abracadabra!" and the cookie should vanish from his hand.

Let's go through one more tutorial using the `While` instruction. In Tutorial 4-6 you will create a `While` instruction that lowers a helicopter to a specified distance above a target.

VideoNote

Using the `While` Instruction to Move an Object

Tutorial 4-6:
Using the `While` instruction to move an object

Here is the problem statement for the world you will create in this tutorial:

Create an Alice world with a scuba diver floating in the ocean. A rescue helicopter hovers in the distance. The helicopter turns to face the scuba diver and then flies to a position above him.

A world named *RescueAtSea* has been created for you to use in this tutorial. The world has the `helicopter` and `scubaDiver` objects shown in Figure 4-58. The `helicopter` object (from the *Vehicles* collection) has a method named `heli blade`, which causes the helicopter's blades to spin continuously. Here is the pseudocode for the algorithm:

```
Do together
    helicopter heli blades
    Do in order
        helicopter turn to face scubaDiver
        helicopter move forward the distance to the scubaDiver
        While helicopter is more than 1/2 meter above the scubaDiver
            helicopter moves down 1/2 meter
        End While
    End do in order
End do together
```

Notice that we have placed the call to the `helicopter` object's `heli blade` method inside of a `Do together` structure. Also inside the `Do together` structure we have placed a `Do in order` structure containing several other instructions. This causes the helicopter's blades to spin at the same time those other instructions are executed.

Figure 4-58 *RescueAtSea* world

A method that is based on this pseudocode has been partially written, and is shown in Figure 4-59. This method has all of the steps except the While instruction, which you will insert.

Step 1: Copy the *RescueAtSea* world from the Student CD to your hard drive and open it.

Figure 4-59 Partially completed method

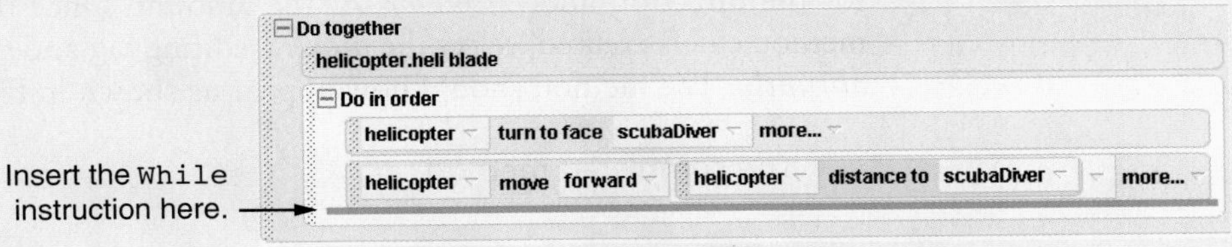

Insert the While instruction here. ——→

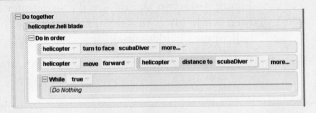

Step 2: Drag the tile for the While instruction into the Method Editor. Drop it inside the Do in order structure at the point indicated in Figure 4-59. A menu appears, allowing you to select a placeholder for the condition. Select *true*. The method should now appear as shown in Figure 4-60.

Figure 4-60 The While instruction placed

Step 3: Now you will replace the placeholder in the While instruction. Select the world object in the Object Tree. From the world's list of functions, drag the tile for the $a > b$ operator and drop it on top of the placeholder. Menus will appear allowing you to select values for a and b. Select *1* as a placeholder for a. Select *0.5* for b. The While instruction should appear as shown in Figure 4-61.

Figure 4-61 The *a > b* operator placed

Step 4: Now you will replace the placeholder for the *a* operand in the *a > b* operator. Select the `helicopter` object and drag the tile for its `distance above` method onto the *1* placeholder. When you drop the tile, a menu appears allowing you to select an object. Select `scubaDiver`, and then select *the entire* `scubaDiver`. The `While` instruction should appear as shown in Figure 4-62.

Figure 4-62 The condition completed

Step 5: Drag the `helicopter` object's tile for the `move` method and drop it inside the `While` instruction. From the menus that appear, select *down* for the direction and *1/2 meter* for the amount. Once the tile for the method call is created, select the *more...* editing tag and change style to *abruptly*. The method should now appear as shown in Figure 4-63.

Figure 4-63 The completed method

Step 6: Save the world and then play it. If your code matches that shown in Figure 4-63 you should see the helicopter fly to the scuba diver, and then gently lower to a rescuing position. While all this is happening, the helicopter's blades should spin.

Step 7: Before closing this world, add appropriate comments to the method and save it.

 Checkpoint

4.17 Why is the `While` instruction considered a conditional loop?

4.18 What causes the `While` loop to stop repeating?

4.19 Why is the `While` loop called a pretest loop?

Review Questions

Multiple Choice

1. The world object's ask user for yes or no function returns this value if the user clicks the *Yes* button.

   a. The string "Yes"
   b. *True*
   c. *False*
   d. The number 1

2. The world object's ask user for yes or no function returns this value if the user clicks the *No* button.

   a. The string "No"
   b. *True*
   c. *False*
   d. The number 0

3. The If/Else instruction tests a condition that must be of this type.

   a. Boolean
   b. Number
   c. String
   d. Any type is allowed

4. An If/Else instruction that has an empty Else part is this type of structure.

   a. Dual-alternative decision structure
   b. Single-alternative decision structure
   c. Null decision structure
   d. Invalid

5. An If/Else instruction that is inside of another If/Else instruction is said to be

   a. Hidden
   b. Packaged
   c. Bundled
   d. Nested

6. This instruction is used to repeat other instructions a specific number of times.

   a. Repeat
   b. While
   c. Loop
   d. If/Else

7. This is a type of variable that the Loop instruction uses internally.

   a. Register
   b. Counter
   c. Conditional
   d. Incremental

8. This is a loop that repeats without ending.

   a. Infinite
   b. Closed

c. Open

d. Nested

9. When a complex condition is created with this logical operator, the operand *a* must be *true* and the operand *b* must be *true* in order for the complex condition to be *true*.

a. `either` *a* `or` *b*, `or both`

b. `both` *a* `and` *b*

c. `not` *a*

d. `union` *a* `and` *b*

10. When a complex condition is created with this logical operator, the operand *a* can be *true*, or the operand *b* can be *true*, or both operands *a* and *b* can be *true* in order for the complex condition to be *true*.

a. `either` *a* `or` *b*, `or both`

b. `both` *a* `and` *b*

c. `not` *a*

d. `union` *a* `and` *b*

11. This instruction is a count-controlled loop.

a. `Repeat`

b. `Count`

c. `Loop`

d. `While`

12. This instruction is a conditional loop.

a. `Repeat`

b. `Count`

c. `Loop`

d. `While`

Short Answer

1. The `If/Else` instruction in Alice has two "slots" in which other instructions may be inserted: the `If` part and the `Else` part. Under what circumstances are the instructions in the `If` part executed? Under what circumstances are the instructions in the `Else` part executed?

2. In Alice what are the two types of decision structures that you can create with the `If/Else` instruction?

3. When working with a `Loop` instruction, what is the difference between the "complicated version" and the "simple version?"

4. Look at the complicated version of the `Loop` instruction shown in Figure 4-64. How many times will this loop repeat?

5. Which looping instruction would you use if you know exactly the number of repetitions that the loop should make?

6. Which looping instruction would you use if you want the loop to execute as long as a certain condition is *true*?

Figure 4-64 Complicated version of a Loop

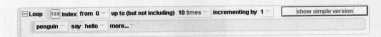

Exercises

1. **Single-Alternative Decision Structure Modification**

   Modify the world that you created in Tutorial 4-1 so it uses the single-alternative decision structure shown in Figure 4-18.

2. *GumdropFish* **Modification**

   Modify the *GumdropFish* world that you created in Tutorial 4-2 so the fish eats both of the gumdrops. First it should eat the gumdrop that is closest (as it currently does), and then it should move to the other gumdrop and eat it. Both gumdrops should have their magical effect on the fish: the red gumdrop should make the fish twice its current size, and the yellow gumdrop should make the fish half its current size.

3. *FanLoop* **Modification**

   Modify the *FanLoop* world on the Student CD so it asks the user for the number of times the fan blades should rotate. Use this value in the Loop statement to control the number of times the roll method is called.

   Hint: Use the ask user for a number function to get the number of rotations. Store the function's return value in a variable, and then use that variable in the Loop statement as the number of times to repeat.

4. **Sea Plane Loop-the-Loop**

   Create a world with a sea plane (from the *Vehicles* collection). Create an infinite loop that causes the sea plane to do a circular loop-the-loop. Adjust the style and duration editing tags to make the animation fast, and as smooth as possible.

5. **Soccer Practice**

   Create a world with a soccer ball from the *Sports* collection and your choice of two people from the *People* collection. Position the ball in front of one of the people. When you play the world, the person object should move one of its legs in a kicking motion, and appear to kick the ball. The ball should move to the other person who kicks it back. Place all of these actions in a loop that repeats five times.

6. **Dragon Guardian**

   VideoNote
   Creating the Dragon Guardian World

   Create a medieval world similar to that shown in Figure 4-65, with a dragon, a knight, and a tent (all found in the *Medieval* collection). The knight should leave his tent and fearlessly approach the dragon. The dragon stands firm until the knight is two meters in front of the dragon. At that point, the dragon turns and flees. The knight goes back to his tent.

Figure 4-65 *Dragon Guardian* world

7. **Roman Numeral Translator**

Create an interactive world that asks the user to enter a number that is at least 1, but not greater than 10. A character of your choice should translate the number to Roman numerals, and say the Roman numerals in a speech bubble. Figure 4-66 shows an example. If the user enters a number outside the range of 1 through 10, the character should say that an invalid number was entered. The method should then ask the user whether he or she wants to enter another number. If the user selects *Yes*, the steps described above should repeat. Otherwise the method should end.

Figure 4-66 Roman numeral translator

8. **The Monkey and the Lollipops**

Mondo the monkey is very fond of red lollipops, but he will not eat lollipops of any other color. Create a world with a `monkey` object (from the *Animals* collection) and at least five `lollipop` objects (from the Food collection, which is inside the *Kitchen* collection). Select two of the `lollipop` objects and change their color properties to *red*. When you play the world, the monkey should move to the lollipops, one after the other. Each time the monkey moves to a lollipop, use an If/Else instruction to test the lollipop's color property. If the lollipop is red, the monkey should eat the lollipop. (To simulate the monkey eating the lollipop, just set the lollipop's isShowing property to false to make it disappear.)

9. **Beam Me Down**

   Create a world with an astronaut positioned inside a transporter, similar to that shown in Figure 4-67. Another astronaut should be positioned outside the transporter at a command console. When you play the world, the astronaut inside the transporter should give the command "Beam me down" and then slowly vanish. (Use a loop that decreases the value of the astronaut's opacity property to make the astronaut vanish.)

Figure 4-67 Beam Me Down world

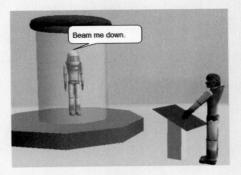

10. **Change for a Dollar Game**

    Use Alice to create a change-counting game that gets the user to enter the number of coins required to make exactly one dollar. The world should have a character that asks the user to enter a number of pennies, nickels, dimes, and quarters. If the total value of the coins entered is equal to one dollar, the character should congratulate the user for winning the game. Otherwise, the character should tell the user whether the amount entered was more than or less than one dollar.

5 Methods, Functions, and More about Variables

TOPICS

5.1 Writing Custom Class-Level Methods

5.2 Saving an Object to a New Class

5.3 Stepwise Refinement

5.4 Passing Arguments

5.5 Using Class-Level Variables as Properties

5.6 Writing Class-Level Functions

5.7 World-Level Methods and Variables

5.8 Using Clipboards

5.9 Tips for Visual Effects and Animation

5.1 Writing Custom Class-Level Methods

CONCEPT: **If a class does not provide a method that you need, you can write your own custom method for an object of that class.**

In addition to the primitive methods that all objects have in Alice, you've seen that some classes in the galleries provide custom methods. For example, the Penguin class has custom methods named wing_flap, walk, jump, and so forth. These methods give objects of the Penguin class unique behaviors that they know how to perform.

Methods that are part of a class are referred to as *class-level methods*. If a class doesn't provide all of the methods that you need, you can easily add your own methods for a particular instance of the class. For example, suppose you have a penguin object and you want it to be able to spin in a circle. As previously mentioned, the Penguin class has numerous custom methods, but none of them causes the object to spin. This is not a problem because you can create your own custom class-level spin method that the penguin object can execute.

You write custom class-level methods in Alice by following these steps:

1. Create an instance of the desired class.
2. Select the instance.

3. In the Details Panel, under the methods tab, click the *create new method* button, as shown in Figure 5-1.
4. A dialog box will appear asking for the new method's name. Enter a name in the dialog box and click the *OK* button. A tile for the new method will appear in the Details Panel, above the *create new method* button.
5. Create the instructions for the method in the Method Editor.

Figure 5-1 The *create new method* button

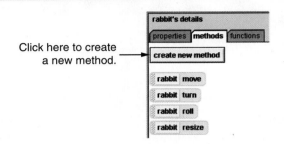

Once you have created the new method, you can call it from other methods in the usual way: you drag the new method's tile into the Method Editor and drop it at the point where you wish to call the method.

In Tutorial 5-1 you will create a world with a Pterodactyl, which is a flying dinosaur. The `Pterodactyl` class has no custom methods, so you will create a custom method that causes an object of the class to flap its wings.

VideoNote
Creating a
Class-Level
Method

Tutorial 5-1:
Creating a class-level method

Step 1:   Start Alice and create a new world. Add an instance of the `Pterodactyl` class (from the *Animals* collection), as shown in Figure 5-2. Change the name of the `world` object's method `my first method` to `animation`.

Step 2:   Select the `pterodactyl` object. In the Details Panel, select the *methods* tab and click the *create new method* button. In the *New Method* dialog box enter `flapWings` as the name of the method, and click *OK*.

You should now see a new tab for the `pterodactyl.flapWings` method appear at the top of the Method Editor, as shown in Figure 5-3. (The `flapWings` method belongs to the `pterodactyl` object, so the method's full name in dot notation is `pterodactyl.flapWings`.) In addition, the tab for `world.animation` is also displayed. The Method Editor allows you to have several methods opened at the same time. You can switch between the methods that are opened by clicking their tabs at the top of the Method Editor. Currently the

Figure 5-2 The `pterodactyl` object

Figure 5-3 The `flapWings` method in the Method Editor

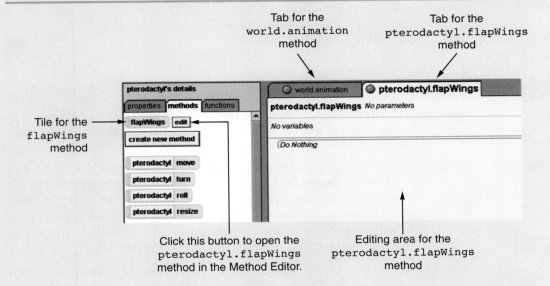

Tab for the
`world.animation`
method

Tab for the
`pterodactyl.flapWings`
method

Tile for the
`flapWings`
method

Click this button to open the
`pterodactyl.flapWings`
method in the Method Editor.

Editing area for the
`pterodactyl.flapWings`
method

`pterodactyl.flapWings` method is selected, so any instructions that are created in the editing area will be placed in that method.

Also, as shown in the figure, a new tile for the `flapWings` method appears in the Details Panel. Notice that a small *edit* button is situated next to the tile. You can open the `flapWings` method in the Method Editor at any time by clicking this button.

TIP: You can close a method in the Method Editor by right-clicking the *methods* tab and then clicking *Close MethodName* on the menu that appears.

Step 3: Complete the `flapWings` method by creating the instructions shown in Figure 5-4.

NOTE: Make sure that the tab for the `pterodactyl.flapWings` method is selected when you create the instructions. You do *not* want to place the instructions in `world.animation`.

Figure 5-4 The completed `flapWings` method

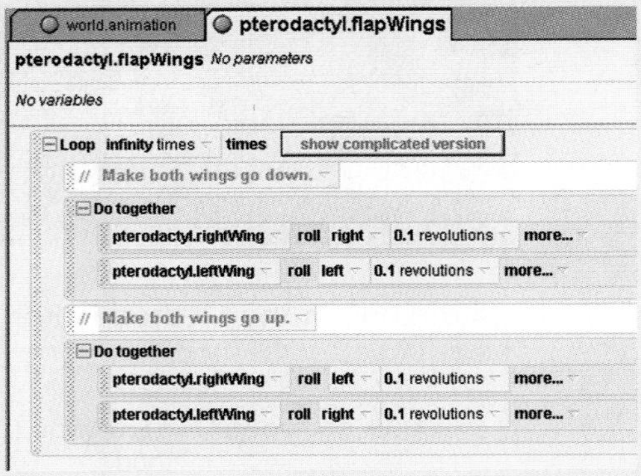

world.animation	● pterodactyl.flapWings

pterodactyl.flapWings *No parameters*

No variables

☐ **Loop** infinity times ⌄ **times** | show complicated version

// Make both wings go down. ⌄

☐ **Do together**

| pterodactyl.rightWing ⌄ | roll right ⌄ | 0.1 revolutions ⌄ | more... ⌄ |
| pterodactyl.leftWing ⌄ | roll left ⌄ | 0.1 revolutions ⌄ | more... ⌄ |

// Make both wings go up. ⌄

☐ **Do together**

| pterodactyl.rightWing ⌄ | roll left ⌄ | 0.1 revolutions ⌄ | more... ⌄ |
| pterodactyl.leftWing ⌄ | roll right ⌄ | 0.1 revolutions ⌄ | more... ⌄ |

Step 4: Although you have written the `pterodactyl` object's `flapWings` method, it will not yet execute when you play the world. (If you click the *Play* button now, nothing will happen in the world.)

To make the `pterodactyl` object's `flapWings` method execute, you need to call the method from the `world.animation` method. In the Method Editor, click the tab for `world.animation`. The method should currently be empty. Drag the tile for the `flapWings` method from the Details Panel and drop it into the Method Editor. After doing that, the method should appear, as shown in Figure 5-5.

Step 5: Save the world and then play it. You should see the `pterodactyl` flapping its wings. (We will return to this world in the next tutorial.)

Figure 5-5 The completed `world.animation` method

● world.animation	○ pterodactyl.flapWings

world.animation *No parameters*

No variables

pterodactyl.flapWings

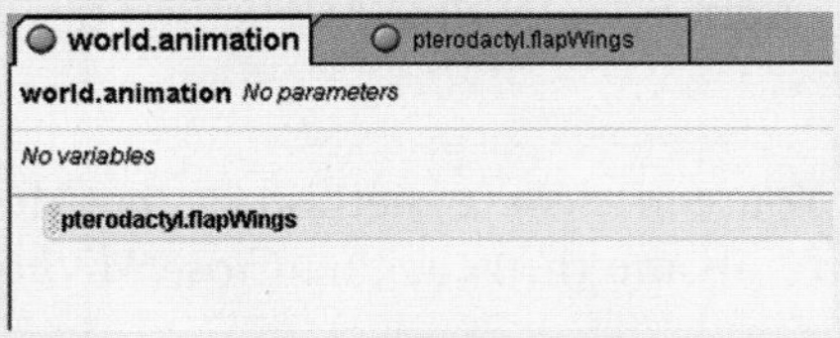

TIP: If you are curious about how any custom method in a class from the galleries works, you can click the *edit* button next to it in the Details Panel. The method will be opened in the Method Editor.

Using Trial-and-Error Experimentation in Method Design

Recall that the `flapWings` method in Tutorial 5-1 simultaneously executed the following instructions to make the `pterodactyl` object's wings go down:

```
pterodactyl.rightWing.roll right 0.1 revolutions
pterodactyl.leftWing.roll left 0.1 revolutions
```

And then the following instructions were simultaneously executed to make the wings go up:

```
pterodactyl.rightWing.roll left 0.1 revolutions
pterodactyl.leftWing.roll right 0.1 revolutions
```

While writing the `flapWings` method you may have wondered how we knew to execute these particular instructions, with the specified arguments. Quite simply, we determined which methods to call and which arguments to provide through a bit of trial and error experimentation.

Recall from Chapter 2 that you can immediately execute any of an object's primitive methods within the Alice environment by right-clicking the object (or its tile in the Object Tree) and then selecting *methods* from the menu that appears. Another menu appears showing a list of all the primitive methods. You select a method from that menu, specify its arguments, and then immediately see the method execute in the World View window. If you are unhappy with the method's results, you can click the *Undo* button to reverse its effects.

This is how we determined the exact method calls and arguments to make the `pterodactyl` object's wings flap. We repeatedly called the wing object's `roll` method with various directions and various values for the amount of revolutions. If a particular set of arguments did not produce the desired result, we clicked the *Undo* button and tried different arguments. After only a few attempts it became clear which values to use.

5.2 Saving an Object to a New Class

CONCEPT: Custom class-level methods are created for a single instance of a class. If you want to create additional objects that have the custom methods, then you must save the object to a new class. Then, all instances of the new class will have the custom methods.

When you create a custom class-level method for an object, you are adding the method to that particular object. The method is not added to the original class that the object was created from.

For example, in Tutorial 5-1 you created a `flapWings` method for the `pterodactyl` object. This custom method was added only to that particular instance of the class, however. If you had created another instance of the `Pterodactyl` class, it would not have had the `flapWings` method.

Quite often, when you add a new class-level method to an object, you will want to create additional objects just like it, each with the new method. To do that you must save the object to a new class. The new class will contain all of the custom methods that you have added to the object. When you create instances of the new class, each will have the custom methods.

To save an object to a new class you follow these steps:

1. Change the name of the object to the name that you wish the new class to have. (There is no need to make the initial letter uppercase; Alice will do this automatically when you save the object.)
2. Right-click the object in the *World View* window or the object's tile in the Object Tree. On the menu that appears select *save object...* A *Save Object* dialog box will appear showing the default file name for the new class. The file name will be the same as the name of the class, and will end with .a2c. (The .a2c extension stands for Alice 2 Class.) Browse to the location on your system where you wish to save the file and click *Save*.

After performing these steps, a file will be created containing the new class. When you want to create an instance of the class, you follow these steps:

1. Click *File*, and then click *Import....*
2. An *Import* dialog box will appear. Browse to the location on your system where the class's .a2c file is located. Select the file and click *Import*. An instance of the class will be created in the world.

In Tutorial 5-2 you will perform these steps to create a new class from the pterodactyl object that has the flapWings method. Then you will create a world and add several instances of the new class.

Tutorial 5-2:
Saving an object to a class

Step 1: Open the world that you created in Tutorial 5-1, in which the pterodactyl object has the flapWings method.

Step 2: Change the name of the pterodactyl object to flyingPterodactyl. (Right-click the pterodactyl object's tile in the Object Tree and then select *rename* from the menu that appears.) You are doing this so that when you save the object, a new class named FlyingPterodactyl will be created.

Step 3: Right-click the tile for the flyingPterodactyl object in the Object Tree. You should see the menu shown in Figure 5-6. Click *save object....* The *Save Object* dialog box shown in Figure 5-7 should appear next. Notice that the name of the file that the class will be saved in is *FlyingPterodactyl.a2c*. Browse to a location on your system where you wish to save the object and then click *Save*.

Step 4: Save the world, and then start a new Alice world.

Figure 5-6 Saving an object

Figure 5-7 *Save Object* dialog box

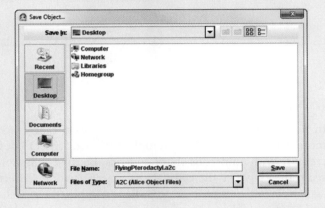

Step 5: Next you will create an instance of the `FlyingPterodactyl` class that you saved in Step 3. Click *File*, and then click *Import....* An *Import* dialog box will appear. Browse to the location on your system where you saved the *FlyingPterodactyl.a2c* file in Step 3. Select the file and click *Import*. An instance of the class will be created in the world.

Step 6: Move the `flyingPterodactyl` object slightly to make room for another instance of the class. Follow the same procedure as in Step 5 to add another instance of the `FlyingPterodactyl` class to the world. Notice that this object is named `flyingPterodactyl2`. The world should appear something like that shown in Figure 5-8.

Step 7: Rename the method `world.my first method` to `world.animate`. Then create the instructions shown in Figure 5-9 in the `world.animate` method. These instructions will simultaneously call both objects' `flapWings` methods.

Step 8: Save the world and then play it. You should see both of the `FlyingPterodactyl` objects flapping their wings.

Figure 5-8 Two `FlyingPterodactyl` objects

Figure 5-9 Instructions in the `world.animate` method

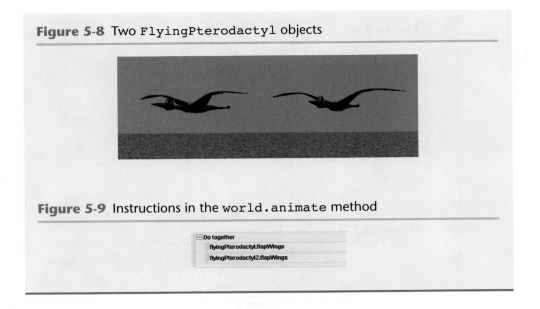

Inheritance

In the real world you can find many objects that are specialized versions of other more general objects. For example, the term "insect" describes a very general type of creature with numerous characteristics. Because grasshoppers and bumblebees are insects, they have all the general characteristics of an insect. In addition, they have special characteristics of their own. For example, the grasshopper has its jumping ability and the bumblebee can sting. Grasshoppers and bumblebees are specialized versions of an insect. This is illustrated in Figure 5-10.

Generalization and specialization are also used in programming. In the previous tutorial you created a `FlyingPterodactyl` class, which is a specialized version of the

Figure 5-10 Generalization and specialization

Insect

All insects have certain characteristics.

In addition to the common insect characteristics, the bumblebee has its own unique characteristics such as the ability to sting.

In addition to the common insect characteristics, the grasshopper has its own unique characteristics such as the ability to jump.

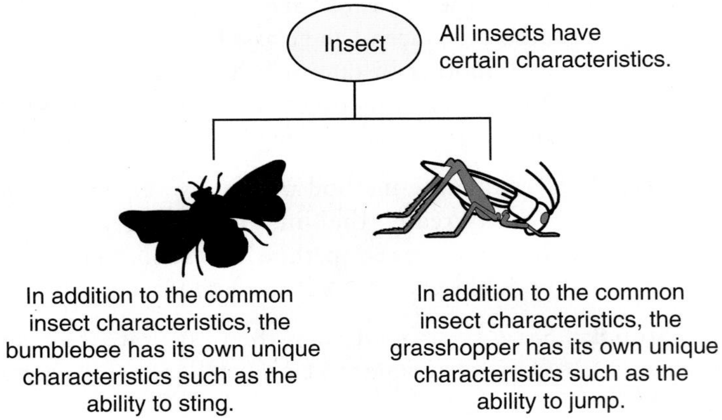

Pterodactyl class. The FlyingPterodactyl class has all of the methods and properties of the Pterodactyl class, plus the flapWings method. Programmers would say that the FlyingPterodactyl class *inherits* all of the Pterodactyl class's methods and properties. Inheritance allows programmers to reuse code. A general class can be created once, and then when a more specialized version of the class is needed, the general class's properties and methods can be inherited instead of created again in the specialized class.

Keep Class-Level Methods Independent of Other Objects

When you write your own class-level methods for an object, keep in mind that the object may be saved to a new class and then imported into other worlds. This means the methods that you write in the object must not be dependent on the existence of other objects. For example, a class-level method in one object should not call a method in another object. If the other object does not exist, an error will occur, and you cannot be sure that the other object will always exist in every world. When you are designing a class-level method, make sure it performs operations only on the object that it belongs to.

 Checkpoint

5.1 Once you have added custom class-level methods to an object, what should you do in order to create other objects like it?

5.2 When you save an object to a new class, what will the new class be named?

5.3 After you have created a new class, how do you add instances of it to an Alice world?

5.4 In inheritance you have a general class and a specialized class. Which of these classes inherits methods and properties from the other?

5.5 Why is it a bad idea to call one object's class-level method from another object's class-level method?

 5.3 Stepwise Refinement

CONCEPT: Sometimes an algorithm that is expressed in pseudocode or flowcharts does not have enough detail to be converted to code. Such an algorithm must be refined, which means it's given more detail. Often, when an algorithm is refined, it becomes several methods.

Because pseudocode and flowcharts are general descriptions of the steps taken in an algorithm, translating them directly into programming instructions isn't always easy. Sometimes a single step that you write in pseudocode or draw in a flowchart requires several programming instructions.

For example, on the Student CD you will find an Alice world named *WorkOut*, which is shown in Figure 5-11. The world has an instance of the `RandomGirl2` class from the *People* collection. The `randomGirl2` object is in an exercise room, and we need to write a method to make her run in place for a total of 10 repetitions. An algorithm for the `runInPlace` method is shown here, in pseudocode:

```
Method runInPlace
   Raise the right leg
   Loop 10 times
      Do together
         Lower the right leg
         Raise the left leg
      End Do together
      Do together
         Lower the left leg
         Raise the right leg
      End Do together
   End Loop
   Lower the right leg
End Method
```

The overall logic of this algorithm makes sense. It gives a general description of the actions that need to take place for the girl to run in place. However, throughout the algorithm we have instructions to **Raise the right leg**, **Lower the right leg**, **Raise the left leg**, and **Lower the left leg**. If we attempt to translate this algorithm into instructions right now, we will find that there are no primitive methods to raise and lower the legs.

This doesn't mean that the algorithm is incorrect. It simply means that the algorithm doesn't have enough detail. To remedy situations such as this, programmers use a process known as *stepwise refinement*. In this process, the programmer goes through each step in the algorithm, refining it as necessary until it has enough detail to be translated into actual instructions.

In refining the `runInPlace` algorithm, we might be tempted to expand the algorithm so that it contains *all* of the steps for raising and lowering each leg. In other words, we might be tempted to replace each occurrence of **Raise the right leg** with the individual steps for raising the right leg. This would mean that we would also replace each occurrence of **Lower the right leg**, **Raise the left leg**, and **Lower the left leg** with the corresponding set of detailed steps. This is not a good approach, however.

Figure 5-11 The *WorkOut* world

If we put too many detailed steps into one method, the method will become large and difficult to understand. A method that performs a complex task should be broken down into several smaller methods. Each of the smaller methods can perform one specific part of the task. The smaller methods can then be executed in the desired order.

For example, to refine the previously shown algorithm for the `runInPlace` method, we will create the following additional methods: `rightLegUp`, `rightLegDown`, `leftLegUp`, and `leftLegDown`. Each of these methods will contain the detailed instructions necessary to raise or lower one of the legs. Then we can call those methods at the appropriate point in the `runInPlace` method, as shown in Figure 5-12. This is a better design than placing all of the code in the `runInPlace` method.

Another benefit of breaking an algorithm into smaller methods is that we can *reuse* some of the code. For example, notice that there are two places in our algorithm where we raise the right leg. Instead of writing the code twice for raising the right leg, we can write it once in a method and then call that method anytime that we need to raise the right leg. The same is true for lowering the right leg. There are two places in the algorithm where we perform that. Instead of writing the code twice to lower the right leg, we write it once in a method and then call that method anytime we need to lower the right leg.

We want the `rightLegUp` method to raise the right leg so it is in the position shown in Figure 5-13. The `randomGirl2` object has a subpart named `rightPantLeg`, which

Figure 5-12 Revised algorithm for the `runInPlace` method

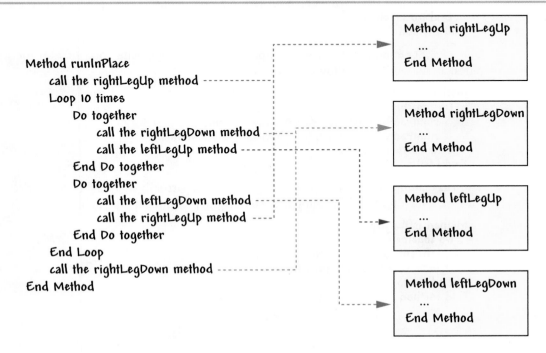

Figure 5-13 Right leg raised

is the entire right leg. The center of the `rightPantLeg` subpart is at the hip. In addition, the `rightPantLeg` object consists of a subpart named `rightShin`, which is the lower part of the leg. The center of the `rightShin` subpart is at the knee. By experimenting with the primitive methods, we find that the following method calls raise the right leg into the position shown in Figure 5-13:

```
rightPantLeg.turn backward 0.2 revolutions
rightPantLeg.rightShin.turn forward 0.2 revolutions
```

Because we want these two actions performed simultaneously, we will put them inside a `Do together` structure. The following pseudocode shows the algorithm for the `rightLegUp` method:

```
Method rightLegUp
    Do together
        rightPantLeg.turn backward 0.2 revolutions
        rightPantLeg.rightShin.turn forward 0.2 revolutions
    End Do together
End Method
```

The `rightLegDown` method will simply perform the opposite rotations on the leg parts, as shown in the following pseudocode:

```
Method rightLegDown
    Do together
        rightPantLeg.turn forward 0.2 revolutions
        rightPantLeg.rightShin.turn backward 0.2 revolutions
    End Do together
End Method
```

The `leftLegUp` and `leftLegDown` methods will be virtually identical to these, except for operating on the left leg subparts. Here is the pseudocode for each:

```
Method leftLegUp
    Do together
        leftPantLeg.turn backward 0.2 revolutions
        leftPantLeg.leftShin.turn forward 0.2 revolutions
    End Do together
End Method
```

```
Method leftLegDown
   Do together
      leftPantLeg.turn forward 0.2 revolutions
      leftPantLeg.leftShin.turn backward 0.2 revolutions
   End Do together
End Method
```

Each of these methods will be called at the appropriate point in the `runInPlace` method. In Tutorial 5-3 you will create and test all of these methods.

Tutorial 5-3:
Completing the *WorkOut* world

Step 1: Copy the *WorkOut* world from the Student CD to your hard drive and open it.

Step 2: First we will write the `rightLegUp` method. Select the `randomGirl2` object, and then select the *methods* tab in the Details Panel. Click the *create new method* button. In the *New Method* dialog box enter `rightLegUp` as the name and click *OK*. Complete the method, as shown in Figure 5-14. Be sure to use the *more...* editing tag to change the duration for each instruction to 0.25 seconds. This will cause the movements to happen faster. (Recall that the default duration for an instruction is one second.)

Step 3: Now create the `rightLegDown`, `leftLegUp`, and `leftLegDown` methods, which are shown in Figures 5-15 through 5-17.

Figure 5-14 The `rightLegUp` method

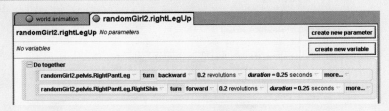

Figure 5-15 The `rightLegDown` method

Figure 5-16 The `leftLegUp` method

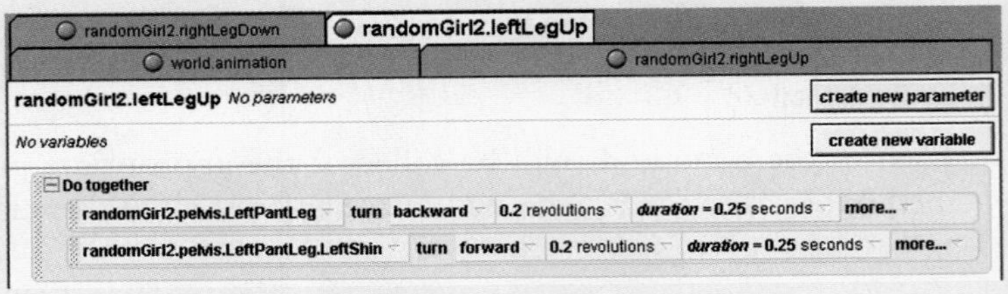

Figure 5-17 The `leftLegDown` method

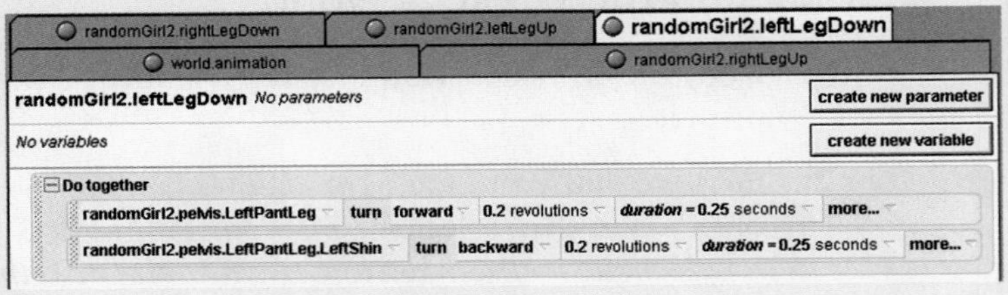

Step 4:   Now that the methods for raising and lowering the legs are created, you can create the `runInPlace` method, as shown in Figure 5-18.

Figure 5-18 The `runInPlace` method

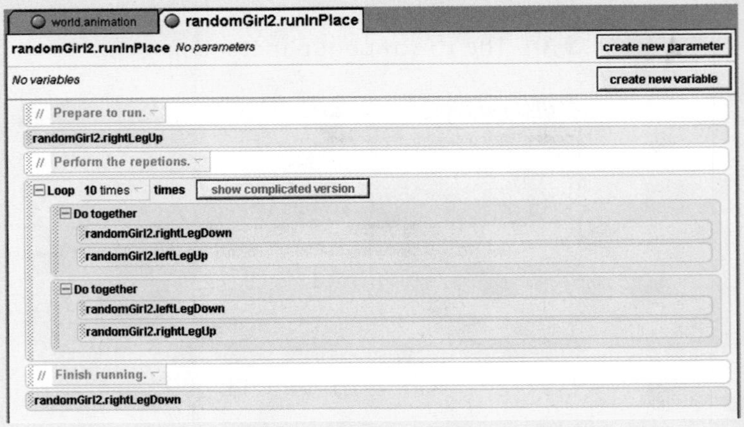

Step 5:   Open the `world` object's `animation` method in the Method Editor. This is the method that will automatically execute when the world is

Figure 5-19 Calling the `runInPlace` method

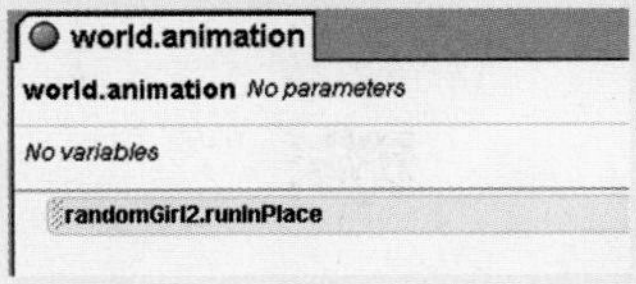

played. Drag the tile for the `randomGirl2` object's `runInPlace` method and drop it into the method. The method should appear, as shown in Figure 5-19.

Step 6: Save the world and then play it. You should see the girl running in place for a total of 10 repetitions.

Step 7: Now you will save the `randomGirl2` object to a new class. Change the object's name to `exerciseGirl`. Then right-click the object and select *save object...* from the menu that appears. Save the object on your system under the file name `ExerciseGirl.a2c`.

Checkpoint

5.6 Why do you sometimes need to refine an algorithm?

5.7 Why should you avoid putting too many instructions in a method?

5.4 Passing Arguments

CONCEPT: **A method may be written so it accepts arguments. Data can then be passed into the method when it is called.**

Some methods require that you pass values as *arguments* when you call them. The arguments are necessary in order for the method to perform its task. You're already familiar with several methods that require arguments. For example, Figure 5-20 shows a call to the primitive move method. When you call the move method, you must specify two arguments: one for the direction and one for the amount. As a result, the method will cause the object to move in the specified direction, the specified amount of meters.

You can also write methods that require arguments to be passed to them when they are called. If you want a method to accept an argument when it is called, you have to

Figure 5-20 A call to the move method

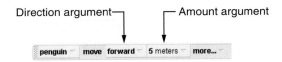

create a parameter in the method. A *parameter* is a special variable that holds the argument being passed into the method.

To create a parameter in a method, you open the method in the Method Editor, and then click the *create new parameter* button, as shown in Figure 5-21. This displays the *Create New Parameter* dialog box, as shown in Figure 5-22. This dialog box is identical to the one that you use to create a local variable. In the dialog box you enter a name for the parameter and select a type. When you click *OK*, the parameter will be created.

Once you create a parameter in a method, an argument will be required anytime the method is called. Inside the method, the parameter will hold the value of the argument. Because the parameter is a variable, you can use it in the method to work with the value that was passed as an argument.

The `runInPlace` method that you created in the `ExerciseGirl` class is a good example of a method that could benefit from a parameter. Currently, the method causes the girl to run in place for 10 repetitions. But what if we want the girl to run for fewer or

Figure 5-21 The *create new parameter* button

Figure 5-22 The *Create New Parameter* dialog box

more repetitions? It would be better for the method to have a parameter for the number of repetitions. That way, when we call the method we have to pass the number of repetitions as an argument. Consequently, we can have the girl do any number of repetitions.

The revised pseudocode for the `runInPlace` method is shown as follows. Note that in the first line, after the name of the method, we have shown a parameter named `repetitions` inside a set of parentheses. In the third line we have replaced the number 10 with the `repetitions` parameter.

```
Method runInPlace(repetitions)
    call the rightLegUp method
    Loop repetitions times
        Do together
            call the rightLegDown method
            call the leftLegUp method
        End Do together
        Do together
            call the leftLegDown method
            call the rightLegUp method
        End Do together
    End Loop
    call the rightLegDown method
End Method
```

In Tutorial 5-4 you will make this modification to the `ExerciseGirl` class.

VideoNote
Passing
Arguments
to a Method

Tutorial 5-4:
Passing arguments to a method

Step 1: Copy the *Gym* world from the Student CD to your hard drive and open it.

Step 2: Import an instance of the `ExerciseGirl` class that you created in Tutorial 5-3.

Step 3: Open the `exerciseGirl` object's `runInPlace` method in the Method Editor.

Step 4: Click the *create new parameter* button. In the *Create New Parameter* dialog box enter `repetitions` as the name of the parameter. (We will name it `repetitions` because it will hold the number of repetitions that the girl is to perform.) Select *Number* as the type, and click *OK*. You should see a tile for the parameter, as shown in Figure 5-23.

Step 5: Currently the loop is written to repeat 10 times. We want to change the loop so it uses the `repetitions` parameter to specify the number of times to repeat. To make this change, drag the tile for the `repetitions` parameter and drop it on top of *10 times* in the loop, as shown in Figure 5-24. After doing this, the `repetitions` parameter will appear as the number of times that the loop will repeat, as shown in Figure 5-25.

Figure 5-23 Parameter created

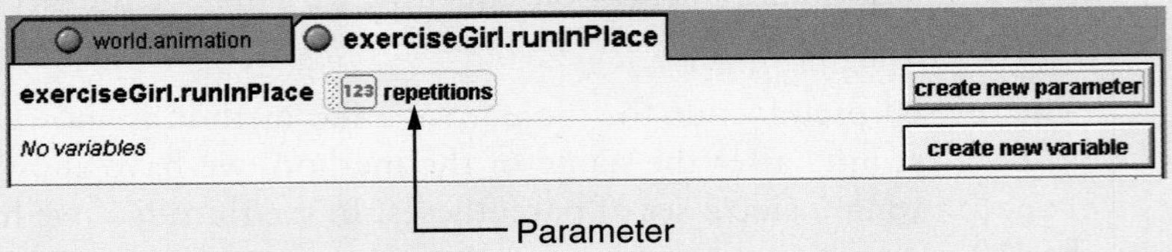

Parameter

Figure 5-24 Modifying the loop

Figure 5-25 The loop updated

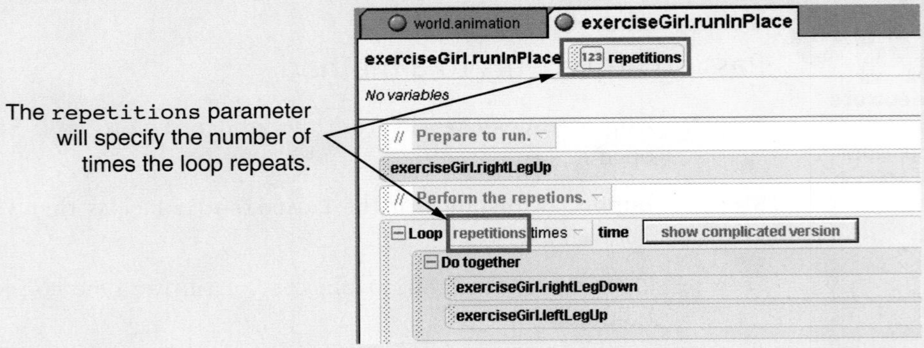

The `repetitions` parameter
will specify the number of
times the loop repeats.

Step 6: Open the `world` object's `animation` method in the Method Editor. This is the method that will automatically execute when the world is played. Drag the tile for the `exerciseGirl` object's `runInPlace` method and drop it into the Method Editor. When you drop the tile, a menu appears allowing you to specify a value for the `repetitions` parameter. Select 2. The tile shown in Figure 5-26 will be created in the method.

Figure 5-26 Method call with argument

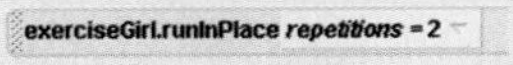

exerciseGirl.runInPlace *repetitions* = 2

Take a moment to think about what will happen when this instruction executes. The `exerciseGirl` object's `runInPlace` method will be called and the value 2 will be passed as an argument to the `repetitions` parameter. As a result, the loop will repeat two times. This is illustrated in Figure 5-27.

Figure 5-27 Passing 2 as the argument

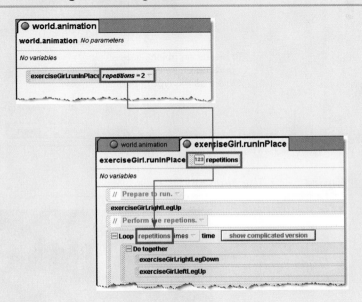

Step 7: Save the world and then play it. You should see the girl run in place for two repetitions. Close the *World Running…* window and then try passing different arguments to the `runInPlace` method. Each time you change the argument, play the world to confirm that the value is being passed to the method. (What happens if you pass 0 to the method?)

Object Parameters

Some methods take an object as an argument, and then perform an operation using that object. For example, the primitive method `turn to face` takes an object as an argument. The method causes an object to turn to face the object that is passed as an argument. The primitive `move to` method also takes an object as an argument. It causes an object to move to the object that is passed as an argument.

You can write your own methods that take objects as arguments. To take an object as an argument you have to create an object parameter. When creating the parameter, you select *Object* as the type, as shown in Figure 5-28. Then, when you call the method you pass an object as an argument for the parameter.

For example, on the Student CD you will find a world named *Bird*, which is shown in Figure 5-29. The world contains an object name `glidingBird`, which is an instance of the `BlueBird` class from the *Animals* collection. Other objects in the world include a `birchTree`, a `bush`, a `flower`, and a `rock`.

Figure 5-28 Select the object type

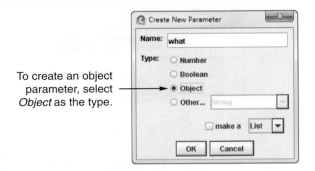

To create an object parameter, select *Object* as the type.

Figure 5-29 The *Bird* world

The `glidingBird` object has a custom class-level method named `glideTo`, which is shown in Figure 5-30. Notice that the method has an Object parameter named `what`, and a Number parameter named `stopAt`.

The `glideTo` method causes the bird to glide to an object, stopping a certain distance away from the object. The first parameter, `what`, is the object that you want the bird to glide to. The second parameter, `stopAt`, is the distance away from the object at which you want the bird to stop.

The `world` object's animation method, shown in Figure 5-31, calls the `glidingBird.glideTo` method four times in succession, passing various objects and stopping distances as arguments. When you play the world, you will see the bird glide to each object that is passed as an argument to the method.

Figure 5-30 The `glideTo` method

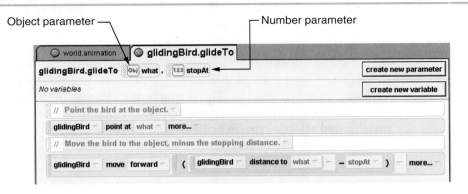

Figure 5-31 The `world.animation` method

 Checkpoint

5.8 What is an argument?

5.9 What is a parameter?

5.10 How do you create a parameter in a method?

5.11 If you create a parameter in a method, what will be required each time you call the method?

5.5 Using Class-Level Variables as Properties

CONCEPT: You can add properties to an object by creating class-level variables. When you save the object to a new class, the class-level variables are saved along with it.

In Chapter 1 you learned that each object in an Alice world has properties, which are values that specify the object's characteristics. Some of the common properties that you have seen are `color`, which specifies the object's color, `opacity`, which determines the transparency of an object, and `isShowing`, which determines whether an object is visible.

A property is really a variable that belongs to an object. Properties hold data about the object that they belong to. Because properties are variables that belong to objects, they are referred to as *class-level variables*.

If you would like to add additional properties to an object, you can do so by clicking the *create new variable* button shown in Figure 5-32. This button appears in the Details Panel, under the *properties* tab. When you click this button, the *Create New Variable* dialog box appears. This dialog box is identical to the one that you see when you create a local variable in a method. In the dialog box you enter a name for the variable and select a type. When you click *OK*, the variable will be created and you will see its tile in the Details Panel, under the *properties* tab.

Figure 5-32 Button to create a class-level variable

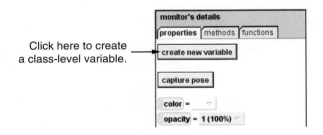

In Tutorial 5-5 you will open the *Office* world, which is on the Student CD. The world contains an instance of the `Monitor` class (from the *Objects* collection), which is a simulated computer monitor. The `monitor` object has a subpart named `screen`, which shows an image that looks like a computer screen.

As it is, the `monitor` object has only the primitive methods and properties that are common to all objects in Alice. You will modify the `monitor` object so it can be turned on or off. When the monitor is turned off, the `screen` subpart's `color` property will be set to black. When the `screen` is black you cannot see the image and it looks like the `monitor` is turned off. To turn the `monitor` on, the screen subpart's `color` property will be set to *no color*, so the image can be seen.

In the tutorial you will add a Boolean property named `isOn` to the `monitor` object. The `isOn` property will be set to *true* when the monitor is on or *false* when the monitor is off. You will also add a class-level method named `turnOnOff` to the `monitor` object. Calling this method will simulate what happens when you press the *power* button on a typical monitor. If the `monitor` is currently on when the method is called, it will turn the `monitor` off. Otherwise, if the `monitor` is off when the method is called, it will turn the `monitor` on.

After making these changes, you will save the `monitor` object to a new class. When you save an object to a new class, any class-level variables and methods that you have added to the object will be saved with it. Then, when you create an instance of the class (by selecting *File*, then *Import...*) the instance will have the additional class-level variables and methods.

Tutorial 5-5:
Adding a property to an object

Step 1: Copy the *Office* world from the Student CD to your hard drive and open it.

Step 2: First you will add a new property (a class-level variable) to the `monitor` object. Select the `monitor` object, and under the *properties* tab in the Details Panel click the *create new variable* button. Next you will see the *create new variable* dialog box. As shown in Figure 5-33, enter `isOn` as the name of the variable, select *Boolean* as the type, and make sure *true* is selected as the value. After doing this you should see a tile for the `isOn` property appear in the Details Panel, as shown in Figure 5-34.

Figure 5-33 Creating a class-level variable

Figure 5-34 New property tile

Tile for the
`isOn` property →

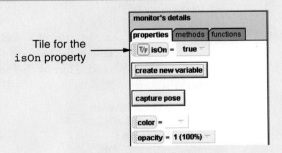

Step 3: Now you will add a class-level method to turn the `monitor` on or off. Here is the pseudocode for the method:

```
Method turnOnOff
    If monitor is on
        screen set color to black
        isOn set to false
    Else
        screen set color to no color
        isOn set to true
    End If
End Method
```

With the `monitor` object selected, click the *methods* tab in the Details Panel and then click the *create new method* button. The *New Method* dialog box will appear next. Enter `turnOnOff` as the name and click *OK*.

Step 4: In the Method Editor, create the instructions shown in Figure 5-35 in the `turnOnOff` method.

Figure 5-35 The `monitor.turnOnOff` method

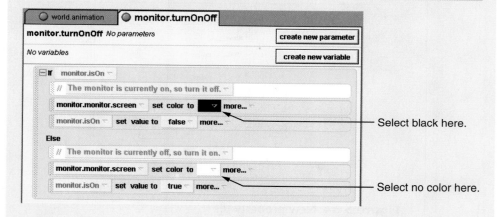

Step 5: Now you use the `world` object's `animation` method to test the `turnOnOff` method. This is the method that will automatically execute when the world is played. Here is the pseudocode for the instructions that you will write.

```
Method world.animation
    monitor turn OnOff
    wait for 1 second
    monitor turn OnOff
End Method
```

Let's take a closer look at the algorithm. First, we call the `monitor.turnOnOff` method. Because the `monitor` object is on to begin with, this instruction will turn it off. Then, we wait for one second. This can be accomplished with the `Wait` instruction. The tile for the `Wait` instruction is located at the bottom of the Method Editor. The `Wait` instruction takes an argument, which is the number of seconds to wait. When the `Wait` instruction executes, the program simply waits, doing nothing, for the specified number of seconds. After waiting for one second, we call the `monitor.turnOnOff` method again. Because the `monitor` will be off when the method is called this time, it will turn the `monitor` on.

Figure 5-36 shows the actual instructions for the `world.animation` method. Open the method in the Method Editor and create the instructions.

Figure 5-36 The `world.animation` method

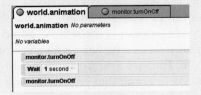

Step 6: Save the world, and then play it. You should see the monitor's screen fade to black. This is the result of the first call to the `monitor.turnOnOff` method. After waiting one second you should see the screen image re-emerge on the monitor. This is the result of the second call to the `monitor.turnOnOff` method. Close the *World Running...* window.

Step 7: Now you will save the `monitor` with the `isOn` property and the `turnOnOff` method to a new class. Change the name of the `monitor` object to `switchableMonitor`, and save it to a new class. After doing this you will be able to add instances of the new class to other Alice worlds.

Checkpoint

5.12 A property is really what type of variable?

5.13 How do you create a class-level variable in an object?

5.6 Writing Class-Level Functions

CONCEPT: In addition to the primitive functions that Alice provides for all objects, you can create your own class-level functions.

In Chapter 4 you learned that a function is a method that returns a value back to the instruction that called the function. All objects in Alice have a set of primitive functions. For example, all objects have a `distance to` function that returns an object's distance from another object, measured in meters.

In the same way that you can write custom, class-level methods for an object, you can also write custom, class-level functions. Sometimes it is useful to write a function that returns some piece of data pertaining to an object.

For example, the way the `ExerciseGirl` class is currently designed, an instance of the class can run in place for an infinite number of repetitions. If she were real, however, she would eventually get tired. We could make the class more realistic by adding a function that tells us whether an instance of the class is tired. That is exactly what you will do in Tutorial 5-6. You will modify the `ExerciseGirl` class by adding a function named `isTired` that returns a Boolean value. If the girl is tired, the function returns *true*. Otherwise, it returns *false*.

TIP: As you go through Tutorial 5-6, it might be helpful if you think about the `isTired` function as a way of asking the object whether she is tired. The value that the function returns is the answer to the question. If she is tired, the answer to the question is *true*. Otherwise, the answer is *false*.

So, how will the function determine whether an `ExerciseGirl` object is tired? It will require that the object keeps two pieces of data: the number of repetitions that makes the object tired and the number of repetitions that the object has done. If the latter value is greater than or equal to the former, then the object is tired.

To keep these two pieces of data we will add two properties to an `ExerciseGirl` object: `getsTiredAt` and `repsDone`. The `getsTiredAt` property will hold the number of repetitions that makes the object tired. The `repsDone` property will keep a count of the number of repetitions that have been done.

After adding these properties to the object, we will modify the object's `runInPlace` method so it increments the `repsDone` property by 1 after each repetition. To *increment* a property or a variable means to add to it. If we increment the object's `repsDone` property by 1 after each repetition, then the `repsDone` property will keep a count of the number of repetitions that the object has performed.

Then we will create the `isTired` function. The `isTired` function will determine whether `repsDone` is greater than or equal to `getsTiredAt`. If it is, then the function returns *true*, indicating that the object is tired. Otherwise the function returns *false*, indicating that the object is not tired.

Tutorial 5-6:
Writing a class-level function

Step 1: Create a new Alice world. As has been our custom, change the name of `world.my first method` to a camelCase name such as `world.animation`.

Step 2: Import an instance of the `ExerciseGirl` class.

Step 3: Select the `exerciseGirl` object and create a new property (a class-level variable) named `getsTiredAt`. For the property's type select *Number*, and for the property's value select *10*. (By giving the property the value 10 we are indicating that the object gets tired at 10 repetitions.)

Step 4: Create another new property named `repsDone`. For the property's type select *Number*, and for the property's value select *0*.

It is *very* important that we give this property the initial value 0. This is because the property will keep a count of the number of repetitions done. When we start the world, the object will have initially done 0 repetitions.

With the *properties* tab selected, the top portion of the Details Panel should appear as shown in Figure 5-37.

Figure 5-37 New properties created

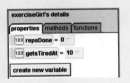

Step 5: Now you will modify the `runInPlace` method so it increments (adds one to) the `repsDone` property after each repetition. Open the method in the Method Editor and drag the tile for the `repsDone` property into the editor. Drop the tile at the location shown in Figure 5-38. (Note that the location is *below* the `Do together` structure, but still inside the loop.)

When you do this, a menu will appear. Select *increment exerciseGirl.repsDone by 1*. This will create the instruction `increment exerciseGirl.repsDone by 1` in the method, as shown in Figure 5-39.

Take a moment to think about the instruction that you just added to the `runInPlace` method. After each complete repetition, the instruction adds 1 to the `repsDone` property. As a result, the property

Figure 5-38 Preparing to increment the `repsDone` property

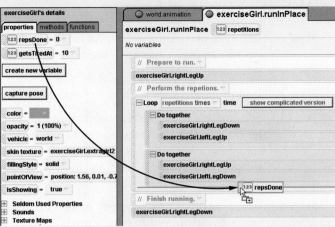

Figure 5-39 The `increment` instruction created

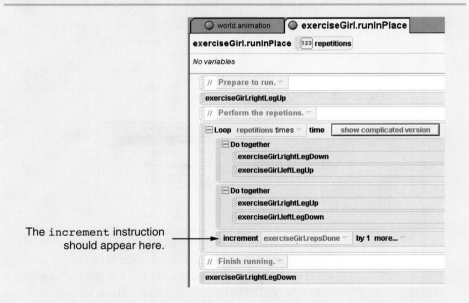

The `increment` instruction should appear here.

will keep a count of the number of repetitions that the object has performed.

Step 6: Now you will create the `isTired` function. With the `exerciseGirl` object still selected, click the *functions* tab in the Details Panel. Then, click the *create new function* button, as shown in Figure 5-40. The *New Function* dialog box will appear next. As shown in Figure 5-41

Figure 5-40 The *create new function* button

Click here to create
a new class-level
function.

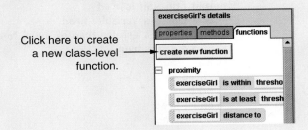

Figure 5-41 The *New Function* dialog box

enter isTired as the name and select *Boolean* as the type. After doing this a function named isTired will be created, as shown in Figure 5-42.

Notice that the function is empty, except for a Return instruction. The Return instruction is required in all functions, and causes a value to be returned from the function. The value that is currently returned is a placeholder that you will replace in a moment.

Figure 5-42 An empty function named isTired

The Return statement is
required in all functions.

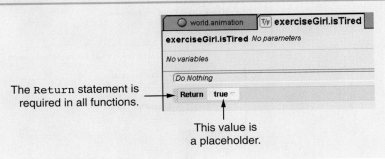

This value is
a placeholder.

Step 7: Now you can complete the isTired function. Here is the pseudocode:

```
Boolean Function isTired
    Local Boolean Variable: tired
    If repsDone is greater than or equal to getsTiredAt
        tired set to true
    Else
        tired set to false
    End If
    Return tired
End Function
```

Let's take a closer look at the algorithm for the function. First of all, we have a local variable named tired. The variable's type is *Boolean*. Then we have an If/Else statement. If the repsDone property is greater than or equal to the getsTiredAt property, then the tired variable is set to *true*. Otherwise, the tired variable is set to *false*. Then the value of the tired variable is returned from the function. When the Return instruction executes, the function ends and the value specified by the instruction is returned from the function.

The actual code for the function is shown in Figure 5-43. Complete the function as shown in the figure. Note that the placeholder value in the Return instruction has been replaced with the tired variable.

Step 8: Now you can test the function. Here is the pseudocode for the world.animation method:

```
Method world.animation
    While exerciseGirl is not tired
        exerciseGirl runInPlace 5 repetitions
        exerciseGirl says the number of reps done
    End While
    exerciseGirl say "I'm Tired. I think I'll take a break."
End Method
```

Figure 5-43 The completed isTired function

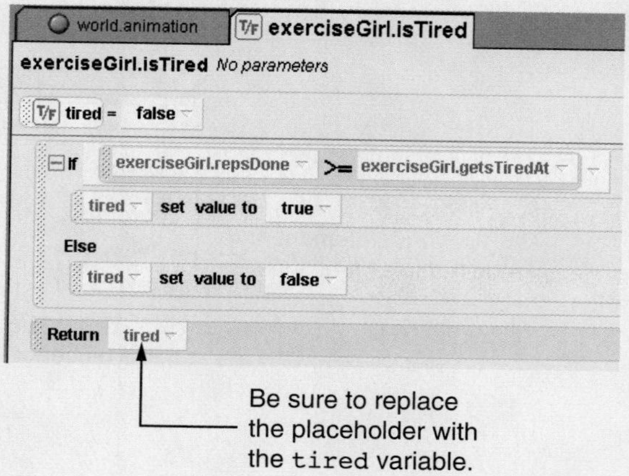

Be sure to replace the placeholder with the tired variable.

Notice that the first line of the loop reads: While exerciseGirl is not tired. How will we implement that logic in code? The function that we wrote is named `isTired` and it returns *true* if the object *is* tired. Do we need to write another function named `isNotTired`?

No, we do not. We can use the not *a* operator with the `isTired` function. Recall from Chapter 4 that the not *a* operator reverses the truth of its operand *a*. The function `exerciseGirl.isTired` returns *true* when the girl is tired, so the expression not `exerciseGirl.isTired` returns *true* when the girl is *not* tired.

If we refine the pseudocode loop to read While not exerciseGirl isTired we will see better how to implement this logic in code. Figure 5-44 shows a flowchart for the method. The actual Alice code for the method is shown in Figure 5-45.

Figure 5-44 Flowchart for the algorithm

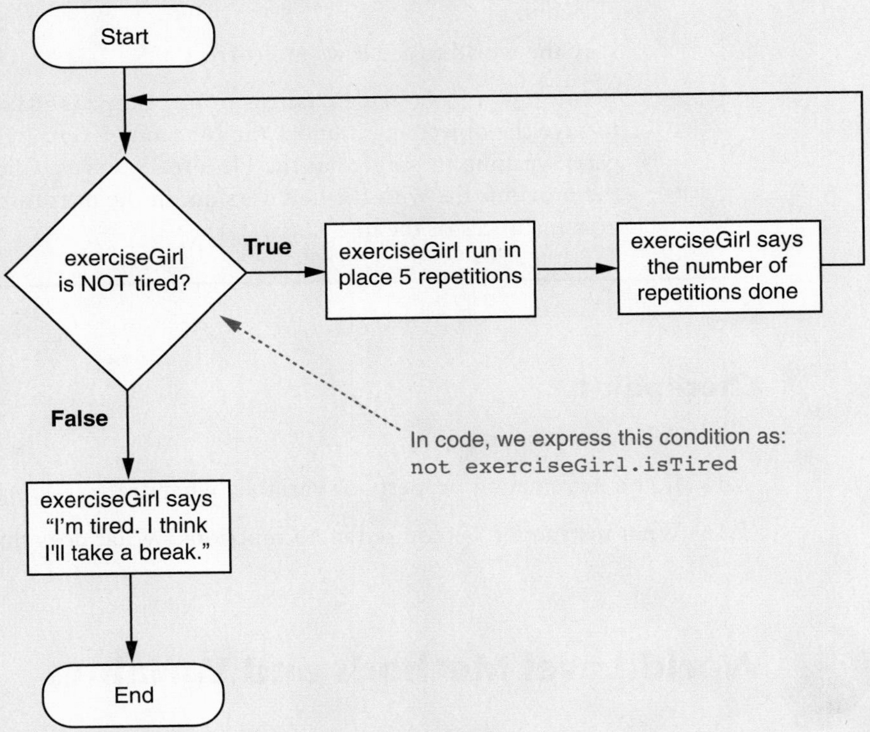

Step 9: Can you predict the number of repetitions that the `exerciseGirl` will perform when you play the world? She should perform a total of 10 repetitions and then stop. Think about it:

- The first time that the loop executes she will do five repetitions. After she does these repetitions, the `repsDone` property will be set to five. The loop executes again because she isn't tired.

Figure 5-45 The `world.animation` method

- The second time the loop executes she will do five more repetitions. After she does these repetitions, the `repsDone` property will then be set to 10. Because `repsDone` is now greater than or equal to `getsTiredAt` property, she is tired and the loop does not execute again.

Play the world to see if we are correct.

Step 10: Because you have made changes to the `exerciseGirl` object, be sure to save the object again under the file name *ExerciseGirl.a2c*. You will get a warning message that the file already exists. Click *OK* to replace the previous file with the new version. In the next tutorial you will import instances of the new class.

 Checkpoint

5.14 What is a function?

5.15 If you increment a property or variable, what are you doing?

5.16 What instruction is required in all functions? What does this instruction do?

 5.7 **World-Level Methods and Variables**

CONCEPT: Instead of creating one long method in the world, you can create several smaller world-level methods that each performs a specific part of the animation. You can then call the smaller methods in the desired order. You can also create world-level variables that act as properties of the world. World-level variables are available to all methods in the world.

World-Level Methods

Previously in this chapter you saw how to write class-level methods for an object. Class-level methods are typically designed to give an object unique behaviors, beyond those that are provided by the primitive methods. You can also write methods in the `world` object. These are called *world-level methods*. You know about world-level methods already because Alice worlds, when they are created, are automatically given a world-level method named `my first method`.

You are not limited to this one method at the world level, however. You can create additional methods in the `world` object. The process of creating a method (or a function) in the `world` object is the same as creating one in any other object. World-level methods are commonly designed in a way that breaks a large, complex algorithm into small manageable pieces. Instead of writing one long world-level method containing all of the instructions necessary to animate the world, you can write several smaller world-level methods that each performs a specific part of the animation. These smaller methods can then be executed in the desired order to make the world do all it is supposed to do. This approach is sometimes called *divide and conquer* because a large problem is divided into several small tasks that are easily performed.

Another reason to divide a problem into several small methods is that it simplifies the program. If a specific task is performed in several different places in a program, a method can be written once to perform that task, and then can be executed anytime it is needed. This is known as *code reuse* because you are writing the code to perform a task once and then reusing it each time you need to perform the task.

Recall that in Tutorial 3-5 (with the snow people) you wrote the `world.animation` method shown in Figure 5-46. The method causes the snowman and snowWoman turn to face each other, the snowman moves over to the snowWoman and then they have a short conversation. This method isn't terribly complex, but we can use it to illustrate how one long method can be broken into smaller methods.

Figure 5-46 `world.animation` method from Tutorial 3-5

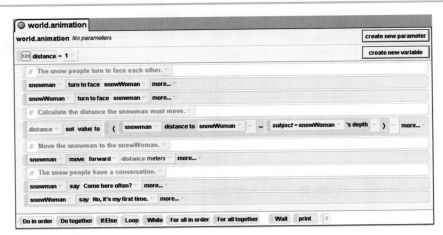

On the Student CD you will find a world named *SnowWorld* which performs the exact same actions. The *SnowWorld* world, however, uses four smaller world-level methods instead of the one long method. As shown in Figure 5-47, the world-level methods in the *SnowWorld* world are `animation`, `faceEachOther`, `getTogether`, and `haveConversation`.

Figure 5-47 World-level methods in *SnowWorld*

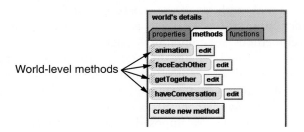

As its name suggests, the `faceEachOther` method causes the snowman and snowWoman to turn and face each other. The `getTogether` method moves the snowman to the snowWoman. In the `haveConversation` method the snowman and snowWoman carry out their dialogue. The `animation` method is still the method that executes when the world starts. It calls all of the other methods, as shown in Figure 5-48.

Figure 5-48 Calling the world-level methods in *SnowWorld*

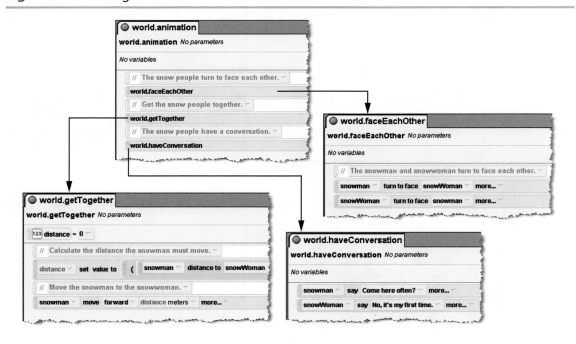

World-Level Variables

A world-level variable is a variable that belongs to the `world` object. Creating a world-level variable is similar to creating a class-level variable. Here are the steps that you take:

1. Select the `world` object in the Object Tree.
2. Select the *properties* tab in the Details Panel.
3. Click the *create new variable* button in the Details Panel, as shown in Figure 5-49.
4. The *Create New Variable* dialog box will appear. In the dialog box you enter a name for the variable and select a type. When you click *OK*, the variable will be created and you will see its tile in the Details Panel, under the *properties* tab.

Just as class-level variables act as properties for an object, world-level variables act as properties for the world. A world-level variable exists as long as the world is running, and is available to all methods in the world.

Figure 5-49 Creating a world-level variable

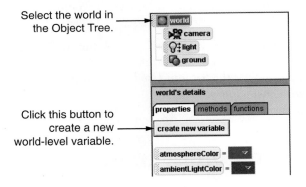

Select the world in the Object Tree.

Click this button to create a new world-level variable.

 Checkpoint

5.17   What is a world-level method?

5.18   What is the process of divide and conquer?

5.19   How can methods help you to reuse code?

5.20   What is a world-level variable? How do you create one?

 5.8 # Using Clipboards

A *clipboard* is a place where you can store a copy of something. In the Alice environment you will see one or more clipboard icons at the right side of the toolbar area, as shown in Figure 5-50.

Figure 5-50 Clipboard icons

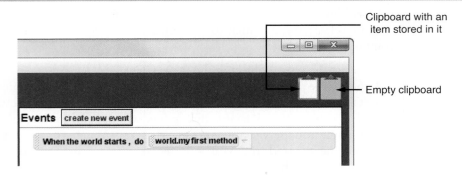

In Alice you can store copies of instructions in a clipboard. This is useful when you want to copy an instruction from one method to another. To store a copy of an instruction in a clipboard you simply click and drag the instruction tile to the clipboard. When a clipboard contains an item, it appears as if it has a white sheet of paper on it. In Figure 5-50 the leftmost clipboard shows an example. To paste the item that is stored in a clipboard, you click and drag the clipboard icon to the location where you want to paste the item. If you want to empty a clipboard, click and drag it to the trashcan.

By default, Alice shows only one clipboard. To change the number of clipboards that are available, click the *Edit* menu, and then click *Preferences*. On the dialog box that appears click the *Seldom Used* tab, and then change the number that appears next to *number of clipboards*.

Tips for Visual Effects and Animation

Billboards

Alice allows you to insert graphical images into your worlds. You can insert images that you have created with a graphics program such as Paint, or pictures that you have taken with a digital camera. Alice supports images in the JPEG, GIF, and TIF file formats.

When you insert an image into an Alice world, you insert it as a *billboard*. You click the *File* menu, and then select *Make Billboard....* A dialog box appears allowing you to browse for image files. You select the desired image and then click the *Import* button. The selected graphics file will be inserted into the world as a billboard.

In an Alice world, billboards are flat, two-dimensional objects. Figure 5-51 shows an Alice world with a three-dimensional snowman object standing in front of a two-dimensional billboard. Although the billboard has height and width, it has no depth. If you view a billboard from the back, it appears as a mirror image. If you view it straight-on from the side, you see nothing (or at the very most, a thin line).

Figure 5-51 A billboard is a 2D object

Billboards can be used for many purposes. For example, they can serve as background scenery or as pictures, as shown in Figure 5-52. They can also present information to the user, as shown in Figure 5-53.

Figure 5-52 A billboard as background scenery or a picture

Figure 5-53 Using a billboard to display information

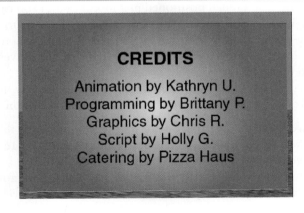

A billboard is an object in an Alice world. When you insert a billboard into a world, a tile for it is created in the Object Tree. The name of the object will be the same as the image's file name. Like any other object in the world, it will have properties and methods. You can use the object's methods to animate the billboard. For example, the turn method can be used to make a billboard rotate.

Fog

Alice has the ability to create a fog effect in the world. Figure 5-54 shows an example of a world that has fog. When a world has fog, a mist appears and objects become less visible as they move into the background.

To turn the fog effect on, you change the world object's fogStyle property to *density*. (The default value is no fog, which turns the effect off.) Then you adjust the world object's fogDensity property until the fog has the desired thickness. The higher the value of the fogDensity property, the thicker the fog will be.

Figure 5-54 A world with fog

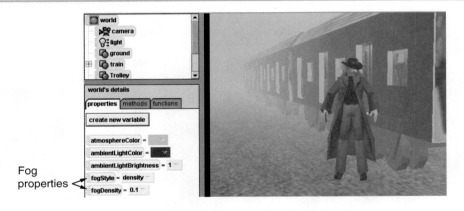

Moving Objects Together with the Vehicle Property

Sometimes it is necessary to move two objects together. For example, Figure 5-55 shows Alice Liddell positioned in a motor boat. (You can find the Motorboat class in the *Vehicles* collection.) Suppose we want the boat to move in the water and carry Alice Liddell along with it. Unless there is some way to "couple" Alice Liddell with the boat, its movements are independent of her movements. One way to make the two objects move together would be to program the boat and Alice Liddell to make the same movements simultaneously. An easier way, however, would be to use the AliceLiddell object's vehicle property, as shown in Figure 5-56.

If we want the AliceLiddell object to move with the Motorboat object, then we make the Motorboat object the vehicle for the AliceLiddell object. Then, any movements that are made by the Motorboat will also be made by AliceLiddell. We do not have to explicitly program AliceLiddell to move along with the Motorboat. She will automatically move with it because it is her vehicle.

Figure 5-55 Alice Liddell in a motor boat

Figure 5-56 The `vehicle` property

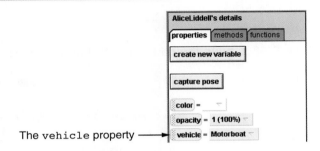

The `vehicle` property ─────▶

Making an Object Circle Another Object

An object's `turn` method can be used to make the object spin around, but it can also be used to make an object move in a circle around another object. To do this, you have to use the `turn` method's *more...* editing tag to change the `asSeenBy` argument.

Normally, the `turn` method causes an object to turn around its own center point. This usually makes the object spin. But you can click the method's *more...* editing tag and change the `asSeenBy` argument to make the object turn around another object's center point.

For example, Figure 5-57 shows the *HawkAndTree* world, which is on the Student CD. There are two objects in the world: `hawk` and `bonzai`. When the world is played, the `hawk` will circle the `bonzai`. As shown in Figure 5-58, this is done by calling the hawk object's `turn` method, specifying right as the direction and 1 revolution as the amount. The `asSeenBy` argument is set to `bonzai`, which causes the `hawk` to turn around the `bonzai` object's center point. As a result, it appears that the `hawk` flies in a circle around the `bonzai`.

When you play the world, the `hawk` circles the `bonzai` quickly, because it makes the entire revolution in one second. You can use the *more...* editing tag to change the `duration` to a higher value. This will slow the `hawk` down, because a higher duration means it will take more time to make the revolution.

Figure 5-57 Hawk circling a tree

Figure 5-58 Calling the `hawk` object's `turn` method

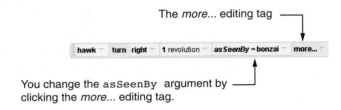

You can also put the `turn` instruction in a loop, to make the `hawk` circle the `bonzai` multiple times. However, the `hawk` will appear to slow down and stop at the end of each revolution and then at the beginning of the next revolution, appear to increase speed gradually. To make the movement appear more realistic, as one continual motion, you can also use the *more...* editing tag to change the `style` argument. The `style` argument specifies how the action should begin and end. By default, the action begins and ends gently. Changing the `style` argument to `abruptly` will cause the action to immediately begin and end.

Figure 5-59 shows an example of a loop that will cause the `hawk` to circle the `bonzai` continuously. The motion looks realistic because the duration is set to a greater value (3 seconds) and the `style` is set to `abruptly`.

Figure 5-59 A loop that causes the `hawk` to circle the `bonzai`

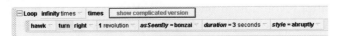

Circling an Invisible Object

In the previous example you saw a world with a `hawk` circling a `bonzai`. The `bonzai` object serves as the center point of the circle that the `hawk` is flying in. What if we want the `hawk` to simply fly in a circle, without the `bonzai`? For the `hawk` to fly in a circle, we still need an object to reference in the `asSeenBy` argument. If we don't want to see the `bonzai` object, we can make it invisible by setting its `isShowing` property to *false*. It will still be present in the world, but it will not be displayed. When we play the world, it will appear as though the `hawk` is simply flying in a circle.

TIP: If you want an object to circle an invisible object, the invisible object can be any object from the gallery.

Capturing Poses

When you use the Scene Editor to put an object into a position, you can capture that position as a *pose*. Poses that have been captured can then be restored during an animation.

For example, suppose we create an instance of the `ToySoldier` class (from the *People* collection), which appears as the image on the left in Figure 5-60. We want to make the soldier salute in an animation, as shown in the image on the right. One way to do this is to write instructions to move the soldier's arm, which are then executed when the world is played. Another way is to move the soldier's arm into the saluting position in the Scene Editor, and then capture the position as a pose. Then we can write a single instruction that will put the soldier in the saluting pose when the world is played.

Figure 5-60 A `toySoldier` object

Once you have placed an object in the desired position, you can capture the position as a pose by clicking the *capture pose* button shown in Figure 5-61. The *capture pose* button is under the *properties* tab in the Details Panel. This creates a tile for the new pose, which will appear just above the *capture pose* button. The tile will show pose as the name of the pose. You will need to change the name to something more meaningful.

Figure 5-61 The *capture pose* button

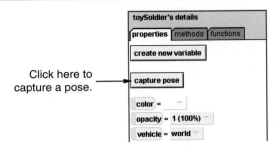

For example, Figure 5-62 shows the tiles for two new poses that we captured for the toySoldier object: atAttention and salute. The atAttention pose is the normal position for the soldier, shown on the left in Figure 5-60. The salute pose is the saluting position shown on the right in Figure 5-60. To put the toySoldier object in either of these positions in an animation, we call the toySoldier.set pose method, passing the name of the desired pose as an argument. Figure 5-63 shows a method with two instructions that will cause the toySoldier to assume these poses. (Load the *SalutingSoldier* world from the Student CD to see this work.)

Figure 5-62 Captured poses

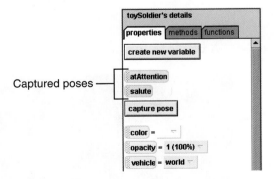

 TIP: When you save an object to a new class, any poses that you have captured for that object will be saved with it. Then, when you import an object using the new class, the object will automatically have the poses.

Figure 5-63 Instructions to set poses

Programming the Camera

You can program the camera in an Alice world just as you can program other objects. It has all of the same primitive methods and functions that other objects have. This can be useful in creating animations. For example, Figure 5-64 shows the *TurnCamera* world, which is on the Student CD. The world has an instance of the BlueBallerina class (from the *People* collection) inside an instance of the Dojo class (from the Web gallery's *Environments* collection). The camera is positioned so it is facing the ballerina. When you play the world, the instructions shown in Figure 5-65 execute. These instructions cause (1) the camera to move forward 10 meters, toward the ballerina, and (2) spin the camera all the way around the ballerina. This technique gives a dramatic visual effect.

Another visual effect that you can accomplish by programming the camera is to make the camera point at a moving object as the object moves. You do this by calling the camera.point at method simultaneously as the object moves.

Figure 5-64 The *TurnCamera* world

Figure 5-65 Instructions to turn the camera around the ballerina

For example, Figure 5-66 shows the *CameraPointAtCar* world, which is on the Student CD. In the world *kelly* (from the *People* collection) is in a `convertibleCorvette` (from the *Vehicles* collection). Her `vehicle` property is set to `convertibleCorvette`, so as the car moves, she moves with it. When the world is played, a loop causes the car to move down the road. As the car moves, the camera's viewpoint changes to follow it. Figure 5-67 shows the instructions that execute when the world is played.

In the *CameraPointAtCar* world, shown in Figure 5-66, the camera itself does not move in the Alice world. Instead, it turns so the car stays in the view. You can also program the camera to move along with an object. This is demonstrated in the *CameraFollowCar* world, also on the Student CD. The objects in this world are identical to those in the *CameraPointAtCar* world. In the *CameraFollowCar* world, the camera's `vehicle` property is set to `convertibleCorvette`, so as the car moves, the camera moves with it.

Figure 5-66 The *CameraPointAtCar* world

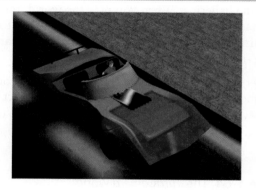

Figure 5-67 Instructions to make the camera point at the car as it moves

TIP: You can also set an object's `vehicle` property to the camera. This will cause the object to move with the camera.

TIP: If you select the camera in the Object Tree, and then switch to quad view, you can see the camera's bounding box in the top, right, and front views. A set of axes is also displayed, indicating the camera's orientation. Figure 5-68 shows an example.

Figure 5-68 In quad view you can see the camera's bounding box

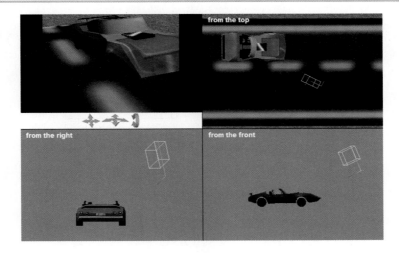

Creating Dummy Objects for the Camera

In the previous discussion we talked about using primitive methods such as move to move the camera around in the world. You can also use dummy objects as an aid in moving the camera. A dummy object is an invisible object that you place at a location in the world. You can then move the camera to the dummy object. These are the steps you can follow to place dummy objects in a world:

1. In scene editing mode, move the camera to the first location that you want the camera to move to when the world plays.
2. Click the *more controls* button, as shown in Figure 5-69. An additional set of controls will appear, as shown in Figure 5-70.
3. Click the *drop dummy at camera* button. This will create a dummy object at the camera's current location. A tile for the dummy object will appear in the Object Tree, as shown in Figure 5-71. (The tiles for all of the dummy objects that you create will be located in a folder named *Dummy Objects* in the Object Tree.)

Figure 5-69 The *more controls* button

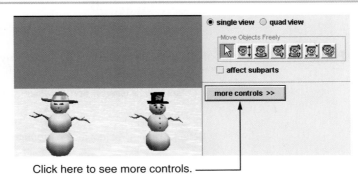

Click here to see more controls. ———

Figure 5-70 Expanded set of controls

Figure 5-71 Tile for a dummy object

Under most circumstances you should change the default name of the dummy object to something that will remind you of the object's purpose, such as firstViewPoint, or sideView.

4. Move the camera to the next location that you want the camera to move to and repeat the process of dropping a dummy object at the camera. Do this for each subsequent location that you want the camera to move to.

5. If you want to start the animation at one of the dummy objects, select the dummy object under *move camera to dummy*, as shown in Figure 5-70.

6. In the method editor you can create instructions to move the camera to any of the dummy objects that you have created. You call the camera.set point of view to primitive method, and pass the desired dummy object as the argument. Figure 5-72 shows an example of such an instruction.

Figure 5-72 Instruction to move the camera to a dummy object

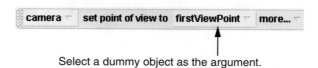

Select a dummy object as the argument.

 **Checkpoint**

5.21 How do you insert a graphical image into an Alice world?

5.22 You have object a and object b in an Alice world. You want object a to move automatically with object b. How do you accomplish this?

5.23 When you execute object a's turn method, and use the *more...* editing tag to set the asSeenBy argument to object b, what effect does this have on the action that is performed?

5.24 What is a pose?

5.25 What is a dummy object?

Review Questions

Multiple Choice

1. If you want to add a new behavior to an object, you add this type of method to it.
   a. Local method
   b. Class-level method
   c. Primitive method
   d. Primitive function

2. After you have saved an object to a new class, you do this to add an instance of it to a world.
   a. Find the class in the local gallery and then add an instance of it to the world
   b. Click *File*, then *Create Instance*
   c. Click *File*, then *Import...*
   d. You cannot add an instance of a class that you have created

3. In this process, the programmer goes through each step in an algorithm, expanding it until it has enough detail to be translated into actual instructions.
   a. Step-wise refinement
   b. Divide and conquer
   c. Incrementation
   d. Inheritance

4. This is a special variable that holds an argument being passed into a method.
   a. Local variable
   b. Class-level variable
   c. Parameter
   d. Property

5. In Alice, a property is really one of these.
   a. A method
   b. A class-level variable
   c. A local variable
   d. A function

6. This instruction is required in all functions.
   a. `Return`
   b. `Terminate`
   c. `SendBack`
   d. `End`

7. This is the process of breaking a long complex algorithm into small manageable pieces.
   a. Virtual composition
   b. Inheritance
   c. Instantiation
   d. Divide and conquer

8. To insert a graphical image into a world, you create one of these.
   a. Flat Panel
   b. Billboard
   c. Frame
   d. ImageView

9. This property specifies that the object will move with another object.
   a. `vehicle`
   b. `movesWith`
   c. `coupledTo`
   d. `joinedWith`

10. You use this primitive method call to move the camera to a dummy object.
    a. `camera.move to dummy object`
    b. `camera.move`
    c. `camera.set point of view to`
    d. You call the dummy object's `restore camera` method

Short Answer

1. When you add custom class-level methods to an object, how can you create other objects like it?

2. When you save an object to a new class, what name will the new class have?

3. Why shouldn't you call one object's class-level method from another object's class-level method?

4. If you have a long series of instructions that you want to execute at the world level, instead of writing one big method, how can you apply the process of divide and conquer?

5. If you have an object named `josie`, sitting on a `horse` object, how would you make `josie` move with the `horse`?

6. In a world where the camera moves around, what would be a simple way to make an object move with the camera?

Exercises

1. **Exercise Competition**

   Three girls, Jenny, Kelly, and Barb, are enrolled in an exercise class. One day after class the three decide to have a friendly competition to see how many sets of 10 repetitions of running in place each can do before getting tired. Barb decides to go first and gets tired at 10 repetitions. Kelly goes next, and she gets tired at 20 repetitions. Jenny, who has been in the exercise class for the longest, goes next. She gets tired at 30 repetitions.

   Create a world that simulates the competition. Each of the girls should be an instance of the `ExerciseGirl` class that you created in this chapter. Set each girl's `getsTiredAt` property to the appropriate value, so the girls get tired at the correct number of repetitions.

2. **ExerciseGirl Modification #1**

   Modify the `ExerciseGirl` class that you created in this chapter's tutorials so she swings her arms in a realistic manner while running in place.

3. **ExerciseGirl Modification #2**

   Add a `jumpingJack` method to the `ExerciseGirl` class. The method should make the object perform jumping jacks, and should have a parameter for the number of repetitions to perform. Be sure to increment the `repsDone` property after each repetition.

4. **Candle Methods**

   Create an instance of the `CandleJar` class (from the *Objects* collection). Add the following class-level methods to the `candleJar` object:

   - `extinguish`—This method should make the candle's flame invisible.
   - `light`—This method should make the candle's flame visible.
   - `flicker`—This method should make the candle's flame appear to flicker for a few seconds.

   Create a scene that demonstrates each of these methods by calling them from the world's method.

5. **Combo Lock Methods**

   Create an instance of the `ComboLock` class (from the *Objects* collection). Add a Boolean class-level variable named `isLocked`, initially set to *True*. The `isLocked` variable will indicate whether the `comboLock` object is locked. Also, add the following class-level methods to the `comboLock` object:

   - `spinRight`—This method should make the lock's dial spin right one revolution.
   - `spinLeft`—This method should make the lock's dial spin left one revolution.
   - `unlock`—If the `comboLock` object is currently locked (`isLocked` set to *True*), this method should make the lock's latch move up so it appears opened, and set the `isLocked` variable to *False*. If the `comboLock` object is currently unlocked, this method should do nothing.

- lock—If the comboLock object is currently unlocked (isLocked set to *False*), this method should make the lock's latch move down so it appears locked, and set the isLocked variable to *True*. If the comboLock object is currently locked, this method should do nothing.

Figure 5-73 shows how the comboLock object should appear in the locked and unlocked positions. Create a scene that demonstrates each of the comboLock object's custom class-level methods.

Figure 5-73 comboLock object in the locked and unlocked positions

Locked   Unlocked

6. **MailBox** Methods

Create an instance of the MailBox class (from the *Objects* collection). Add the following class-level variables to the mailBox object:

- doorOpen, a Boolean variable initially set to *False*. The doorOpen variable will indicate whether the mailbox's door is open.

- flagUp, a Boolean variable initially set to *False*. The flagUp variable will indicate whether the mailbox's flag is up.

Also, add the following class-level methods to the mailBox object:

- openDoor—If the mailbox's door is currently closed (the doorOpen variable set to *False*), this method should open the mailbox's door, and set the doorOpen variable to *True*. If the mailbox's door is already open (the doorOpen variable set to *True*), this method should do nothing.

- closeDoor—If the mailbox's door is currently open (the doorOpen variable set to *True*), this method should close the mailbox's door, and set the doorOpen variable to False. If the mailbox's door is already closed (the doorOpen variable set to False), this method should do nothing.

- raiseFlag—If the mailbox's flag is currently down (the flagUp variable set to *False*), this method should raise the mailbox's flag, and set the flagUp variable to *True*. If the mailbox's flag is already raised (the flagUp variable set to *True*), this method should do nothing.

- `lowerFlag`—If the mailbox's flag is currently raised (the `flagUp` variable set to *True*), this method should lower the mailbox's flag, and set the `flagUp` variable to *False*. If the mailbox's flag is already lowered (the `flagUp` variable set to *False*), this method should do nothing.

Create a scene that demonstrates each of these methods.

7. **Orbiting Spaceships**

Create a world that shows two spaceships orbiting Earth. For Earth, use an instance of the `Globe` class (from the *Objects* collection). After you insert an instance of the class, delete all of the subparts except for the `GlobeBall`. You can find a variety of spaceships in the Web gallery's *Space* collection.

One of the spaceships should be closer to Earth than the other one. The spaceship that is closest to Earth should orbit faster than the spaceship that is farther away.

8. **Marcello the Magician**

Marcello the magician has finally mastered his disappearing act. To perform the act, he places several items on a table in front of him. He stands with his right arm extended over an item. He says the magic words "Alakazam, Alakazee" and the object disappears. He repeats this procedure for each object on the table.

Create a world in which Marcello (an instance of the `Magician` class, from the *People* collection) demonstrates his new act, as shown in Figure 5-74. In the `magician` object you should create two new class-level methods: `sayMagicWords`, and `makeDisappear`. The `sayMagicWords` should cause Marcello to say the magic words. The `makeDisappear` method should have an Object parameter. It should cause Marcello to turn to face the object, say the magic words (by calling the `sayMagicWords` method), and then make the object disappear by setting its `isShowing` property to *false*.

After you have created and tested the methods, save the `magician` object to a new class so you can use it in other worlds.

Figure 5-74 Marcello performing his act

9. **More Tricks for Marcello**

Give Marcello the Magician (from Exercise 8) the ability to do more magic tricks. For example, you could write a method named `levitate`, which would take an object as an argument. The method would cause the object to levitate in the air.

You could also write a method named `transform` that would take two objects as arguments. The method would cause the first object to "transform" into the other. To set that method up, one of the objects would have to be invisible (opacity set to 0), and both objects would have to be placed in the same location. When the method is called, the visible object would be made invisible and simultaneously the invisible object would be made visible.

10. **Karate Moves**

Create a world with an instance of the `EvilNinja` class (from the *People* collection). Modify the `EvilNinja` object so it can do at least one kind of karate kick and a karate punch. Write the necessary class-level methods to make the `EvilNinja` make these moves. Save the `EvilNinja` to a new class named `KarateNinja`, and then import an instance of the new class into a world with a `Dojo` object (from the Web gallery's *Environments* collection). Write a world-level method that makes the `KarateNinja` object demonstrate how it can kick and punch.

TIP: If you want to make your ninja movements authentic, you can search the Web for sites that give short tutorials on basic kicks and punches.

11. **Old West**

The opening scene of a western movie shows a woman standing in front of a saloon. The sheriff rides his horse up to the woman and says "Howdy Ma'am."

Create an old west themed world that recreates this scene, as shown in Figure 5-75. The world should have the following objects: a `saloon`, a `sheriff`, and a `westGirl` (all from the *Old West* collection), and a `horse` (from the *Animals* collection). Position the `sheriff` so he is sitting on the `horse`. Set the sheriff's properties such that when the `horse` moves, the `sheriff` should move with it.

In the `sheriff` object, create a method named `greetWoman`. This method should cause the `sheriff` to say "Howdy Ma'am." Also, create the necessary methods in the `horse` object to make the horse walk forward. These methods should cause the horse's front and rear legs to move in a walking motion. (You might consider capturing poses with the legs in different positions.)

Figure 5-75 *Old West* world

Figure 5-76 *Graveyard tour* world

12. **Graveyard Tour**

    Create a spooky world with a church (from the *City* collection) and a graveyard. To create the graveyard, use a gate and tombstones (from the *Spooky* collection) and fence pieces (from the Web gallery's *Buildings* collection). You can also use other items, such as a statue (from the *City* collection). Figure 5-76 shows an example of the world.

    When the world is played, the camera should move through the world, and a candlestick (from the *Objects* collection) should move along with the camera. This will give the effect that you are walking through the world, carrying the candlestick. To make the candlestick move with the camera, set the candlestick's `vehicle` property to the camera.

    The camera should first move to the gate. When the camera reaches the gate, the gate doors should slowly swing open. Once the doors are opened, the camera should move through the graveyard toward the church. When the camera gets close to the church doors, the candle's flame should go out and the world should become dark. (Use the flame's opacity property to make it go out. The world has a light object, which controls the amount of light in the world. Set the light object's brightness property to *0* to make the world dark.)

13. **Search and Rescue**

    Create a sea world with two `scubaDiver` objects (from the *People* collection) adrift, as shown in the left image in Figure 5-77. Create a `helicopter` (from the *Vehicles* collection), and position it off-screen. The image on the right in Figure 5-77 shows the `helicopter`. Create two life preservers as instances of the `Torus` class (from the *Shapes* collection) and position them just below the `helicopter`'s runners. Set the torus objects' `vehicle` property to the `helicopter` so they will move with the `helicopter`.

    Write a method in the `helicopter` object named `locate`. The `locate` method should take an object as its argument. The method should cause the `helicopter` to turn to face the object that was passed as an argument, move to a position that is 10 meters away from the object, and then circle the object one time.

Figure 5-77 *Search and Rescue* world

Write two more methods named `dropLeftPreserver` and `dropRightPreserver`. These methods should cause the left and right life preservers to drop to the surface of the water. To do this, each method should first set the appropriate torus's `vehicle` property to the `world`, and then move the torus down the distance that the torus is above the `ground` object (which in this case is the water).

When the world is played, the `helicopter` should move to the first scuba diver, circle it, drop one of the life preservers, move to the second scuba diver, circle it, and then drop the other life preserver.

6 Events

TOPICS

6.1   Responding to Events
6.2   Handling Key Press and Mouse Events
6.3   Using Events in Simulations and Games
6.4   Tips for Games and Simulations

6.1   Responding to Events

CONCEPT: An event is an action that takes place while an Alice world is playing. Alice worlds are capable of detecting events and responding to them. You write methods known as event handlers to perform the actions that you want to take place in response to an event.

An event is an action that takes place while a program is running. When Alice worlds are running, they are capable of detecting several different types of events. For example, an event occurs when the user clicks an object with the mouse. An event also occurs when the user types a key on the keyboard. Table 6-1 describes all of the events that an Alice world can detect while it is running.

When any of the events listed in Table 6-1 occur, your Alice world can perform an action in response to the event. In fact, all of the Alice worlds that you have created so far respond to the When the world starts event. This event occurs as soon as you click the *Play* button to run a world.

In the Alice environment, at the top right of the screen, you see an area labeled *Events*, as shown in Figure 6-1. Recall that this area is called the *Events Editor*. When you create an Alice world, a tile appears in the Events Editor that reads as follows:

```
When the world starts, do world.my first method
```

Table 6-1 Events that Alice can detect

Event	Description
When the world starts	This event occurs immediately when the world is started. It happens only once, each time the world is played.
While the world is running	This event occurs as long as the world is running.
When a key is typed	When the user types a key on the keyboard, this event occurs when the key is released.
While a key is pressed	This event occurs while the user holds down a key.
When the mouse is clicked on something	This event occurs when the user clicks an object in the world with the mouse.
While the mouse is pressed on something	When the user clicks an object with the mouse, this event occurs while the user holds down the mouse button.
While something is true	When a condition that you have specified becomes *true*, this event occurs as long as the condition remains *true*.
When something becomes true	This event occurs when a condition that you have specified becomes *true*.
When a variable changes	This event occurs when a variable's value changes.
Let the mouse move <objects>	This event allows the user to move an object in the world by clicking and dragging it with the mouse.
Let the arrow keys move <subject>	This event allows the user to move an object in the world by typing the arrow keys on the keyboard.
Let the mouse move the camera	This event allows the user to move the camera through the world by clicking and dragging the mouse.
Let the mouse orient the camera	This event allows the user to change the camera's orientation (the direction in which it is pointing) by clicking and dragging the mouse.

This tile specifies that when the world starts, the method `world.my first method` will be executed. The left portion of the tile shows the name of an event, `When the world starts`, and the right portion of the tile is a drop-down box that shows the name of the method that will be executed when the event occurs. You can click the down-arrow on the drop-down box to select a different method. Any method that is selected in this tile will be automatically executed when the world starts.

Figure 6-1 The Events Editor

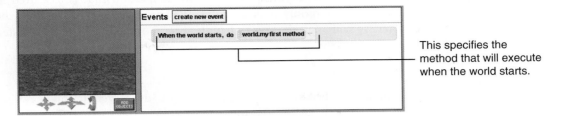

This specifies the method that will execute when the world starts.

The process of responding to an event is commonly called *handling the event*. In order for an Alice world to handle an event, a tile for that event must appear in the Events Editor. When a world is first created, the only tile that appears in the Events Editor is for the When the world starts event. If you want the world to handle any other events, you must create a new tile for the event in the Events Editor. To create a new event tile, you click the *create new event* button, as shown in Figure 6-2. A menu of available events will appear next, as shown in Figure 6-3. You select the event that you want to handle from this menu. A tile for the event will then be created in the Events Editor.

Figure 6-2 The *create new event* button

Click here to create a new event tile.

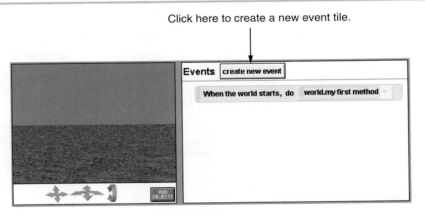

Figure 6-3 Menu of available events

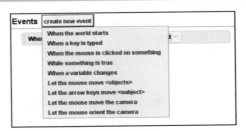

Most event tiles require that you specify additional arguments, such as the method that you want to execute in response to the event. A method that is executed in response to an event is commonly referred to as an *event handler*. Throughout the rest of this chapter we will explore ways to handle several of the events that are listed in Table 6-1.

NOTE: We will not use the `Let the mouse move <object>` event in this chapter. That event requires knowledge of lists, so we will explore it in Chapter 7.

Specialized Events

Perhaps you noticed that some of the events listed in Table 6-1 do not appear on the events menu shown in Figure 6-3. Some of the events in the table are more specialized versions of other general events. To create one of these specialized events, you have to create the general event first, and then right-click the event tile and select *change to* on the menu. This allows you to change the event to a more specialized event.

Table 6-2 lists the specialized events and describes how to create them. As we progress through the chapter we will take a closer look at these.

Table 6-2 Specialized events and how to create them

Event	How to Create It
`While the world is running`	Create a tile for the `When the world starts` event; right-click the tile and select *change to*.
`While a key is pressed`	Create a tile for the `When a key is typed` event; right-click the tile and select *change to*.
`While the mouse is pressed on something`	Create a tile for the `When the mouse is clicked on something` event, right-click the tile and select *change to*.
`When something becomes true`	Create a tile for the `While something is true` event, right-click the tile and select *change to*.

NOTE: Events are also used in many of the traditional programming languages. For example, in Java and Visual Basic, events occur when the user performs actions such as clicking a button.

Checkpoint

6.1 What is an event?

6.2 When an Alice world is first created, what event tile(s) appear in the Events Editor?

6.3 How do you specify a different method to be automatically executed when the world starts?

6.4 How do you create a new event tile in the Events Editor?

6.5 What is an event handler?

6.2 Handling Key Press and Mouse Events

CONCEPT: **In Alice you can detect when the user has pressed a key on the keyboard and when the user has clicked an object. You can use these capabilities to build sophisticated interactions in your worlds.**

So far, the Alice worlds that you have developed have had only limited interactivity with the user. For example, you have learned to use the `ask` functions to read numeric input, string input, and yes or no responses. In this section you will learn how to use events to detect key presses and mouse clicks. By handling these events you will be able to create worlds in which the user can interact with objects by typing keys and clicking the mouse.

Key Press Events

One of the events that an Alice world can handle is `When a key is typed`. This event is triggered when the user types a key on the keyboard and then releases the key. To create a tile for the event you click the *create new event* button in the Events Editor, and then select `When a key is typed` from the menu that appears. The tile shown in Figure 6-4 will be created in the Events Editor.

Figure 6-4 Event tile

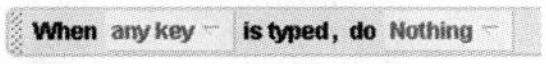

```
When any key ˅  is typed, do Nothing ˅
```

The event tile, as it is shown in Figure 6-4, is not yet complete. We still have to specify a key, and a method to execute when the key is typed. When you click the down-arrow next to the *any key* placeholder, a menu appears showing all of the keys that you can select for this event. The available keys are the [Spacebar], the [Enter] key, [↑], [↓], [←], and [→] keys, the letter keys, the number keys, or any key.

After you select a key, you can do one of the following things to specify a method to execute in response to the event:

- Click the down-arrow ˅ next to *Nothing*. This causes a menu to appear showing all of the methods that you have created in the world. Select the method that you want to execute when the key is typed.
- Drag the tile for an object's primitive method from the Details Panel and drop it on top of the *Nothing* placeholder.

Figure 6-5 shows an example of a completed `When a key is typed` event tile. This tile specifies that when the [↑] key is pressed, a method named `world.moveUp` will be executed.

Figure 6-5 Completed event tile

When | ↑ | is typed, do | world.moveUp |

> **TIP:** If you want to execute an object's primitive method in response to an event, you can drag the tile for the desired primitive method and drop it on top of the *Nothing* placeholder.

Tutorial 6-1 will take you through the process of creating event tiles and handlers that respond when designated keys are pressed.

VideoNote

Handling Key Press Events

Tutorial 6-1:
Handling key press events

On the Student CD you will find a world named *Faeries*, which is shown in Figure 6-6. The creature on the left is an instance of the `MabHazelnut` class, and the creature on the right is an instance of the `GossamerFlameGlimmer` class. Both of these classes are from the *Fantasy > Faeries* collection.

Figure 6-6 The *Faeries* world

Both of these objects have several custom, class-level methods for making facial expressions, flapping their wings, and so forth. In this tutorial you will give both objects a class-level method named `fly`, which will cause the creatures to flap their wings while moving up in the air, then back down. Then you will create event tiles that call each object's `fly` method when a designated key is pressed.

Step 1: Copy the *Faeries* world from the Student CD to your hard drive and open it.

Step 2: First you will create a `fly` method for the `gossamerFlameGlimmer` object. Select the `gossamerFlameGlimmer` object and click the *create new method* button in the Details Panel, under the *methods* tab. Name the method `fly`.

Step 3:   In the `gossamerFlameGlimmer.fly` method, create the instruction shown in Figure 6-7.

Figure 6-7 The `fly` method

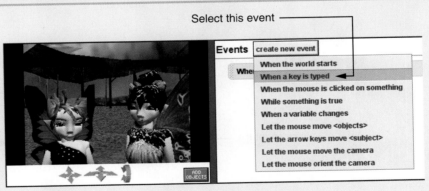

Step 4:   We want the `gossamerFlameGlimmer.fly` method to execute when the user presses the Ⓖ key. Now you will create an event tile to make that happen. In the Events Editor, click the *create new event* button. From the menu that appears, select *When a key is typed*, as shown in Figure 6-8. This should create a tile for the `When a key is typed` event, as shown in Figure 6-9.

Figure 6-8 Creating a new event tile

Select this event

```
Events  create new event
                        When the world starts
        Whe                When a key is typed
                        When the mouse is clicked on something
                        While something is true
                        When a variable changes
                        Let the mouse move <objects>
                        Let the arrow keys move <subject>
                        Let the mouse move the camera
                        Let the mouse orient the camera
```

ADD OBJECTS

Figure 6-9 The Events Editor showing the new event tile

```
Events  create new event
   When the world starts,  do  world.animation
   When  any key  is typed,  do  Nothing
```

Step 5: To complete the event tile that you just created, you need to specify a key and a method. Click the down-arrow ▽ next to *any key*, then from the menu select *letters*, and then select G. This is shown in the image on the left in Figure 6-10. Then, click the down-arrow ▽ next to *Nothing*. From the menu that appears, select gossamerFlameglimmer, then select fly, as shown in the image on the right in Figure 6-10. This should create the tile shown in Figure 6-11.

Figure 6-10 Completing the event tile

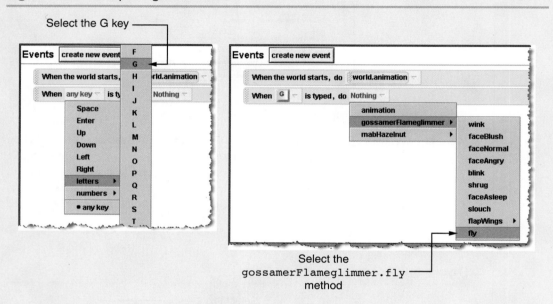

Select the G key ———

Select the
gossamerFlameglimmer.fly ———
method

Figure 6-11 The new tile in the Events Editor

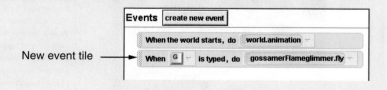

New event tile ———▶

Step 6: Save the world, and then play it. Any time that you press the Ⓖ key, you should see the gossamerFlameglimmer object flap her wings and briefly fly. Close the *World Running...* window when you are finished testing.

Step 7: Select the mabHazelnut object and create the fly method, as shown in Figure 6-12.

Figure 6-12 The `mabHazelnut.fly` method

```
● mabHazelnut.fly
mabHazelnut.fly No parameters
No variables

 //  Simultaneously flap wings and move up.
 ⊟ Do together
     mabHazelnut.flapWings duration = 1    amount = 0.25
     mabHazelnut    move  up    0.5 meters    more...

 //  Simultaneously flap wings and move down.
 ⊟ Do together
     mabHazelnut.flapWings duration = 1    amount = 0.25
     mabHazelnut    move  down    0.5 meters    more...
```

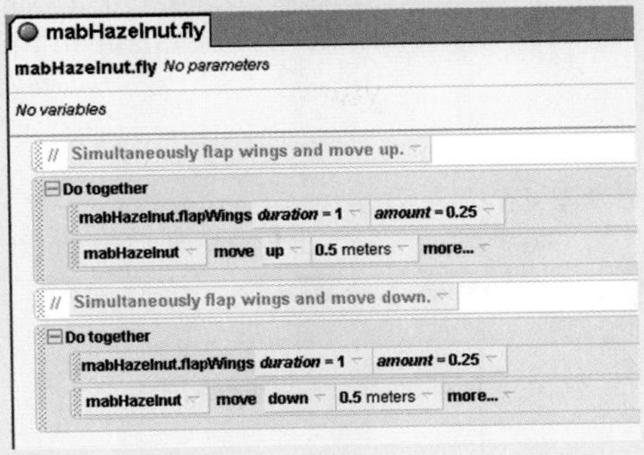

Step 8: Create an event tile that executes the `mabHazelnut.fly` method when the Ⓜ key is typed. Figure 6-13 shows how the tile should appear.

Figure 6-13 Event tile

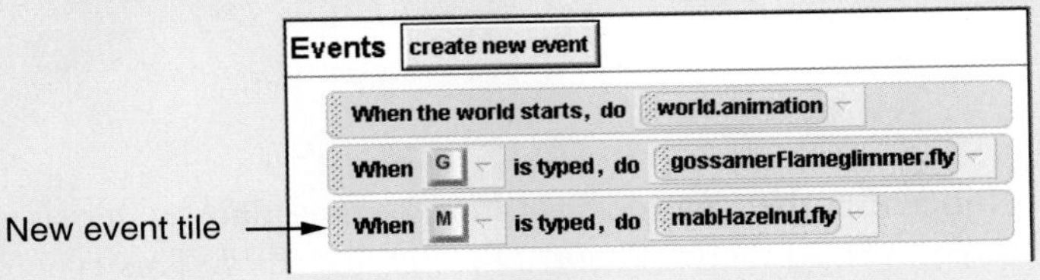

```
Events  create new event

        When the world starts, do   world.animation

        When  G   is typed, do    gossamerFlameglimmer.fly

New event tile →  When  M   is typed, do    mabHazelnut.fly
```

Step 9: Save the world, and then play it. Any time that you press the Ⓜ key, you should see the `mabHazelnut` object flap her wings and briefly fly. Close the *World Running...* window when you are finished testing.

> **TIP:** Alice can simultaneously handle multiple events. For example, if you press the Ⓖ key, and then quickly press the Ⓜ key, you will see the `gossamerFlameglimmer` and the `mabHazelnut` objects fly at the same time.

Handling the `While a key is pressed` Event

Recall that one of the specialized events that you can handle is the `While a key is pressed` event. This event occurs as long as the user holds down a key. This is different from the `When a key is typed` event, which occurs only when the user releases a key.

This is how you create a tile for the `While a key is pressed` event: First, create a tile for the `When a key is typed` event. Then, right-click the tile and from the menus that appear select *change to > While a key is pressed*, as shown in Figure 6-14. After doing this, the event tile will be changed to appear as shown in Figure 6-15.

Figure 6-14 Changing an event tile

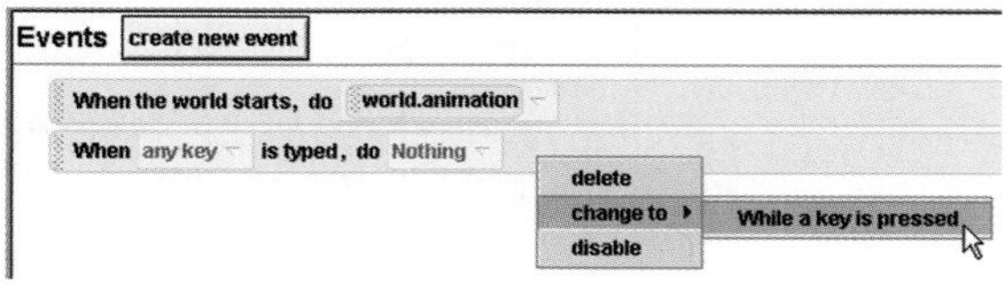

Figure 6-15 Tile for the `while a key is pressed` event

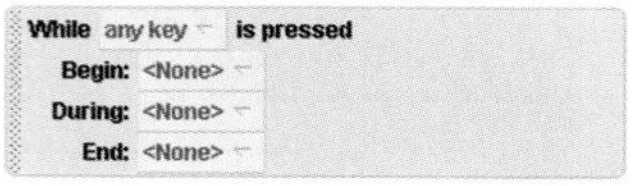

Notice that the new tile has four different placeholder slots: one for the key, and then three others labeled *Begin*, *During*, and *End*. This type of event is referred to as a *BDE* event. When you create a BDE event, you specify an action to take place at the beginning of the event (the moment that the event occurs), an action to take place during the event (the time during which the event is taking place), and an action to take place at the end of the event (the moment that the event stops occurring).

Although you are not required to provide actions in each of these slots, they allow you to create a powerful event handling mechanism. Tutorial 6-2 will show you how to handle one of these events.

Tutorial 6-2:
Handling the `while a key is pressed` event

On the Student CD you will find a world named *SpaceJet*, which is shown in Figure 6-16. The spaceship is an instance of the `GrayJumpJet` class, and the pilot is an instance of the `Scientist_Woman` class. Both of these classes are from the *SciFi* collection.

In this tutorial you will use the `While a key is pressed` event to fly the spaceship while the user holds down the Spacebar. The action will work like this:

Figure 6-16 The *SpaceJet* world

```
While the spacebar is pressed
   Begin:   grayjumpjet move up 15 meters
   During:  grayjumpjet move forward 30 meters abruptly
   End:     grayjumpjet move down 15 meters
```

Step 1: Copy the *SpaceJet* world from the Student CD to your hard drive and open it.

Step 2: Click the *create new event* button in the Events Editor, and select *When a key is typed* from the menu. This will create a tile for the `When a key is typed` event.

Step 3: Right-click the `When a key is typed` event tile that you just created. On the menu that appears, select *change to > While a key is pressed*. The tile should now appear as shown in Figure 6-17.

Figure 6-17 Event tile

```
While  any key ▾  is pressed
   Begin:  <None> ▾
  During:  <None> ▾
     End:  <None> ▾
```

Step 4: Change the event tile's placeholders as follows:
- Change the *any key* placeholder to the *Space* key
- Select the `grayjumpjet` object and drag the tile for its `move` method onto the *<None>* placeholder in the *Begin* section, as shown in Figure 6-18. When you drop the tile, select *up* for the direction, and specify *15 meters* for the amount.

Figure 6-18 Dragging the `grayjumpjet.move` tile to the *Begin* section

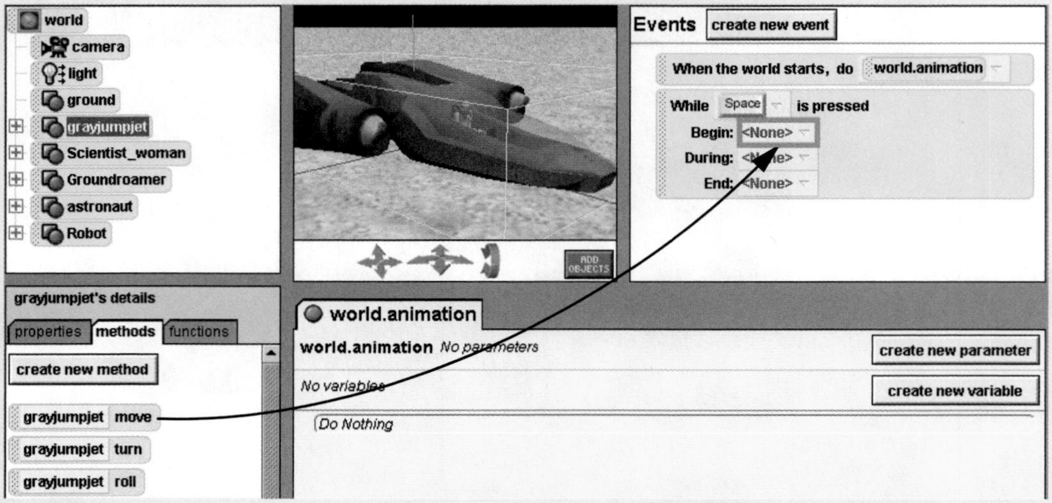

![Figure 6-18 screenshot showing the Alice interface with the object tree, a grayjumpjet spaceship, and the Events panel with the grayjumpjet.move tile being dragged to the Begin section]

- Drag the tile for the `grayjumpjet` object's move method and drop it onto the *<None>* placeholder in the *During* section. Select *forward* for the direction, and specify *30 meters* for the amount. Use the *more...* editing tag to change the `style` argument to *abruptly*.
- Drag the tile for the `grayjumpjet` object's move method and drop it onto the *<None>* placeholder in the *End* section. Select *down* for the direction, and specify *15 meters* for the amount.

After doing all this, the tile should appear as shown in Figure 6-19.

Figure 6-19 The completed event tile

Step 5: Save the world and then play it. To test the event handling code, hold down the ⎵Spacebar⎵. You will see the spaceship rise straight upward (because of the *Begin* portion of the event tile), and then fly forward (because of the *During* portion of the event tile). When you release the spacebar the spaceship will stop moving forward and will move down to the surface (because of the *End* portion of the event tile).

Notice that as the spaceship moves, the camera moves with it because the camera's vehicle property is set to the `grayjumpjet` object.

Mouse Events

Another event that an Alice world can handle is `When the mouse is clicked on something`. This event is triggered when the user clicks the mouse on an object in the world. To create a tile for the event you click the *create new event* button in the Events Editor, and then select *When the mouse is clicked on something* from the menu that appears. The tile shown in Figure 6-20 will be created in the Events Editor.

Figure 6-20 Event tile

To complete the tile you click the down-arrow next to *anything*, and a menu appears showing all of the objects in the world. After you select an object, you can click the down-arrow next to *Nothing*. This causes a menu to appear showing all of the methods that you have created in the world. Select the method that you want to execute when the mouse is clicked on the selected object.

In Tutorial 6-3 you will add an event tile for handling mouse clicks to an Alice world.

VideoNote
Handling a
Mouse Click
Event

Tutorial 6-3:
Handling a mouse click event

Figure 6-21 shows the *Fridge* world from the Student CD. The world contains an object named `fridge`, which is the refrigerator. In this tutorial you will modify the world so the user can open the refrigerator door by clicking it with the mouse.

Step 1: Copy the *Fridge* world from the Student CD to your hard drive and open it.

Figure 6-21 The *Fridge* world

Step 2: We want the `fridge` object's door to open when the user clicks on it. The `fridge` object has a subpart named `fridgeDoor`, which is the refrigerator door. To open the door, we will execute the `fridgeDoor` object's primitive `turn` method in response to a mouse click on the `fridge` object.   .

In the Events Editor, click the *create new event* button. From the menu that appears, select *When the mouse is clicked on something*. This should create a tile for the `When a key is typed` event, as shown in Figure 6-22.

Figure 6-22 Event tile

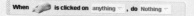

Step 3: In the event tile that you just created, click the down-arrow that appears next to *anything*. On the menu that appears, select *fridge*, then select *fridgeDoor*, and then select *the entire fridgeDoor*.

Step 4: Select the `fridgeDoor` object and drag the tile for its `turn` method onto the *Nothing* placeholder in the event tile. When you drop the turn method's tile, select *left* for the direction and *0.25 revolutions* for the amount. After doing this, the event tile should appear similar to the one shown in Figure 6-23.

Figure 6-23 Completed event tile

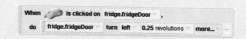

Step 5: Save the world and play it. When you click the refrigerator door, it should swing open, revealing a six-pack of grape soda inside!

Handling the `While the mouse is clicked on something` Event

One of the specialized events that you can handle is the `While the mouse is clicked on something` event. This event occurs as long as the user holds down the mouse button with the pointer positioned over an object. This is different from the `When the mouse is clicked on something` event, which occurs only when the user clicks an object with the mouse.

This is how you create a tile for the `While the mouse is clicked on something` event: First, create a tile for the `When the mouse is clicked on something` event. Then, right-click the tile, and from the menus that appear select *change to* > *While the mouse is clicked on something*. After doing this, the event tile will be changed to appear as shown in Figure 6-24.

Figure 6-24 Event tile

`While the mouse is clicked on something` is a BDE event. The tile has four different placeholder slots: one for an object and three others labeled *Begin*, *During*, and *End*. You specify an action to take place at the beginning of the event (the moment that the mouse is clicked on the object), an action to take place during the event (the time during which the mouse button is held down), and an action to take place at the end of the event (the moment that the mouse button is released).

On the Student CD you will find a world named *Globe* that demonstrates the `While the mouse is clicked on something` event. The world contains an instance of the `Globe` class (from the *Objects* collection). When you click the globe it starts spinning. As long as you hold down the mouse button it will continue to spin. Figure 6-25 shows the event tile that creates this action.

Figure 6-25 The *Globe* world

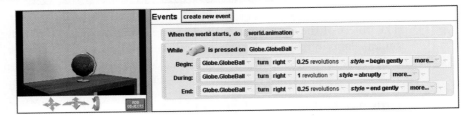

 Checkpoint

6.6 What is the difference between a `While a key is pressed` event and a `When a key is pressed` event?

6.7 How do you create a `While a key is pressed` event?

6.8 In a BDE event, what does B, D, and E stand for?

6.9 What is the difference between a `While the mouse is clicked on something` event and a `When the mouse is clicked on something` event?

6.3 Using Events in Simulations and Games

CONCEPT: You can have numerous event handlers working in a program, responding to various user interactions and internal events in the program.

In this section we will examine an Alice world that simulates a helicopter rescue mission. You will find it in the *IslandRescue* world on the Student CD. The world consists of the helicopter shown in Figure 6-26, which is positioned over an aircraft carrier at sea. Both the `Helicopter` and the `Carrier` classes are in the *Vehicles* collection. The red ring that is hanging from the helicopter is an instance of the `Torus` class, from the *Shapes* collection.

Figure 6-26 Helicopter in the *IslandRescue* world

The object of the simulation is to maneuver the helicopter to a man who is stranded on an island in front of the carrier, and pick him up with the ring as shown in Figure 6-27. The `Man` class is in the Web gallery's *People* collection. When the ring comes

Figure 6-27 Picking up the man

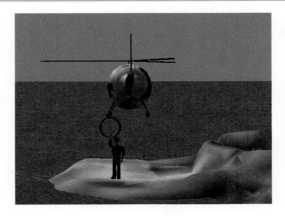

within one meter of the man's hand, he will automatically become attached to the ring. Then you bring the man back to the carrier and drop him on the orange circle, as shown in Figure 6-28. (The circle and the cones are from the *Shapes* collection.) When the man comes within 10 meters of the circle, he will automatically let go of the ring and will drop to the center of the circle.

Figure 6-28 Bringing the man back to the carrier

To maneuver the helicopter, you use the ⬆ and ⬇ keys and the Spacebar. Instructions for flying the helicopter are shown on the billboard when the world is started, as shown in Figure 6-29. To start the simulation you click anywhere in the window with the mouse.

Figure 6-29 Instructions for flying the helicopter

> **Welcome to Island Rescue!**
>
> Use the ring to pick the man up, then bring him back to the ship and drop him on the orange circle.
>
> Hold the ⬆ and ⬇ keys to move the helicopter up and down.
> Hold the ⬅ and ➡ keys to turn the helicopter left and right.
> Hold the spacebar to move the helicopter forward.
>
> Click anywhere to begin!

Everything that happens in this world is driven by events. Let's take a look at each event to see how the simulation works. First, Figure 6-30 shows what happens when the world starts. The `world.animation` method is called, which starts the helicopter blades.

Figure 6-31 shows the next event tile, for the `When the mouse is clicked on anything` event. This tile causes the `IslandRescueInstructions` billboard to become invisible when the user clicks the mouse on anything in the world.

Figure 6-30 `When the world starts` event

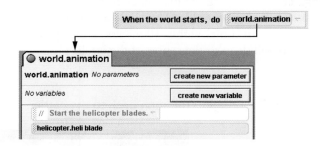

Figure 6-31 The `When the mouse is clicked on anything` event

Figure 6-32 shows the next event tile, for the `While the world is running` event. This event calls the `world.updateCamera` method, which is also shown in Figure 6-32. The `world.updateCamera` method has an `If/Else` instruction that determines whether the helicopter is more than 15 meters away from the camera. If this is true, then the camera is simultaneously pointed at the helicopter and moved to a position that is 15 meters away from the helicopter. As a result, the camera continuously follows the helicopter.

Figure 6-32 The `while the world is running` event

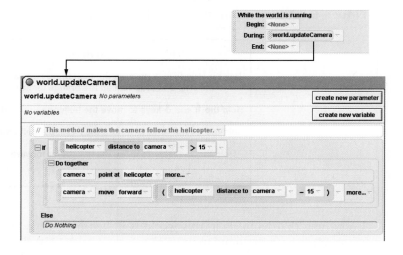

Figure 6-33 shows the tiles for the next five events. These tiles handle the key press events, which are used to maneuver the helicopter. After these, the next tile is the `When something is true` event, as shown in Figure 6-34. This event occurs when the `Man` object's right palm is within one meter of the `ring` object. When this happens,

Figure 6-33 Tiles for the key press events

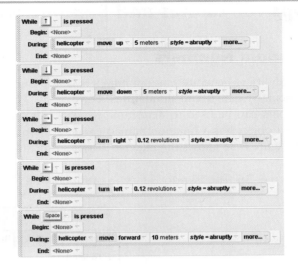

Figure 6-34 A `when something is true` event

the `Man` object's `vehicle` property is set to the `ring` object. This causes the man to be picked up by the helicopter.

The last event tile is the `When something is true` event shown in Figure 6-35. This event occurs when the `Man` object is within 10 meters of the `dropZone` object (the orange circle on the carrier). When this happens, the `world.moveManToDropZone` method, also shown in Figure 6-35, is executed. This method sets the `Man` object's `vehicle` property to the `world`, moves the `Man` object to the center of the `dropZone` object, and lowers the `Man`'s right arm.

Figure 6-35 Another `when something is true` event

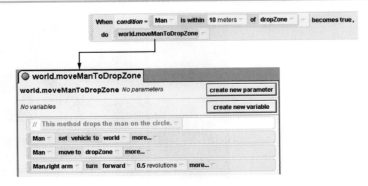

6.4 Tips for Games and Simulations

Random Numbers

The ability to generate random numbers is important for some types of applications, particularly games and simulations. For example, in a computer card game, random numbers can be used to determine which cards are dealt to the user. In Alice, the world object has a function named random number, which returns a random number. Figure 6-36 shows the random number function's tile in the Details Panel.

Figure 6-36 The random number function tile

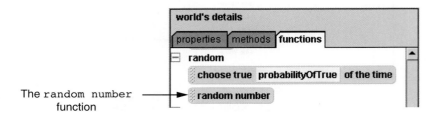

The random number function returns a fractional number between 0 and 1. You can alter this behavior by using the function's *more...* editing tag. The editing tag has the following arguments:

- minimum: You can use the minimum argument to specify a minimum value for the random number that is returned.
- maximum: You can use the maximum argument to specify a maximum value for the random number that is returned. (The random number will be a value up to the maximum, but not including it.)
- integerOnly: If you set the integerOnly argument to *true*, the function will return only whole numbers.

To demonstrate how random numbers can be used to make an object do different things, look at the *RandomBee* world, which is on the Student CD. Figure 6-37 shows the world, which has an instance of the Bee class (from the Web gallery's *Animals* collection) and three instances of the Flower class (from the *Nature* collection).

Figure 6-37 The *RandomBee* world

When you play the world, the bee flies to the flowers randomly. The program generates a random number to determine which flower that the bee will fly to, and assigns the number to a variable named `selectedFlower`. Figure 6-38 shows the instruction that does this.

Figure 6-38 Instruction to get a random number

Notice that the `minimum` argument is set to *1*, the `maximum` argument is set to *4*, and the `integerOnly` argument is set to *true*. This means that the function will return an integer random number from *1* up to, but not including, *4*. So, this function will return *1*, *2*, or *3*.

Figure 6-39 shows the `world.animation` method, which is called when the world is started. This method generates a random number, and then uses a series of nested `If/Else` instructions to test the random number. If the number is 1, then the bee flies to the `flower` object. Otherwise, if the number is 2, then the bee flies to the `flower2` object. Otherwise, if the number is 3, then the bee flies to the `flower3` object.

Figure 6-39 The `world.animation` method

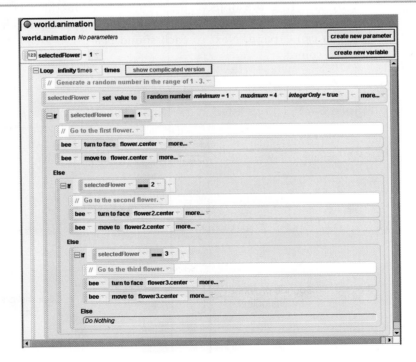

Playing Audio

Several of the classes in the Alice galleries come with sounds that can be played when the world is running. For example, the Lion class, which is in *Animals* collection, has two sounds: lionroar and wimper. You can see a list of a class's sounds by clicking the class's thumbnail in the gallery and looking at its *class information* window. Figure 6-40 shows the *class information* window for the Lion class.

Figure 6-40 The Lion class

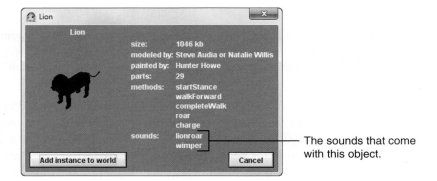

The sounds that come with this object.

If you have already added an object to the world, you can see the sounds that it has by selecting the object and then looking in the Details Panel under the *properties* tab. As shown in Figure 6-41, the *properties* tab has a *Sounds* section that you can expand. Next to each sound is a green arrow that you can click to play the sound.

Figure 6-41 Sounds listed in the Details Panel

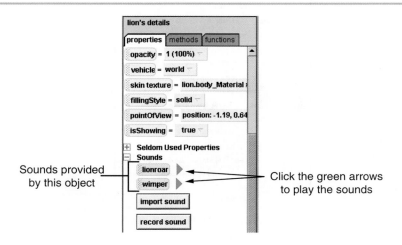

Sounds provided by this object

Click the green arrows to play the sounds

You can also write instructions to play sounds while a world is running. To play a sound, you call an object's primitive play sound method. When you call the play sound method you specify the name of the sound that you wish to play as an argument. Figure 6-42 shows an instruction tile that calls the play sound method to play the lion object's lionroar sound. The number that appears inside parentheses next to the sound's name is the amount of time that the sound plays. In Figure 6-42 the lionroar sound plays for 0.909 seconds.

Figure 6-42 Calling the play sound method

lion   play sound   lion.lionroar (0:00.909)   more...

Importing and Recording Sounds

If you have a previously recorded sound, stored in either the .wav or .mp3 formats, you can import it into an object. Look back at Figure 6-41 and you will see an *import sound* button in the Detail Panel. When you click this button, you see an *import* dialog box. Use the dialog box to locate and select the sound file that you wish to import.

Just below the *import sound* button is the *record sound* button. If you have a microphone attached to your computer you can click this button to record a new sound. After you record the sound it will be imported into the object.

The Character Builders

The Alice galleries provide several different characters in the *People* collection. In addition to the existing characters in these collections, Alice provides powerful character building tools that you can use to design your own people objects. These tools are called *hebuilder* and *shebuilder*, and are located in the local gallery's *People* collection. Figure 6-43 shows the gallery thumbnails for the tools. You use the *hebuilder* tool to create a male character and the *shebuilder* tool to create a female character. To start one of these character building tools, click the desired thumbnail.

Figure 6-43 The *hebuilder* and *shebuilder* tools

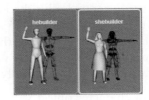

When designing a character, you select the following characteristics:

- You design the body by selecting head, torso, and leg types
- You design the face by selecting a skin color, eyes, and mouth
- You design the hair by selecting a hair style and color
- You design the clothing by selecting a shirt, pants, and shoes

Figure 6-44 shows the interface for the *hebuilder* tool. The icons across the top of the window allow you to navigate to the different sections of the tool. Each section allows you to select a set of characteristics for the character you are building. At the bottom of the window you see a box labeled *Name* and a box labeled *Created By*. You enter a name for the character in the *Name* box, and your own name (if you wish) in the *Created By* box. When you click the *OK* button, the character will be generated and added as an object to the world. The name of the object will be the name that you provided for the character.

Figure 6-44 The *hebuilder* interface

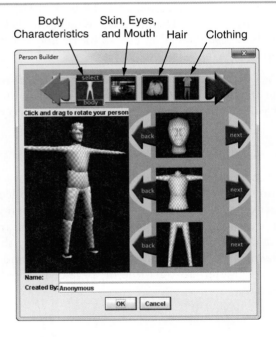

Characters that are generated with the *hebuilder* and *shebuilder* tools have several custom, class-level methods. Figure 6-45 shows a list of the methods as displayed in the Details Panel. These methods cause the character to exhibit various gestures and expressions. Of particular interest is the walk method, which causes the character to articulate its body movements realistically as if he or she were walking.

Once you create a character object with the *hebuilder* or *shebuilder* tools, you can save the object to a new class, and then import it to other worlds.

Figure 6-45 Custom methods in a *hebuilder* or *shebuilder* character

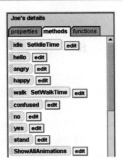

Debugging with the `print` Statement

When a program is not performing correctly, programmers will sometimes write statements in the program that display *diagnostic messages* on the screen. For example, if the programmer suspects that a variable is being assigned an incorrect value, diagnostic messages can be displayed at various times in the program's execution showing the variable's value. While the program is running, the programmer can watch these diagnostic messages and determine at what point the variable is being set to the wrong value. This helps the programmer to see what is going on "under the hood" while the program is running.

In Alice you can use the `print` instruction to display diagnostic messages. As shown in Figure 6-46, the `print` instruction's tile is located at the bottom of the Method Editor. Like all the other Alice instructions, you drag the tile and drop it into a method at the point where you want the instruction to execute.

As shown in Figure 6-46, creating a `print` instruction in a method causes a menu to appear. The menu allows you to enter a text string to print, or select an object. To display the contents of a variable, you select *object*, and then select *expressions*, and then select the desired variable. When the `print` instruction executes, it displays its output in an area known as the *text console*, which is at the bottom of the *World Running…* window.

Figure 6-46 Location of the `print` instruction

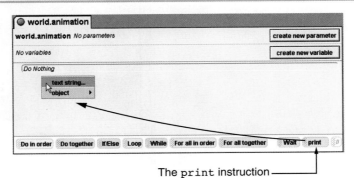

The `print` instruction

Recall that earlier in this section we examined the *RandomBee* world, in which a bee flies to randomly selected flowers. The program generates a random number to determine which flower the bee will fly to, and assigns the number to a variable named selectedFlower. Suppose we want to see the numbers that are being assigned to the variable so we can verify that the algorithm is working properly.

On the Student CD you will find a world named *PrintingRandomBee*. This world is a modified version of the *RandomBee* world shown earlier in this section. As shown in Figure 6-47, the *PrintingRandomBee* world has a print instruction that displays the contents of the selectedFlower variable, just after a random number has been assigned to it. Figure 6-48 shows the world as it is running. The messages displayed in the text console area at the bottom of the window allow us to see the contents of the selectedFlower variable as the world runs.

Figure 6-47 The print instruction in the *PrintingRandomBee* world

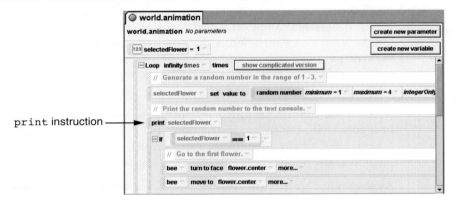

Figure 6-48 Messages displayed in the text console

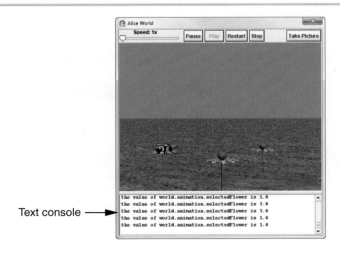

Review Questions

Multiple Choice

1. This is what the process of responding to an event is called.

   a. Triggering the event
   b. Suppressing the event
   c. Handling the event
   d. Killing the event

2. When an Alice world is first created, this is the event for which the only tile appears in the Events Editor.

   a. `When the world starts`
   b. `When a key is typed`
   c. `When the mouse is clicked on something`
   d. `When something is true`

3. This is an event handler.

   a. An object that triggers events
   b. A method that is executed in response to an event
   c. A tile in the Object Tree representing an event
   d. A method that prevents events from occurring

4. This is what BDE stands for.

   a. Basic Duration Event
   b. Before, During, Event
   c. Begin, During, End
   d. Balanced Dual Event

5. This `world` function returns a random number.

   a. `rand`
   b. `randNum`
   c. `getRandom`
   d. `random number`

6. By default, a random number is between these two values.

   a. 1 and 10
   b. 0 and 1
   c. 0 and 100
   d. −1 and 1

7. Which of the following characteristics do you *not* specify with the *hebuilder* or *shebuilder* tools.

   a. Hat
   b. Hair color
   c. Head
   d. Pants

8. You use this statement to display messages in the text console area while a world is running.
   a. `display`
   b. `message`
   c. `print`
   d. `console`

Short Answer

1. How do you specify a different method to be automatically executed when the world starts?

2. Which event would you handle if you wanted to perform an action as long as the user holds down a key?

3. How do you create a tile for the `While a key is pressed` event?

4. How do you create a tile for the `While the world is running` event?

5. How do you create a tile for the `When something becomes true` event?

6. How do you generate integer random numbers?

Exercises

VideoNote
Creating the
Jumping Fish
World

1. **Jumping Fish**

   Create a *sea* world with an island and a fish. The fish should swim around the island. (Part of the fish's body should be above the water's surface, so you can see it swimming.) When you press the (Spacebar), the fish should jump up, out of the water, and then come back down.

2. **Ice Skater**

   Create a world with an instance of the `Lake` class (from the *Environments* collection) and an instance of the `IceSkater` class (from the *People* collection). Program the `iceSkater` so she skates around in a circle on the lake. When you press the (S) key, she should spin around. When you press the (J) key, she should jump.

3. **Couch Color Tester**

   Create a tool that an interior designer can use to visualize how a couch of different colors will look in a room. Create a world with a room and an instance of the `Couch` class (from the *Furniture* collection). The world should also have four balls (spheres from the *Shapes* collection), each a different color. When the user clicks one of the balls, the couch should turn the same color as the ball.

   The world should also have a `Lightswitch` (from the *Controls* collection). When the user clicks the switch with the mouse, it should turn the lights off or on in the room. To turn the lights off, set the `world` object's `ambientBrightness` property to *0*. To turn the lights on, set the `world` object's `ambientBrightness` property to *1*.

4. **First Steps on the Moon**

   Create a world that recreates astronaut Neil Armstrong's first steps on the moon on July 20, 1969. Create a *moon* world with a lunar lander and an astronaut (from the *Space* collection). When you click the lunar lander with the mouse, the astronaut should descend the lunar lander's ladder. When the astronaut reaches the moon's surface, you should play the sound file *step.wav*, which is on the Student CD. This sound file, which is courtesy of NASA, will play the famous words that Armstrong said as he set foot on the moon.

5. **Haunted House**

   Create a world with a haunted house. Use the `Let the mouse move the camera` event to allow the user to move the camera freely through the world. Have at least two scary creatures that stay hidden until the camera gets within a certain distance of them. When that happens, the creatures should jump out to frighten the user.

6. **Boat Obstacle Course**

   Create a game that has a motorboat (from the *Vehicles* collection) with a driver and several large partially submerged torus objects (from the *Shapes* collection). Figure 6-49 shows an example. The world should also have several obstacles floating in the water. Use events in such a way that the user can drive the boat and control its speed. Each time the user drives the boat through a torus, he earns points and the torus should sink underwater. Each time the user comes very close to an obstacle, he loses points and the obstacle should sink underwater. When either all of the torus objects or all of the obstacles have sunk, the game is over and the number of points that the user has earned should be displayed.

Figure 6-49 Boat obstacle course

7. **Circle Track**

   Create a round race track like the one shown in Figure 6-50. The track in the figure was created with two circles (from the *Shapes* collection). Place a car on the track, and place a two-button switch (from the *Controls* collection) in the foreground. When the user clicks the *green* button, the car should drive around the track. When the user clicks the *red* button, the car should stop.

Figure 6-50 Circle track

8. **Amusement Park Rides**

The *Amusement Park* collection contains several classes for amusement park rides, and many of these classes have custom methods that animate the rides. Create a world with three rides and three button switches (from the *Controls* collection). Each button switch should turn on one of the rides when it is clicked by the user.

9. **Shark Pursuit**

Create an *undersea* world with a shark and any other type of fish. The shark should swim toward the other fish, but when the shark gets within one meter of the fish, it quickly swims away. The shark continues to pursue the fish, but each time the shark gets within one meter, the fish swims away. Your world should generate a random number to indicate the direction that the fish will swim to escape the shark, and the distance.

10. **Who Wants to Dance with Bob?**

Use the *hebuilder* and *shebuilder* tools to design several different characters. Place them in a world where a party is taking place. Name one of the characters Bob, and give him a method named askToDance. The method should take an object as an argument. When you click any of the other characters, Bob should approach that character and ask if they want to dance. Only one of the other characters should be programmed to accept. The others should politely decline. When Bob asks the person who accepts his invitation, they should do a simple dance.

11. **Freeze Dance**

Freeze Dance is a party game where the participants perform funny dance moves in a dark or dimly lit room while music is played. One person is in charge of turning the lights on and off at various intervals. When the lights are turned on, everyone in the room immediately "freezes" in their current position. When the lights are turned off, or dimmed, everyone resumes making funny dance moves.

Create an Alice world that simulates the game of Freeze Dance. Start by using the character builders to create one female and one male character. In each of the character objects, write methods that cause them to perform a few funny dance moves. (You might consider capturing poses that can be used to make the dance moves.) Once the characters have started dancing, you should be able to stop them at any point, and they should maintain their current position.

After you have created these character objects, save them as new classes. Then, import several instances of the classes into a world that simulates a party where the game will be played. While the world is running, the user should be able to turns the lights on or off by pressing the [Spacebar]. When the user turns the lights off, the characters should dance. When the user turns the lights on, the characters should freeze in their current positions.

TIP: To simulate the lights turning off, you can change the world's `ambientLightBrightness` property. For example, you could set the property to *0* to simulate the lights going out, and then set it to *5* to simulate the lights turning on.

7 Lists and Arrays

TOPICS

7.1 Lists
7.2 Arrays

7.1 Lists

CONCEPT: A list holds a group of items. Items may be added to a list and removed from a list while the world is running.

Data Structures

This chapter introduces two data structures that are provided by Alice. A *data structure* is a mechanism for storing data and organizing it in some way. The data structures that you can use in Alice are lists and arrays. They are similar to the list and array data structures that are provided by most traditional programming languages. In this section we will look at lists.

Lists

Lists are common in everyday life. Before you go to the grocery store, you probably make a list of items to purchase. During a busy morning of running errands, you might make yourself a list of things to do. When you plan to throw a party, it's usually a good idea to prepare a list of guests to invite. A list is simply a group of items that are stored together for some purpose.

Lists are also used by programmers. To the programmer, a *list* is a container that holds a group of items. The items in a list are stored in a sequence where one item is considered to come after the other. Each item's position in the list is numbered. The first item in the list is at position 0, the second item is at position 1, and so forth. These position numbers are commonly referred to as *indexes*. Lists also have a size, which is the number of items that are stored in the list.

Figure 7-1 illustrates the concept of a list in Alice. In the figure, there are four objects, each is an instance of the skaterGirl class (from the *People* collection). The names of the objects are jenny, karen, katie, and lynn. These objects are all items in a list named girlList. The jenny object is at position 0, the karen object is at position 1, the katie object is at position 2, and the lynn object is at position 3. The size of the list is four because it contains four items.

> **TIP:** Notice that the size of the list in Figure 7-1 is four, but the position number of the last item in the list is three. The position number of the last item in a list is always one less than the size of the list because the position numbers start at zero.

A list is a dynamic data structure. This means that after you have created a list, the world can execute code that adds items to it and/or removes items from it. The list automatically expands as items are added to it, and it automatically shrinks as items are removed from it.

Figure 7-1 A list of objects

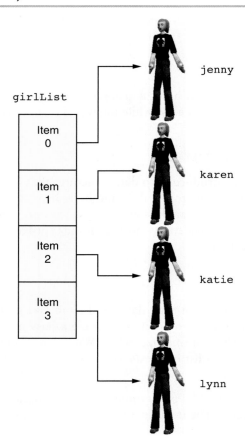

Creating a List in Alice

Lists can hold items of any type. You can have lists of numbers, lists of Boolean values, lists of strings, lists of objects, and so forth. If you want to create a list of objects, then you must first create the objects that you want to store in the list.

In Alice a list is considered a special type of variable, so you can create a list anywhere that you see a *create new variable* button. For example, you can select any object (or the world) in the Object Tree and then create a list in the Details Panel, under the *properties* tab. You can also open a method in the Method Editor and create a list inside the method.

To create a list, click the *create new variable* button. In the *create new variable* dialog box, enter a name for the list and select the type of items that will be stored in the list. As shown in Figure 7-2, select *List* from the drop-down menu that appears in the *Value* area, and check the *make a* option. When you check the *make a* option, the dialog box expands as shown in Figure 7-3. The area at the bottom of the dialog box is known as the *Collection Editor*.

Figure 7-2 Creating a list

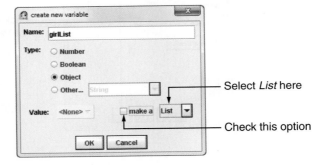

Figure 7-3 The *new item* button

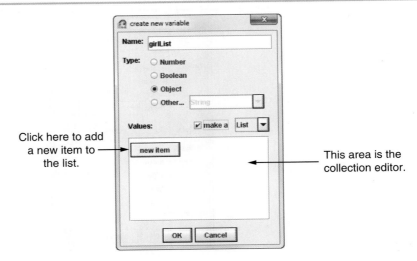

As shown in Figure 7-3, the Collection Editor has a *new item* button that allows you to add items to the list. When you first click this button, a tile for item 0 is added, as shown in Figure 7-4. To set the value of item 0 you click the area next to the tile that reads *<None>*.

Each time you click the *new item* button, a new item tile will be added to the list. Figure 7-5 shows the dialog box after four items have been added to a list, and a value has been selected for each item.

Figure 7-4 Item 0 added to the list

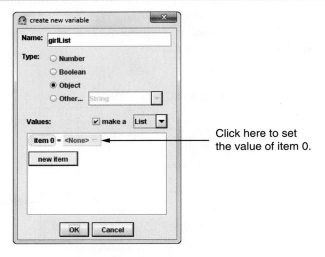

Click here to set the value of item 0.

Figure 7-5 Four items added to the list

Some Simple List Processing Instructions

Once you have created a list, Alice provides two simple instructions for processing the items in the list. Figure 7-6 shows the tiles for the `For all in order` and `For all together` instructions. These instructions are special loops that allow you to perform the same operation on each item in a list.

The `For all in order` instruction steps through the list, one item at a time, performing the same operation on each item. The `For all together` instruction performs the same operation on all the items in a list simultaneously. In Tutorial 7-1 you will use both of these instructions on a list and see the difference in the way they perform.

Figure 7-6 List processing instructions

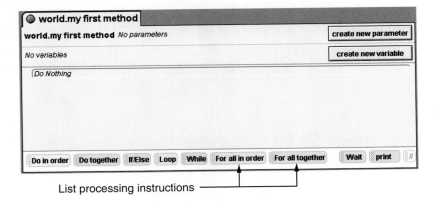

List processing instructions

VideoNote

Creating a List and Using the *For all in order* and *For all together* Instructions

Tutorial 7-1:

Creating a list and using the *For all in order* and *For all together* instructions

On the Student CD you will find a world named *FourSkaters*, which is shown in Figure 7-7. The world has four instances of the `iceSkater` class (from the *People* collection). The objects' names are `firstSkater`, `secondSkater`, `thirdSkater`, and `fourthSkater`. In this tutorial you will add the four objects to a list, and then use the `For all in order` and `For all together` instructions to make them perform an operation.

Step 1: Copy the *FourSkaters* world from the Student CD to your hard drive and open it.

Step 2: Now you will create a list at the world level. Select the `world` in the Object Tree, and then select the *properties* tab in the Details Panel. Click the *create new variable* button that appears in the Details Panel.

Figure 7-7 The *FourSkaters* world

Step 3: In the *create new variable* dialog box enter *skaterList* as the name and select *Object* as the type. Select *List* from the drop-down menu that appears in the *Value* area, and check the *make a* option. The dialog box should now appear as shown in Figure 7-8.

Figure 7-8 The *create new variable dialog* box

Step 4: Click the *new item* button. A tile that reads *item 0 = <None>* will be created just above the button. Click the part of the tile that reads *<None>*, and then select *firstSkater* and the *entire firstSkater* from the menus that appear. This sets the value of *item 0* to the firstSkater object. The tile should now appear as shown in Figure 7-9.

Figure 7-9 Tile for item 0 added

Step 5: Repeat the procedure that you performed in Step 4 to add tiles for *item 1*, *item 2*, and *item 3*. Set the value of *item 1* to the `secondSkater` object, the value of *item 2* to the `thirdSkater` object, and the value of *item 3* to the `fourthSkater` object. The *create new variable* dialog box should now appear as shown in Figure 7-10. (If you make a mistake creating any of the tiles, you can delete them by dragging them to the trash can, and then start over.) Click the *OK* button to close the dialog box.

Figure 7-10 Four items added to the list

Step 6: With the `world` still selected, you should see a tile for the `skaterList` in the Details Panel, under the *properties* tab. As shown in Figure 7-11, the items in the list are shown on a button. (You will probably have to resize the Details Panel to see the list completely.) Clicking this button brings up the Collection Editor. You can use the Collection Editor any time you need to add more items to the list or remove items from the list.

Figure 7-11 The completed list

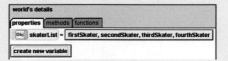

TIP: If the `world` object is selected and you don't see the `skaterList` tile in the Details Panel under the *properties* tab, then it's possible that you clicked the wrong *create new variable* button in Step 2. If this is the case, click the *Undo* button, then go back and repeat Steps 2 through 6.

Step 7: Now you will create an instruction that will cause each of the skaters in the list, one after the other, to spin left one revolution. Of course you could write four different instructions, calling the `turn` method for each object, but that's unnecessary because you have added the objects to a list. Instead, you can create one `For all in order` instruction that does this for you.

Make sure the `world` object's `animate` method is open in the Method Editor. Drag the tile for the `For all in order` instruction and drop it into the method. (Refer to Figure 7-6 for the location of the `For all in order` instruction tile.) When you drop the tile into the Method Editor, a menu will appear. Select *expressions*, and then select `world.skaterList`. This should create the instruction shown in Figure 7-12.

Figure 7-12 The `For all in order` instruction

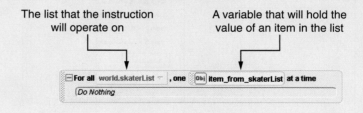

In the instruction, `world.skaterList` is the list that the instruction will operate on, and `item_from_skaterList` is a variable that will contain the value of a different item each time the loop performs its actions. During the first loop iteration, `item_from_skaterList` will contain the value of item 0; during the second iteration, it will contain the value of item 1, and so forth.

Step 8:   In the `For all in order` instruction that you just created, drag the `item_from_skaterList` tile and drop it on top of the *Do Nothing* area inside the `For all in order` instruction, as shown in Figure 7-13. When you drop the tile, a menu will appear. Select `item_from_skaterList turn`, and then select *left* for the direction and *1 revolution* for the amount. The method should now appear as shown in Figure 7-14.

Figure 7-13 Dragging the `item_from_skaterList` tile

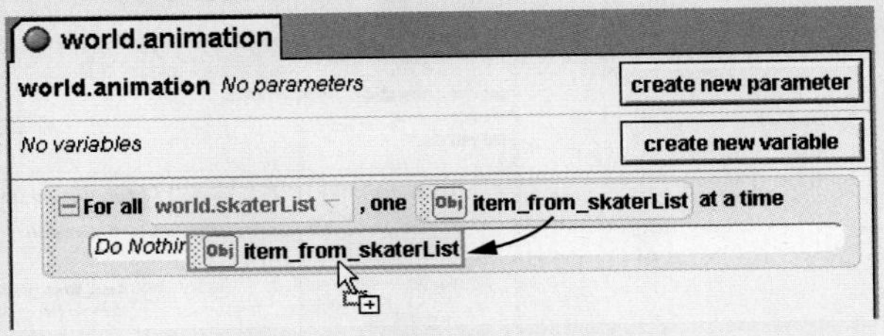

Figure 7-14 The completed instruction

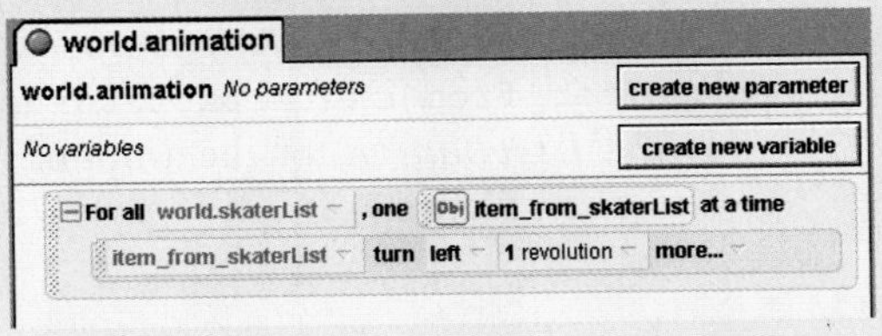

Take a moment to think about the instruction that you just created. The instruction is a loop that will repeat once for each item in `skaterList`. The first time that the loop executes, the `item_from_skaterList` variable will hold the object that is item 0 in the list. That object's `turn` method will be called, causing it to turn left one revolution.

The second time the loop executes, `item_from_skaterList` will hold the object that is item 1 in the list. That object's `turn` method will be called, causing it to turn left one revolution. This continues for each object in `skaterList`.

Step 9: Save the world and then play it. You should see each of the skaters turn, one after the other. When the world has stopped playing, close the *world running...* window.

Step 10: Now you will create a `For all together` instruction so you can see the difference between it and the `For all in order` instruction. Drag the tile for the `For all together` instruction and drop it into the method. (Refer to Figure 7-6 for the location of the `For all together` instruction tile.) When you drop the tile into the Method Editor, a menu will appear. Select *expressions*, and then select `world.skaterList`. The `world.animation` method should now appear as shown in Figure 7-15.

Figure 7-15 The `For all together` instruction added

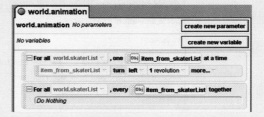

Step 11: In the `For all together` instruction that you just created, drag the `item_from_skaterList` variable tile and drop it inside the `For all together` instruction. When you drop the tile, a menu will appear. Select `item_from_skaterList` turn, and then select *left* for the direction and *1 revolution* for the amount. The method should now appear as shown in Figure 7-16.

Figure 7-16 The completed instruction

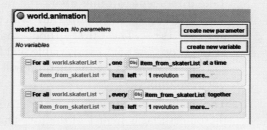

Step 12: Save the world and then play it. First you should see each of the skaters turn, one after the other. This is the `For all in order` instruction executing. Then you should see all of the skaters turn simultaneously. This is the `For all together` instruction executing.

A More Complex Example

The *FourSkaters* world that you completed in Tutorial 7-1 performs a simple list operation. In Tutorial 7-2 you will complete a world that performs a more complex operation on the items in a list. You will create a `For all together` instruction that passes each item in a list as an argument to a method. The method, which you will also write, will manipulate a subpart of the list items that are passed to it as an argument.

Tutorial 7-2:
More complex list processing

On the Student CD you will find a world named *KarateClass*, which is shown in Figure 7-17. The objects in the world are `coach`, `girl`, `madScientist`, and `evilNinja` (all from the *People* collection). These objects are inside an instance of the `Dojo` class (from the Web gallery's *Environments* collection). In this tutorial you will complete the world so it performs the actions in the following problem description:

> *The evil ninja has started teaching karate classes to his three students. Create a world that shows the ninja commanding his students to practice kicking. Each time the ninja says "Kick!" the students will simultaneously kick with their right legs. The ninja commands them to kick five times.*

Step 1: Copy the *KarateClass* world from the Student CD to your hard drive and open it.

Figure 7-17 The *KarateClass* world

Step 2:   First you will write a world-level method that will accept an object as its argument and make the object kick its right leg. Select the `world` in the Object Tree, then, under the *methods* tab of the Details Panel click the *create new method* button. Name the method `kick`. In the Method Editor, create a parameter named `who`. The parameter's type should be `Object`. The `kick` method should now appear as shown in Figure 7-18.

Figure 7-18 The `kick` method with an object parameter

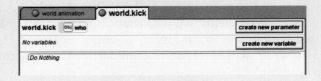

Step 3:   Here is the pseudocode for the `kick` method:

```
Method kick(who)
    who's right leg turn backward 1/4 revolution
    who's right leg turn forward 1/4 revolution
End Method
```

When this method is called, an object is passed into the `who` parameter. The `who` parameter's right leg subpart is then moved backward and forward to make a kicking motion. Figure 7-19 shows how this method should appear when it is complete. In order to create the instructions shown in the figure, however, there are a number of steps you must take.

Figure 7-19 The completed `kick` method

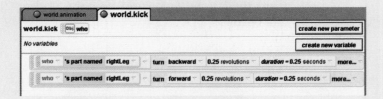

To create the first instruction in the method, expand the `madScientist` object in the Object Tree and select its `rightLeg` sub-part. Drag the tile for the `rightLeg`'s `turn` method and drop it into the method. Select *backward* as the direction and ¹/₄ revolution as the amount. The instruction should appear as shown in Figure 7-20.

Figure 7-20 The first instruction

madScientist.rightLeg turn backward   0.25 revolutions   more...

Step 4:   As it is now, the instruction that you just created turns the
          `madScientist` object's `rightLeg` subpart. You must modify the state-
          ment so it turns the `rightLeg` subpart of any object passed to the `who`
          parameter.

          Select the `madScientist` object and click the *functions* tab in the
          Details Panel. Scroll down to the end of the list of functions until you
          see the *other* category. As shown in Figure 7-21, drag the tile for the
          `madScientist's part named` function and drop it on top of
          `madScientist.rightLeg` in the instruction. This will change the
          instruction to appear as shown in Figure 7-22.

Figure 7-21 Dragging the part named function into the method

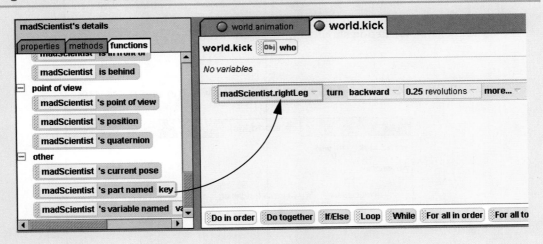

Figure 7-22 The modified instruction

madScientist   's part named   turn backward   0.25 revolutions   more...

Step 5:   Click the area shown in the top image in Figure 7-23. (Make sure you
          do not click the down-arrow. Click the area to the left of the down-
          arrow.) This will expand the tile as shown in the bottom image in
          the figure. In the expanded area, type *rightLeg* (be sure to spell it ex-
          actly as shown here) and press Enter. The instruction should now ap-
          pear as shown in Figure 7-24.

Figure 7-23 Entering the name of the part

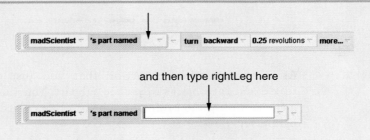

madScientist
's part named
turn
backward
0.25 revolutions
more...
and then type rightLeg here
madScientist
's part named

Figure 7-24 The modified instruction

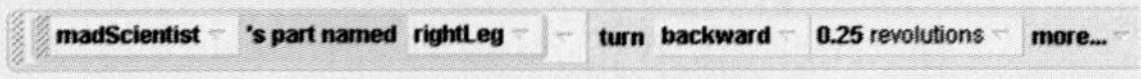

madScientist
's part named
rightLeg
turn
backward
0.25 revolutions
more...

Step 6: Next, drag the tile for the `who` parameter to the instruction and drop it on top of `madScientist`, as shown in Figure 7-25. After doing this, change the instruction's *duration* to *0.25 seconds*. The completed instruction should appear as shown in Figure 7-26.

Figure 7-25 Replacing `madScientist` with the `who` parameter

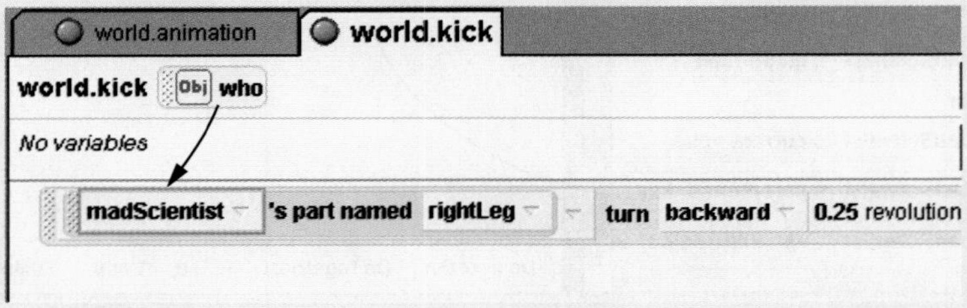

world.animation
world.kick
world.kick
Obj
who
No variables
madScientist
's part named
rightLeg
turn
backward
0.25 revolution

Figure 7-26 The completed instruction

who
's part named
rightLeg
turn
backward
0.25 revolutions
duration = 0.25 seconds
more...

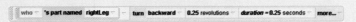

Step 7: The instruction that you just created will turn the `rightLeg` subpart of the `who` parameter backward 1/4 revolution. You need to create another instruction similar to this one to turn the `who` parameter's `rightLeg` subpart forward 1/4 revolution. Repeat the process you went through in Steps 3 through 6 to create the second instruction shown in Figure 7-27.

NOTE: The `kick` method expects that the object passed to the who parameter has a subpart named `rightLeg`. If you pass an object without a subpart named `rightLeg` to the method, an error will occur.

Figure 7-27 The completed `kick` method

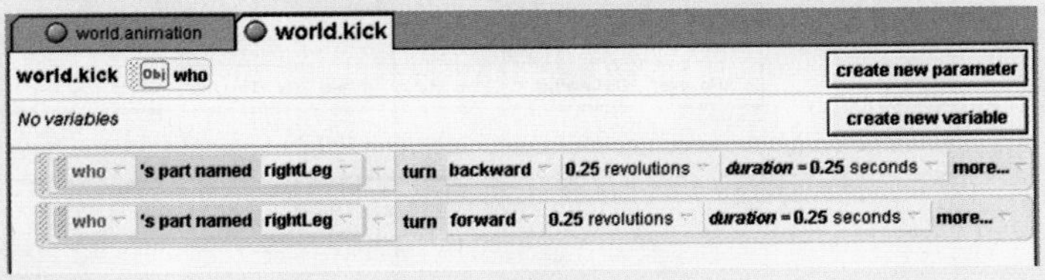

Step 8: At the world level, create a list named `studentList`, and add the `coach`, `girl`, and `madScientist` objects to it. Figure 7-28 shows how the list's tile should appear.

Figure 7-28 The `studentList` list

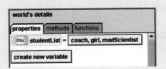

Step 9: The last step is to complete the `world.animation` method, which executes when the world is played. Here is the pseudocode for the method:

```
Loop 5 times
    evilNinja say "Kick!"
    For all items in studentList together
        kick(item from the list)
    End For
End Loop
```

Complete the method by creating the instructions shown in Figure 7-29.

Step 10: Save the world and then play it. You should see the evil ninja give the command to kick, and then the three students should kick their right legs simultaneously. This will happen five times.

Figure 7-29 The completed `world.animation` method

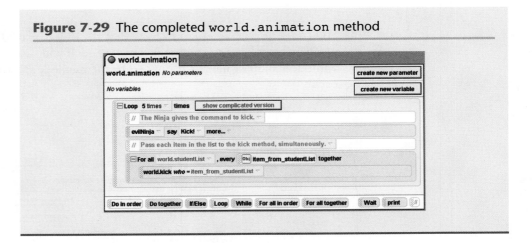

Methods for Modifying a List

We've discussed how items can be added to a list or removed from a list using the Collection Editor. Alice also provides various methods that allow you to store items in a list and remove items from a list. These methods can be called while the world is running, allowing an Alice program to modify the contents of a list.

When you drag a list's tile and drop it into the Method Editor, a menu appears showing a list of the methods that you can call to modify the list. Figure 7-30 shows an example. In the figure, the tile for a list named `myList` is being dragged and dropped into the Method Editor. Table 7-1 gives a description of each of these methods.

For example, take a look at *Fish World*, which is on the Student CD. This world contains three fish objects named `blueminnow`, `fish`, and `goldfish`. The `world` object

Figure 7-30 List modification methods

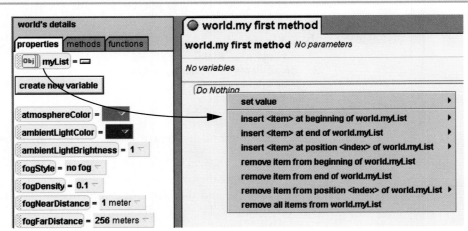

Table 7-1 Methods for inserting and removing list items

Command	Description
`Insert <item> at beginning of list`	Inserts an item at the beginning of a list, which is position 0. The other items are shifted toward the end of the list.
`Insert <item> at end of list`	Inserts an item at the end of the list.
`Insert <item> at position <index> of list`	Inserts an item at a specific position, indicated by `index`. The item currently at that position, and all subsequent items, will be shifted toward the end of the list.
`remove item from beginning of list`	Removes the item at position 0 from the list. (This item is not removed from the world, only from the list.) The remaining items are shifted toward the beginning of the list.
`remove item from position <index> of list`	Removes the item at a specific position, indicated by `index`. (This item is not removed from the world, only from the list.) The subsequent items are shifted toward the beginning of the list.
`remove all items from list`	Removes all items from the list. (The items are not removed from the world, only from the list.)

also has a list named `fishList`. The list is empty because no items were added to it with the Collection Editor. The `world.animation` method has the three instructions shown in Figure 7-31. These instructions add the `blueminnow`, `fish`, and `goldfish` objects to the end of the `fishList` list. After these instructions execute, the `blueminnow` object will be item 0, the `fish` object will be item 1, and the `goldfish` object will be item 2.

Figure 7-31 Instructions in *FishWorld*

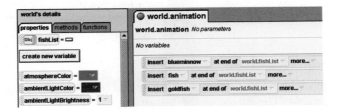

List Functions

Alice provides a number of functions that return information about a list, or return an item from a list. Table 7-2 describes these functions.

When you drag a list tile and drop it on top of a placeholder in an instruction, a menu will appear showing some of these list functions. The list functions that will appear in the menu will be those with a return type that is compatible with the placeholder.

Table 7-2 List functions

Function Name	Return Type	Description
`size of list`	Number	Returns the size of the list, which is the number of items stored in the list.
`first index of`	Number	You pass an argument to this function and it returns the position of the first occurrence of the argument in the list. If the argument does not appear in the list, the function returns −1.
`last index of`	Number	You pass an argument to this function and it returns the position of the last occurrence of the argument in the list. If the argument does not appear in the list, the function returns −1.
`is list empty`	Boolean	Returns *true* if the list is empty, or *false* otherwise.
`list contains`	Boolean	You pass an argument to this function and it returns *true* if the argument is in the list, or *false* otherwise.
`first item from list`	Same type as the items in the list	Returns the first item in the list (the item in position 0). If the list is empty, this function returns the special value none.
`last item from list`	Same type as the items in the list	Returns the last item in the list. If the list is empty, this function returns the special value none.
`random item from list`	Same type as the items in the list	Returns a random item from the list. If the list is empty, this function returns the special value none.
`ith item from list`	Same type as the items in the list	You specify an index number (a position number) as an argument and the function returns the item stored at that position in the list. If the list is empty, this function returns the special value none.

For example, suppose that `myList` is a list of objects, and the variable x is a Number variable. The image at the top of Figure 7-32 shows an instruction that assigns the value 1 to the variable x. If we drag the tile for `myList` and drop it on top of the value 1, we will see a menu showing the list functions that return a Number. The image at the bottom of Figure 7-32 shows the menu that will appear.

As another example, suppose that `myList` is a list of objects, and that we have the `If/Else` instruction shown in the top image in Figure 7-33. If we drag the tile for `myList` and drop it on top of the *true* placeholder, we will see a menu showing the list functions that return a Boolean value. The image at the bottom of Figure 7-33 shows the menu that will appear.

Figure 7-32 A list function menu

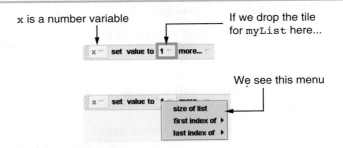

Figure 7-33 A list function menu

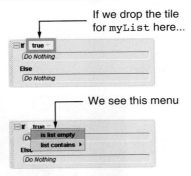

Finally, let's look at one more example. The last four functions shown in Table 7-2 return an item from a list. These functions are `first item from list`, `last item from list`, `random item from list`, and `ith item from list`. To call any of these functions, drop the list's tile on top of a placeholder that is of the same type as the items in the list.

For example, suppose that `myList` is a list of objects, and the variable `obj` is an object variable. The image at the top of Figure 7-34 shows an instruction that assigns the `ground` object as a placeholder to the variable `obj`. If we drag the tile for `myList` and drop it on top of `ground`, we will see a menu showing the list functions that return an item from the list. The image at the bottom of Figure 7-34 shows the menu that will appear.

Figure 7-34 A list function menu

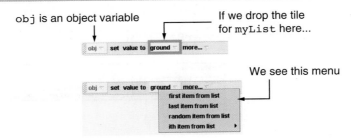

An Example World That Uses List Methods and Functions

Let's look at an example world that was created for the following problem description:

A soccer player practices by lining up five soccer balls in front of a goal, and kicking them one at a time toward the goal. Create a world that demonstrates the soccer player practicing.

On the Student CD you will find a world named *SoccerPractice*, which is shown in Figure 7-35. The girl is an object named `soccerPlayer` and was created using the *shebuilder* tool, which is discussed in Chapter 6. The soccer balls and the goal are from the *Sports* collection.

Figure 7-35 The *SoccerPractice* world

Take a moment to load the world and play it. You will see the `soccerPlayer` turn to face the rightmost ball, walk to the ball, and then kick it. Then she steps back to her starting position and repeats these steps for the remaining balls. Some of the balls go into the goal when she kicks them, and some do not.

Before examining the methods in this world, let's look at how the algorithm was developed. First, the five soccer ball objects are stored in a world-level list named `soccerBalls`, as shown in Figure 7-36.

Figure 7-36 The `soccerBalls` list

Here is the original pseudocode for the `world.animation` method, which executes when the world is played:

```
Method world.animation
    Loop number of times = size of the soccerBalls list
        targetBall = first item in the soccerBalls list
        soccerPlayer goes to targetBall and kicks it
        Remove the first item from the soccerBalls list
        soccerPlayer steps back to the starting position
    End Loop
    soccerPlayer turns to face the camera
End Method
```

This pseudocode describes the steps in the algorithm, but we need more detail to actually implement it with Alice instructions. If we use the process of stepwise refinement, which is described in Chapter 5, we can expand the algorithm as shown in Figure 7-37. The refined algorithm has three world-level methods: `animation`, `kickTheBall`, and `goBack`.

The `world.kickTheBall` method is shown in Figure 7-38. First, notice that the method has an object parameter named `whichBall`. When the method is called, the soccer ball that the `soccerPlayer` is to kick is passed as an argument. The figure points out the following four items:

Figure 7-37 Pseudocode for the world methods

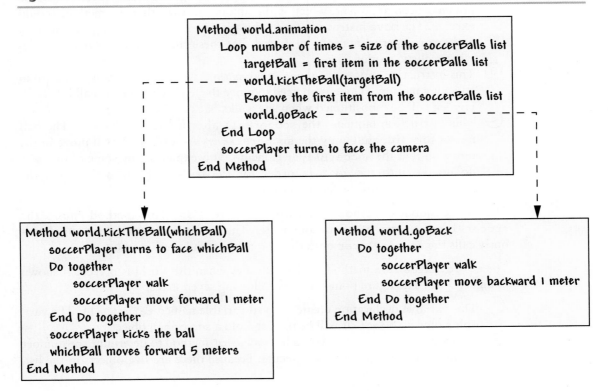

Figure 7-38 The `world.kickTheBall` method

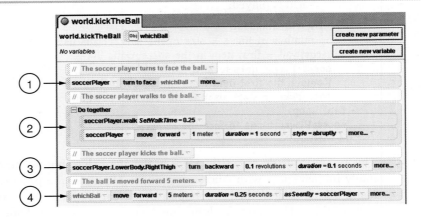

① This instruction causes the `soccerPlayer` to turn to face the ball that was passed as an argument to the method.

② This `Do together` instruction causes the `soccerPlayer` to walk to the ball that was passed as an argument to the method. It simultaneously calls the `soccerPlayer` object's `walk` method and `move` method. The `move` method moves the `soccerPlayer` forward a distance of one meter. The way the world was set up, the `soccerPlayer` is roughly one meter away from each ball.

The `walk` method was generated by the *shebuilder* tool, and it causes the object to move her legs as if she is walking. We specify 0.25 seconds as the `SetWalkTime` argument, which is the amount of time that the method should execute. The `move` instruction uses a duration of 1 second. Through a little trial and error experimentation, we found that these timing values produce somewhat realistic motion.

③ This instruction causes the `soccerPlayer` object's right leg to move forward in a kicking motion. (There is no need to move the leg back after the ball is kicked. Her leg will be repositioned when she walks back to the starting position.)

④ This instruction launches the `soccerBall` after it has been kicked. The ball moves forward, `asSeenBy` the `soccerPlayer`. As a result, it will move in the direction that the `soccerPlayer` is facing. This explains why some of the balls do not go into the goal. In order for the balls to go into the goal, the `soccerPlayer` must be facing the goal.

The `world.goBack` method is shown in Figure 7-39. This method causes the `soccerPlayer` to step backward one meter. The `Do together` structure simultaneously calls the `soccerPlayer` object's `walk` method and `move` method.

The `world.animation` method, which executes when the world is played, is shown in Figure 7-40. The figure points out the following seven items:

① This variable declaration creates a local variable named `targetBall`. The variable's type is `Object`. It will be used to hold a soccer ball object.

② This loop uses the `soccerBalls` list's `size of` method to determine the number of times that the loop should execute. Because there are five objects in the list, the loop will execute five times.

Figure 7-39 The world.goBack method

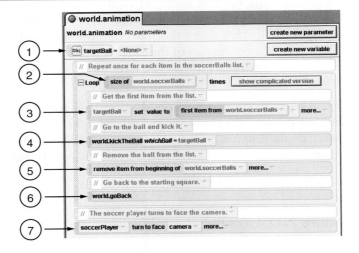

(Figure 7-39 image)

Figure 7-40 The world.animation method

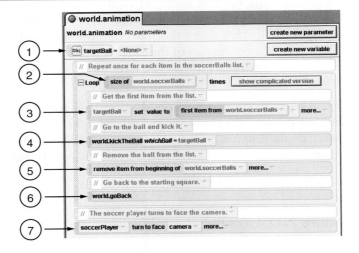

③ This instruction calls the soccerBalls list's first item from list method to get the first item in the list and assign it to the targetBall variable.

④ This instruction calls the world.kickTheBall method, passing targetBall as an argument.

⑤ This instruction removes the first item from the soccerBalls list. The other items in the list will be shifted toward the front of the list. As a result, the item that was previously second in the list will become the first item in the list.

⑥ This instruction calls the world.goBack method.

⑦ This instruction turns the soccerPlayer so she is facing the camera.

Using the Let the mouse move <objects> Event

One of the events that you can use in an Alice world is Let the mouse move <objects>. This event allows the user to move objects in a running Alice world by clicking and dragging them with the mouse. We covered events in Chapter 6, but we did not discuss this particular event because it requires a list. When you create a tile for this event, you specify a list containing the objects that the user will be able to move.

Figure 7-41 Creating the `Let the mouse move <objects>` event

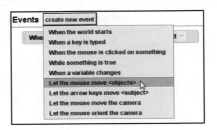

To create a tile for this event, click the *create new event* button in the Events Editor, and then select `Let the mouse move <objects>` from the menu, as shown in Figure 7-41. After doing this, the event tile shown in Figure 7-42 will be created. When you click on the part of the tile that reads *Any Object*, you will see a menu that allows you to select a list that you have already created in this world, or to create a new list.

If you select an existing list from the menu, the user will be able to move the objects that are in that list by clicking and dragging them while the world is running. If you select *create new list...* from the menu, you will see the *Create new list* dialog box shown in Figure 7-43. This dialog box allows you to create a new list and add items

Figure 7-42 Event tile

Figure 7-43 The *Create new list* dialog box

to it. After you create the list, the user will be able to move the objects that are in the list by clicking and dragging them while the world is running.

While the world is running, this event allows you to move an object by performing the following actions:

- To move an object horizontally within the world, simply click and drag it.
- To move an object straight up or down, hold down the [Shift] key while clicking and dragging the object.
- To rotate an object left or right, hold down the [Ctrl] key while clicking and dragging the object.
- To tumble an object (rotate it left, right, forward, backward, or any combination of these directions), hold down the [Ctrl] and [Shift] keys while clicking and dragging the object.

Tutorial 7-3 demonstrates how easy it is to implement this event.

VideoNote
Using the
Let the
mouse move
<objects>
Event

Tutorial 7-3:
Using the `Let the mouse move <objects>` event

Step 1: Copy the *MovableFurniture* world from the Student CD to your hard drive and open it. This world is a room with various items of furniture, as shown in Figure 7-44.

Figure 7-44 The *MovableFurniture* world

Step 2: Click the *create new event* button in the Events Editor, and then select `Let the mouse move <objects>` from the menu (refer to Figure 7-41).

Step 3: A tile should be created for the event (refer to Figure 7-42). Click the part of the tile that reads *Any Object*. On the menu that appears, select *create new list...* and you should see the *Create new list* dialog box. As shown in Figure 7-45, enter moveableObjects as the name

Figure 7-45 The *Create new list* dialog box

and select Object as the type. Add the items shown in the figure and then click the *OK* button.

Step 4: Save the world and then play it. You should be able to move the furniture objects by clicking and dragging them. Try the different key and mouse click combinations previously described to move, turn, and tumble the objects.

Storing Non-Visual Data In a List

All of the examples that we have looked at so far use lists of visual objects. You can also store non-visual data, such as numbers, strings, and Boolean values, in a list. For example, look at the *HamletList* world on the Student CD. As shown in Figure 7-46 this world contains an instance of the HandsomePrince class, from the *People* collection.

Figure 7-46 The *HamletList* world

The `world` object contains a list, named `script`, which contains four strings. The strings are lines from Shakespeare's *Hamlet*. Figure 7-47 shows the list opened in the Collection Editor. When you play the world, the `world.animation` method executes a `For all in order` instruction that causes the `handsomePrince` to say the lines in the list. Figure 7-48 shows the method.

Figure 7-47 The `script` list

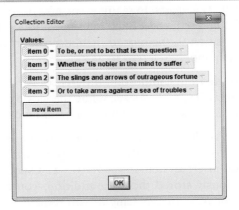

Figure 7-48 The `world.animation` method

 **Checkpoint**

7.1 What is a data structure?

7.2 What is the position number of the first item in a list?

7.3 What is the size of a list?

7.4 Describe the `For all in order` and `For all together` instructions.

7.5 Describe the methods that Alice provides for inserting items into a list.

7.6 Describe the methods that Alice provides for removing items from a list.

7.7 When you drag a list tile and drop it on top of a placeholder in an instruction, a menu will appear. What will be on the menu?

7.2 Arrays

CONCEPT: An array is similar to a list, in that it holds a group of items. An array's size is fixed, however, so you cannot add more items to an array than it can hold while the world is running. Also, arrays do not support the same insertion and removal methods that lists support.

An array is a container that holds a group of items. The items in an array are commonly called *elements*. In many ways, arrays are similar to lists. The items in an array are stored in a sequence. Each item's position in the array is numbered, with the first item at position 0, the second item at position 1, and so forth. These position numbers are commonly referred to as indexes.

There are also some important differences between arrays and lists. One difference is that an array has a fixed size. While the world is running, the size of an array cannot be changed. Consequently, you cannot add more items to an array than it can hold.

Another way that an array is different from a list is that the items stored in an array do not automatically shift their positions when an item is inserted into the array. When you insert an item into an array at a specific position, it replaces any item that was previously stored there. In addition, you can only remove an item that is currently in an array by replacing it with some other value.

Figure 7-49 illustrates the concept of an array in Alice. In the figure, there are four objects, each an instance of the Lion class (from the *Animals* collection). The names

Figure 7-49 An array of objects

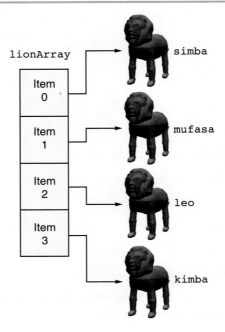

of the objects are `simba`, `mufasa`, `leo`, and `kimba`. These objects are all items in an array named `lionArray`. The `simba` object is at position 0, the `mufasa` object is at position 1, the `leo` object is at position 2, and the `kimba` object is at position 3. The size of the array is four because it contains four items.

 TIP: The position number of the last item in an array is always one less than the size of the array because the position numbers start at zero.

Creating an Array in Alice

To create an array in Alice, you follow the same procedure that was given earlier for creating a list. You click the *create new variable* button in the object or method where you want to create the array. In the *create new variable* dialog box, enter a name for the array and select the type of items that will be stored in the array. As shown in Figure 7-50, select *Array* from the drop-down menu that appears in the *Values* area, and check the *make a* option. When you check the *make a* option, the dialog box expands, as shown in the figure, to display a Collection Editor. You click the *new item* button to add items to the array. In Figure 7-50 four items have been added to the array. When you click the *OK* button, the array is created.

Figure 7-50 Creating an array

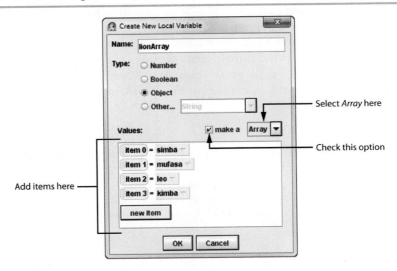

An array will appear as a tile in the object or method where it was created. Figure 7-51 shows an example. Notice that an asterisk (*) appears on the tile, indicating that it is an array. As shown in the figure, the items in the array appear on a button. Clicking this button brings up the Collection Editor. You can use the Collection Editor any time you need to add more items to the array or remove items from the array.

On the Student CD you will find a world named *LionArray*, containing `Lion` objects and the `lionArray` discussed here. You will find the `lionArray` in the `world` object.

Figure 7-51 An array tile

You can create instructions that work with the individual items in an array. For example, if you open the `world.animation` method in the *LionArray* world you will see the instructions shown in Figure 7-52 in the topmost part of the method. These instructions cause the items in the array to move forward 0.5 meters, one at a time, beginning with the item at position 0.

Figure 7-52 Instructions that operate on array items

Notice that in Figure 7-52 there is one instruction for each item in the array. The first instruction operates on item 0, the next instruction operates on item 1, and so forth. A better way to do this would be with a looping structure. Unfortunately, the `For all in order` and `For all together` instructions that work with lists do not work with arrays. If you wish to step through an array, performing an operation on each item, you have to create a `Loop` instruction that executes once for each item in the array. You use the complicated version of the loop, and you use the loop's `index` variable to specify an array item. For example, if you look at the bottom of the `world.animation` method in the *LionArray* world you will see the loop shown in Figure 7-53.

Figure 7-53 A loop that steps through the items in an array

Notice that the instruction inside the loop uses the `index` variable to specify an item in the array. The first time the loop executes, the `index` variable will be set to 0, so item 0 will move forward. The second time the loop executes the `index` variable will be set to 1, so item 1 will move forward. This continues for each item in the array.

> **TIP:** Refer to Chapter 4 for a detailed discussion of the complicated version of the `Loop` instruction.

Tutorial 7-4 leads you through the steps for creating an array and a `Loop` instruction that steps through the array.

Tutorial 7-4:
Creating an array and a loop that steps through it

On the Student CD you will find a world named *FourSkatersArray*, which is shown in Figure 7-54. This world is a copy of the *FourSkaters* world that you completed in Tutorial 7-1. In this tutorial you will add the four skater objects to an array, and then create a `Loop` instruction that makes them perform an operation.

Figure 7-54 The *FourSkatersArray* world

Step 1: Copy the *FourSkatersArray* world from the Student CD to your hard drive and open it.

Step 2: In the `world` object, create an array named `skaterArray`. Add four items to the array. Set the value of item 0 to the `firstSkater` object, the value of item 1 to the `secondSkater` object, the value of item 2 to the `thirdSkater` object, and the value of item 3 to the `fourthSkater` object. The tile for the array should appear as shown in Figure 7-55.

Figure 7-55 The `skaterArray` array

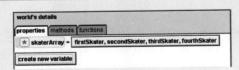

(You will probably have to resize the Details Panel to see the array completely, as shown in the figure.)

Step 3: Now you will create an instruction that will cause each of the skaters in the array, one after the other, to turn left one revolution. Make sure the `world` object's `animate` method is open in the Method Editor. Drag the tile for the `Loop` instruction and drop it into the method. When you drop the tile into the Method Editor, a menu will appear, allowing you to select the number of times that the loop should execute. You want the loop to execute once for each item in the array, so specify 4. This should create a tile for the `Loop` instruction. Click the *show complicated version* button. The tile should now appear as shown in Figure 7-56.

Figure 7-56 The `Loop` instruction

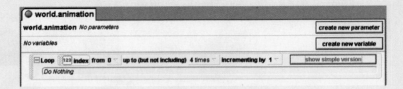

Step 4: Inside the `Loop` instruction we want to access an item from the array and execute its `turn` method. Drag the `skaterArray` tile from the Details Panel and drop it inside the loop, as shown in Figure 7-57. When you drop the tile, make the following selections from the menus that appear: *item responses > item 0 > item 0 from* `world.skaterArray` *turn > left > 1 revolution (all the way around)*. Figure 7-58 shows these menu selections.

Figure 7-57 Drop the `skaterArray` tile onto the `Loop` instruction

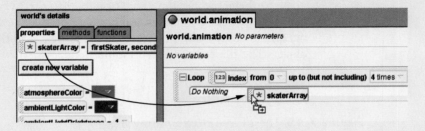

Step 5: The instruction that you just created inside the `Loop` causes item 0 to turn left 1 revolution. If you were to play the world now, you would see the skater object in item 0 turn four times. That's not what we had

Figure 7-58 Menu selections

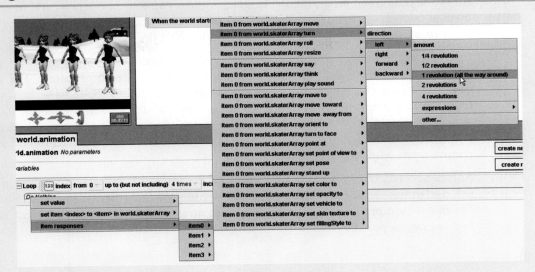

in mind. Instead, we want all of the skater objects to turn, one after the other. To make that happen you need to change item 0 to *item index* in the Loop instruction. As shown in the top image in Figure 7-59 drag the tile for the index variable and drop it on top of the 0. This will change the instruction so it appears as the bottom image in the figure.

Figure 7-59 Changing item 0 to item index

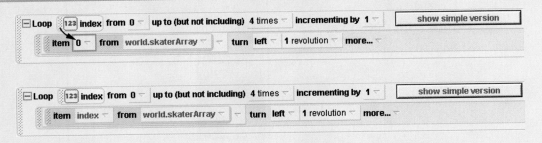

Take a moment to think about how this loop will work. The first time that the loop executes, the index variable will be set to 0. This will cause item 0 to turn. The next time the loop executes, the index variable will be set to 1, This will cause item 1 to turn. This continues to repeat as long as the index variable contains a value that is up to, but not including, 4.

Step 6: Save the world and then play it. One at a time, you should see the skaters turn left one revolution.

Arrays versus Lists

All of the traditional programming languages allow you to create arrays, and most of them allow you to create lists. When programmers have the choice of using either an array or a list, they choose the data structure that best fits the application.

One of a programmer's primary considerations when deciding between an array and a list is whether the size of the data structure needs to be fixed or dynamic. The size of a list is dynamic, which means that items can be added to the list and removed from the list while the program is running. The list automatically expands and shrinks to accommodate these operations. An array's size, however, cannot change while the program is running. Programmers choose lists when they need to add and remove items while the program is running.

Another consideration is the desired speed of the program. Because of the way that lists and arrays work internally, programs can usually process arrays faster than lists. For this reason programmers typically choose arrays for applications that must perform as fast as possible.

Using an `ArrayVisualization` Object

The Alice local gallery provides a class that is useful for visualizing how an array works. The class is named `ArrayVisualization`, and it is found in the *Visualizations* collection. The thumbnail for the class is shown in Figure 7-60. Figure 7-61 shows an example of an `ArrayVisualization` object. The object has numbered squares that represent the elements in the array. You can add other objects to the elements in the `ArrayVisualization` and they will appear in the squares. This gives you a way of seeing how an array works.

Figure 7-60 The `ArrayVisualization` class

Figure 7-61 An `ArrayVisualization` object

NOTE: The `ArrayVisualization` class is designed as an aid for learning how arrays work. Because it is a unique tool provided by Alice, you will not find anything quite like it in a traditional programming language.

When you create an instance of the `ArrayVisualization` class, the *Initialize array* dialog box shown in Figure 7-62 is displayed. This dialog box works like a Collection Editor. You click the *new item* button to add items to the `ArrayVisualization` object, just as if it were an array. Unlike a regular array, however, you can add only objects to an `ArrayVisualization` object.

After you add objects to the `ArrayVisualization`, they are moved to the appropriate square. For example, Figure 7-63 shows the *ArrayVisualization* world, which is on the Student CD. This world has an `ArrayVisualization` object containing the four skater objects that you worked with in Tutorial 7-4. If you select the `ArrayVisualization` object, and then look under the *properties* tab in the Details Panel, you will see an array named `elements`, as shown in Figure 7-64. This array holds the skater objects.

Figure 7-62 The *Initialize array* dialog box

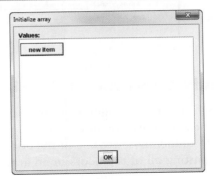

Figure 7-63 The *ArrayVisualization* world

Figure 7-64 The `elements` array

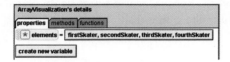

The `world.animation` method is shown in Figure 7-65. This method has a loop that steps through the `elements` array, executing each of the skater object's `turn` method. To see the method execute, just play the world.

Figure 7-65 The `world.animation` method

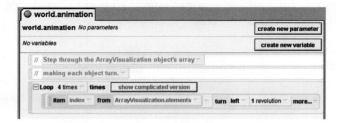

Randomly Selecting an Item in an Array

In some applications you might want to randomly select an item in an array. For example, suppose you are creating a game that presents different doors to the user. You want to randomly select one of the doors to put a treasure behind. You could do this by putting all of the doors in an array and then randomly selecting one of them.

You might recall that in Alice lists have a function that returns a random item from the list (the name of the function is `random item from list`). Arrays, however, have no such function. To randomly select an item in an array you have to generate a random number that you can use as an index. To do this you use the world-level `random number` function, which we discussed in Chapter 6, and you use the *more...* editing tag to set the following arguments:

- Set the `minimum` argument to *0* so the value that is returned will not be less than 0
- Set the `maximum` value to the size of the array so the value that is returned will be up to, but not including, the size of the array
- Set the `integerOnly` argument to *true* so the value that is returned will be an integer

In Tutorial 7-5 you will modify the *ArrayVisualization* world by adding a method that randomly selects an item in the array.

Tutorial 7-5:
Randomly selecting an array element

Step 1: Copy the *ArrayVisualization* world from the Student CD to your hard drive and open it.

Step 2: In the `world` object, create a new method named `randomMove`. In the `randomMove` method, create a Number variable named `index`. The method should appear as shown in Figure 7-66.

Figure 7-66 The `randomMove` method at this point

Step 3: The `randomMove` method will randomly select an item in the `ArrayVisualization`, and call its `turn` method. Here is the pseudocode for the method:

> Method randomMove
>   Set the index variable to a random number
>   Call the turn method on the object at the random index
> End Method

Figure 7-67 shows the code for the method. Complete the method as shown in the figure.

Figure 7-67 The completed `randomMove` method

TIP: The last instruction shown in the method can be created by dragging the tile for the `ArrayVisualization` object's `elements` array and dropping it into the Method Editor. When you drop the tile, make the following selections from the menus that appear: *item responses > item 0 > item 0 from `ArrayVisualization.elements` turn > left > 1 revolution (all the way around)*. This will create an instruction that turns the object stored at item 0. To change the instruction so it turns a randomly selected object, drag the tile for the `index` variable and drop it on the 0. That should change the instruction to appear as shown in Figure 7-67.

Step 4: Open the `world.animation` method in the Method Editor. Below the existing instructions in the method, create the additional instructions shown in Figure 7-68.

Step 5: Save the world and play it. First you should see the skater objects each turn, one at a time. Then you should see four randomly selected skater objects turn.

Figure 7-68 The completed `world.animation` method

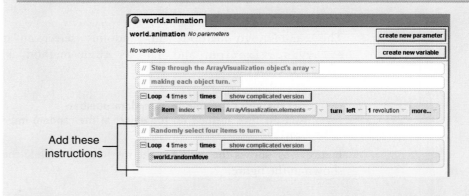

Add these instructions

 Checkpoint

7.8 In what ways are arrays and lists similar?

7.9 In what ways are arrays and lists different?

7.10 What two instructions does Alice provide for lists, but not for arrays?

7.11 If you wish to step through an array, performing an operation on each item, what type of instruction would you create?

7.12 What is an `ArrayVisualization` object? How is it useful for learning to program with arrays?

7.13 How do you randomly select an item in an array?

Review Questions

Multiple Choice

1. The first item in a list or array is stored at this position.

   a. 1
   b. 0
   c. −1
   d. You can pick any starting position

2. This is the size of a list or an array.

   a. The number of items stored in the list or array
   b. The amount of memory used by the list or array
   c. The number of items in the list or array plus 10
   d. Twice the number of items in the list or array

3. This is always the position number of the last item in a list or an array.

   a. 0
   b. One more than the size of the list or array
   c. One less than the size of the list or array
   d. The same as the size of the list or array

4. This instruction steps through a list, one item at a time, performing the same operation on each item in the list.

   a. `For all in order`
   b. `For all together`
   c. `For each item`
   d. `For all one at a time`

5. This instruction steps through a list, simultaneously performing the same operation on each item in the list.

   a. `For all in order`
   b. `For all together`
   c. `For each item`
   d. `For all at the same time`

6. A list has one or more methods for this.

   a. Inserting an item at the beginning of the list
   b. Inserting an item at the end of the list
   c. Inserting an item at a specific position in the list
   d. All of the above

7. A list has one or more methods for this.

   a. Removing an item at the beginning of the list
   b. Removing an item at the end of the list
   c. Removing an item at a specific position in the list
   d. All of the above

8. This event uses a list of objects.

   a. `While the mouse is pressed on something`
   b. `When the mouse is clicked on something`
   c. `Let the mouse move <objects>`
   d. `Let the arrow keys move <subject>`

9. This is true for the size of an array.

   a. It cannot change while the world is running
   b. It can change while the world is running
   c. It is always twice the number of items stored in the array
   d. It is always one more than the number of items stored in the array

10. This is a dynamic data structure.

    a. Array
    b. List
    c. Both list and array
    d. Neither list nor array

Short Answer

1. What is a data structure?

2. Which automatically grows in size as you add items to it, lists or arrays?

3. When you drag a list tile and drop it on top of a placeholder in an instruction, a menu will appear. What will be on the menu?

4. How do you create an instruction that steps through an array, performing an operation on each item?

5. How do you randomly select an item in a list? How do you randomly select an item in an array?

6. What is an `ArrayVisualization` object?

7. If you are writing a program that will add items to data structure while the program is running, would you choose a list or an array as the data structure?

8. If you are writing a program that needs to access items in a data structure and execute as fast as possible, would you choose a list or an array as the data structure?

Exercises

VideoNote
Creating the
School of
Fish World

1. **School of Fish**

   Create an undersea world with a school of at least five fish. The fish should always swim together in the same direction. At intervals, the school should turn in a random direction. Write the algorithm in such a way that the school of fish is never completely off screen.

2. **Magic Blocks**

   Create a world with a child and a set of at least five building blocks. Initially, the world should appear as shown in the left image in Figure 7-69. The blocks should all be on the ground. These are magic blocks, however. When the world is played, they should stack themselves as shown in the image on the right in the figure. (The child in the figure is an instance of the `LittleBrother` class, in the *People* collection, and the building blocks are instances of the `BuildingBlock` class in the *Objects* collection.)

Figure 7-69 *Magic blocks* world

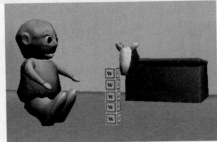

3. Dominoes

Create a world with at least ten objects arranged like dominoes. Figure 7-70 shows an example, using instances of the Box class, from the *Shapes* collection. These items should all be in a list or an array. When the user clicks anything in the world, the first item should fall over and strike the second item, which should fall over and strike the third item, and so forth.

Figure 7-70 *Dominoes* world

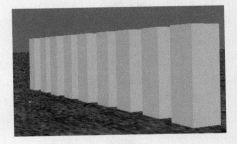

4. Bug Zapper Game

Create a world with a list or an array that contains bugs. (You can find various bugs in the *Animals > Bugs* collection.) When the world is played, the bugs should all move quickly in different random directions. When the user successfully clicks a bug, it vanishes. The game should continue until all of the bugs are gone.

5. Bug Zapper Modification

This exercise assumes that you have completed Exercise 4, Bug Zapper Game. Modify the world so that at first the bugs are moving slowly. Each time the user clicks a bug, the remaining bugs should move a little faster.

6. Shark Escape

This exercise assumes that you have completed Exercise 1, School of Fish. Modify the world to also include a shark (from the *Animals* collection) that initially is positioned away from the school of fish, but slowly swims toward it. When the shark gets close to the school, they should all swim away, faster than the shark, to a safe distance.

7. **Cooking Show**

Create a world that simulates a TV cooking show. You should have a kitchen with various items from the *Kitchen* collection. When you play the world, the host of the show should put the ingredients for a recipe, one at a time, into a bowl. You can use items from the *Kitchen > Food* collection for the ingredients and use the Dome class in the *Shapes* collection to create a bowl. Put the ingredients in a list or an array. The action of the host putting each item into the bowl should be the result of an instruction that steps through each item in the list or array. As the host places each ingredient into the bowl, he or she should name the ingredient.

8. **Airport**

Create a world that simulates an airport with a control tower and a runway. A group of airplanes should be lined up, ready for take-off. Store the airplane objects as items in a list or an array. One at a time, the airplanes should take off and fly away into the distance.

9. **Honor Guard**

Create a world with a stadium (from the *City* collection) and a group of toy soldiers (from the *People* collection) lined up at one end of the field. The soldiers should simultaneously march to the 50 yard line (the middle of the field), stop, salute, turn around, and march back to the end of the field.

10. **Karate Class Modification**

Modify the *KarateClass* world, presented earlier in this chapter, so the evil ninja commands the students to practice their karate chops five times. Each time the evil ninja says "Chop!" the students should make a karate chop motion.

11. **Dance Class**

A group of dance students have just learned their first dance step. In class, they practice along with their instructor by repeating the dance step five times. Create a world that simulates the dance class.

Hint: This world is similar in many ways to the *KarateClass* world presented earlier in this chapter.

12. **Soccer Practice**

Modify the *SoccerPractice* world that was presented earlier in this chapter so the soccer player always shoots the balls toward the goal. Create another character that acts as a goalie, trying to block the balls from entering the goal. You should also have a coach standing to the side watching the practice.

Each time the soccer player kicks a ball, the world should generate a random number to determine whether the goalie will successfully block the ball. You can do this by generating a random integer in the range of 0 through 1. If the number is 0, the goalie will block the ball. If the number is 1, the goalie will not block the ball and it will enter the goal. Each time the soccer player kicks a ball, the coach should announce whether it was blocked or entered the goal.

8 Recursion

TOPICS

8.1 Introduction to Recursion
8.2 Problem Solving with Recursion

8.1 Introduction to Recursion

CONCEPT: **A recursive method is a method that calls itself.**

In many of the worlds that you've examined in the previous chapters, you've seen how one method can call another method. Alice also supports *recursion*, which means that a method can call itself. Let's look at an example. On the Student CD you will find a world named *EndlessRecursion*. As shown in Figure 8-1, the world has a boy object (from the *People* collection) sitting in the passenger seat of a convertibleCorvette object (from the *Vehicles* collection). When you play the world the world.animation method executes. As you can see from Figure 8-1 the method calls another method, world.boyAskQuestion. The world.boyAskQuestion method is shown in Figure 8-2.

Let's look at the instructions in the world.BoyAskQuestion method. First, the boy says "Are we there yet?" Then the Wait instruction causes the method to pause for half a second. Then, the method calls itself. Each time it calls itself, these instructions are repeated. Can you see a problem with the method? There's no way to stop the recursive calls. This method is like an infinite loop because there is no code to stop it from repeating.

Like a loop, a recursive method must have some way to control the number of times it repeats. To see how the world.boyAskQuestion method can be modified so it does not repeat indefinitely, look at the *Recursion* world, also on the Student CD. Figure 8-3

Figure 8-1 The *EndlessRecursion* world

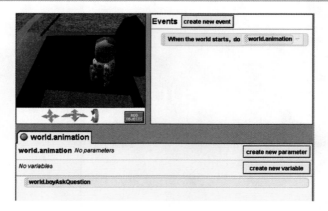

Figure 8-2 The `world.boyAskQuestion` method

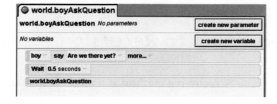

Figure 8-3 The revised `world.boyAskQuestion` method

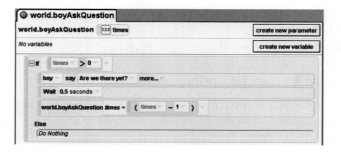

shows the `world.boyAskQuestion` method in the *Recursion* world. This version of the method accepts an integer argument, which is the number of times the method should call itself.

This method contains an `if` statement that controls the repetition. As long as the `times` parameter is greater than zero, the boy asks "Are we there yet," then the `Wait` instruction executes, and then the method calls itself again. Each time it calls itself, it passes `times` — 1 as the argument. Figure 8-4 shows the `world.animation` method in this world.

The `world.animation` method in this world calls the `world.boyAskQuestion` method with the argument 5, which causes the method to call itself five times. The first time the method is called, the `boy` asks the question, the `Wait` instruction executes, and then the method calls itself with 4 as the argument. Figure 8-5 illustrates this.

The diagram in Figure 8-5 illustrates two separate calls of the `world.boyAskQuestion` method. Each time the method is called, a new instance of the `times` parameter is created in memory. The first time the method is called, the `times` parameter is set to 5. When the method calls itself, a new instance of `times` is created, and the value 4 is passed into it. This cycle repeats until finally, zero is passed to the method. This is illustrated in Figure 8-6.

As you can see from Figure 8-6, the method is called a total of six times. The first time it is called from the `world.animation` method, and the other five times it calls itself. The number of times that a method calls itself is known as the *depth of recursion*. In this example, the depth of recursion is five. When the method reaches its sixth

Figure 8-4 The `world.animation` method

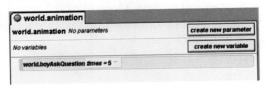

Figure 8-5 First two calls of the method

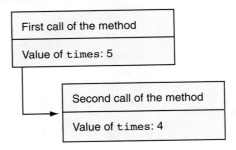

Figure 8-6 Total of six calls to the `world.boyAskQuestion` method

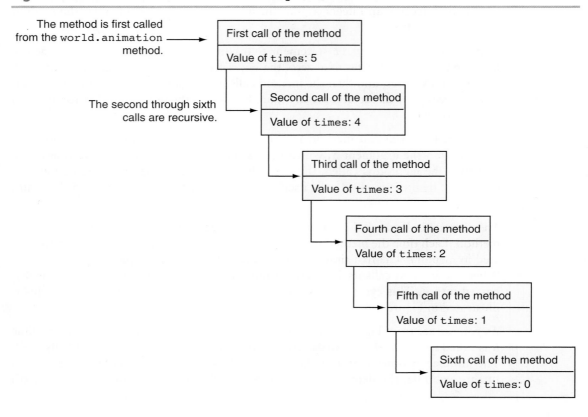

The method is first called from the `world.animation` method.

First call of the method

Value of `times`: 5

The second through sixth calls are recursive.

Second call of the method

Value of `times`: 4

Third call of the method

Value of `times`: 3

Fourth call of the method

Value of `times`: 2

Fifth call of the method

Value of `times`: 1

Sixth call of the method

Value of `times`: 0

call, the `times` parameter is set to 0. At that point, the `if` statement's condition is false, so the method returns. Control of the program returns from the sixth instance of the method to the point in the fifth instance directly after the recursive method call. This is illustrated in Figure 8-7.

Figure 8-7 Control returns to the point after the recursive method call

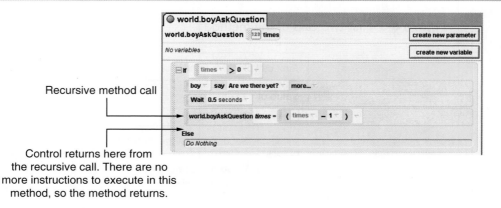

Recursive method call

Control returns here from the recursive call. There are no more instructions to execute in this method, so the method returns.

Tutorial 8-1 leads you through the process of creating a recursive method in an Alice world.

Tutorial 8-1:
Creating a recursive method

Step 1: Start Alice and create a snow world with an instance of the `IceSkater` class (from the *People* collection), as shown in Figure 8-8. As has been our custom in this text, change the name of `world.my first` method to `world.animation`, or any name that meets the camelCase naming convention.

Figure 8-8 *Snow* world with an `IceSkater`

Step 2: Next you will create a world-level method named `skaterSpin`. Here is the pseudo code for the method:

```
Method skaterSpin(times)
    If times > 0
        skater set pose to pose4
        skater turn left 1 revolution
        skater set pose to original pose
        skaterSpin(times − 1)
    End If
End Method
```

The purpose of the method is to make the `skater` perform a spin maneuver a specified number of times. The `times` parameter will hold the number of times that the `skater` should perform the maneuver. If `times` is greater than 0, the method sets the `skater`'s pose to `pose4`, turns the `skater` left one revolution, and then sets the `skater`'s pose back to the original pose. Then the method calls itself passing `times` − 1 as an argument.

Select the `world` object and create a new method named `skaterSpin`. In the method, create a Number parameter named `times`. Create the instruction shown in Figure 8-9 in the method.

Figure 8-9 Starting the `world.skaterSpin` method

Step 3:   Now you will create the recursive method call. Drag the tile for the world's `skaterSpin` method and drop it in the Method Editor at the location shown by the green line in Figure 8-10. When you drop the tile, by releasing the mouse button, a pop-up menu will appear allowing you to select a value for the `times` parameter. Select expressions, and then select `times`. After doing this you should see the dialog box shown in Figure 8-11. This dialog box warns you that you are about to

Figure 8-10 Creating a recursive method call

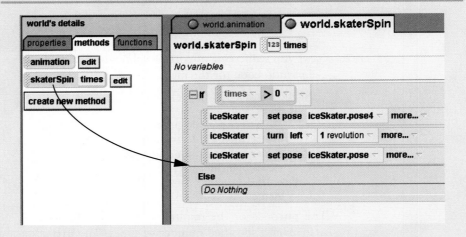

Figure 8-11 Recursion Warning

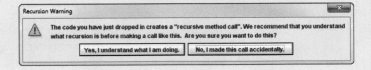

create a recursive method call. Click the button that reads "Yes, I understand what I am doing." The method should now appear as shown in Figure 8-12.

Figure 8-12 The world.skaterSpin method so far

Step 4: The instruction that you created in the last step recursively calls the world.skaterSpin method, passing times as the argument. Modify the instruction so it passes times − 1 as the argument, as shown in Figure 8-13. (To make this modification, click the down-arrow ⌄ that appears next to *times* = times, then select *math*, then select *times* −, then select *1*.) This completes the world.SkaterSpin method.

Figure 8-13 The completed world.skaterSpin method

Step 5: Open the world.animation method in the Method Editor. Drag the tile for the world.SkaterSpin method and drop it into the world.animation method. Specify 3 as the argument. The world.animation method should appear, as shown in Figure 8-14.

Figure 8-14 The completed `world.animation` method

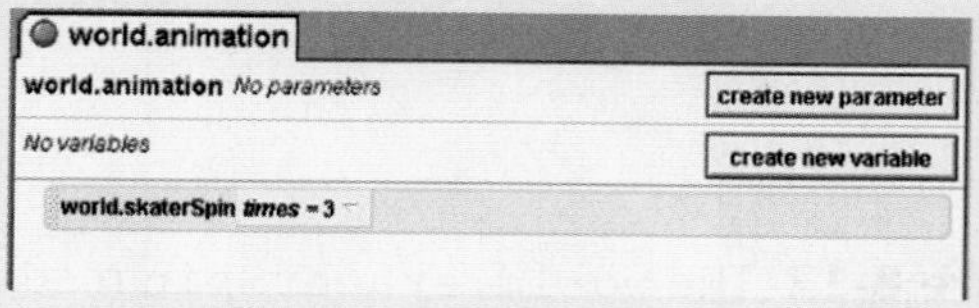

Step 6: Save the world and then play it. You should see the `skater` perform three spins.

8.2 Problem Solving with Recursion

CONCEPT: A problem can be solved with recursion if it can be broken down into successive smaller problems that are identical to the overall problem.

The Alice worlds that you studied in the previous section demonstrate the mechanics of a recursive method. Recursion can be a powerful tool for solving repetitive problems and is commonly studied in computer science courses. It might not be clear to you yet how to use recursion to solve a problem.

First, it should be noted that recursion is never absolutely required to solve a problem. Any problem that can be solved with recursion can also be solved with a loop. Some repetitive problems, however, are more easily solved with recursion than with a loop. Often, programmers who understand recursion find that they can use it more easily than loops to design certain algorithms.

In general, a recursive method works as follows:

- If the problem can be solved now, without recursion, then the method solves it and returns
- If the problem cannot be solved now, then the method reduces it to a smaller but similar problem and calls itself to solve the smaller problem

In order to apply this approach, first, we identify at least one case in which the problem can be solved without recursion. This is known as the *base case*. Second, we determine a way to solve the problem in all other circumstances using recursion. This is called the *recursive case*. In the recursive case, we must always reduce the problem to a smaller version of the original problem. By reducing the problem with each recursive call, the base case will eventually be reached and the recursion will stop.

In Tutorial 8-2 you will use the recursive problem solving approach in another Alice world.

Tutorial 8-2:
Recursive problem solving in animation

On the Student CD you will find a world named *Circles*, which is shown in Figure 8-15. This is similar to the *HawkAndTree* world in Chapter 5. There are two objects in the world: hawk and bonzai. In this tutorial you will create a recursive method that makes the hawk fly in circles around the bonzai. The method will accept an argument that specifies the number of times that the hawk should circle the bonzai.

Figure 8-15 The *Circles* world

Step 1: Copy the *Circles* world from the Student CD to your hard drive and open it.

Step 2: Select the world object and create a new method named flyCircles. In the method, create a Number parameter named times. Here is the pseudocode for the method:

```
Method world.flyCircles(times)
    If times > 0
        hawk turn right 1 revolution around bonzai
        world.flyCircles(times − 1)
    End If
End Method
```

The times parameter will hold the number of times that the hawk should fly in a circle around the bonzai. This algorithm's recursive case is when times is greater than 0. When this condition is true, the method calls the hawk object's turn method to make it fly around the bonzai. Then the method recursively calls itself passing times − 1 as an argument.

When the times parameter is 0, the method has reached its base case and it does not perform a recursive call.

Figure 8-16 shows the actual code for the method. Complete the method as shown in the figure.

Figure 8-16 The completed `world.flyCircles` method

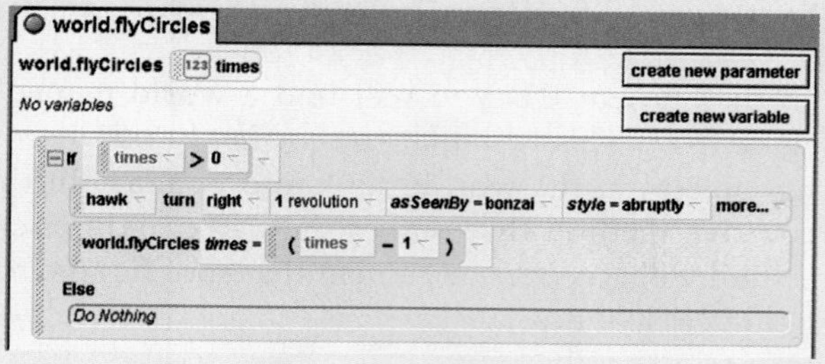

Step 3:   The `world` already has a method named `animation`, which executes when the world is played. Open this method in the Method Editor and complete it as shown in Figure 8-17. This will call the `world.flyCircles` method, passing 5 as the argument.

Figure 8-17 The completed `world.animation` method

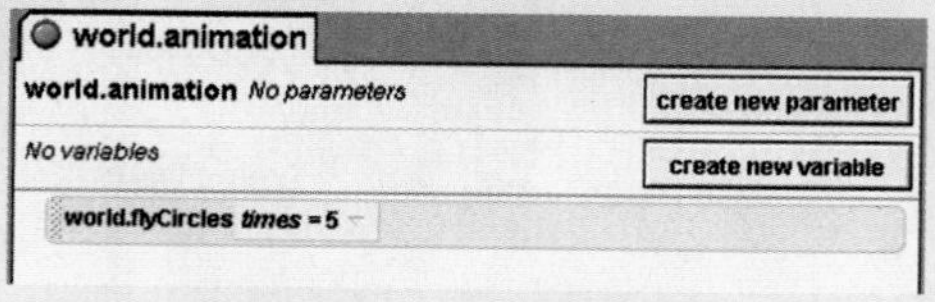

Step 4:   Save the world and then play it. You should see the `hawk` fly around the `bonzai` five times. If you wish to experiment, try changing the `world.animation` method so it passes other values to the `world.flyCircles` method, and then play the world to see the results.

Using Recursion in Mathematical Problems

Let's take an example from mathematics to examine an application of recursion. In mathematics, the notation $n!$ represents the factorial of the number n. The factorial of a non-negative number can be defined by the following rules:

$$\text{If } n = 0 \text{ then } n! = 1$$
$$\text{If } n > 0 \text{ then } n! = 1 \times 2 \times 3 \times \ldots \times n$$

Let's replace the notation $n!$ with factorial(n), which looks a bit more like the computer code for a function, and rewrite these rules as follows:

$$\text{If } n = 0 \text{ then factorial}(n) = 1$$
$$\text{If } n > 0 \text{ then factorial}(n) = 1 \times 2 \times 3 \times \ldots \times n$$

These rules state that when *n* is 0, its factorial is 1. When *n* is greater than 0, its factorial is the product of all the positive integers from 1 up to *n*. For instance, factorial(6) is calculated as $1 \times 2 \times 3 \times 4 \times 5 \times 6$.

When designing a recursive algorithm to calculate the factorial of any number, first we identify the base case, which is the part of the calculation that we can solve without recursion. That is the case where *n* is equal to 0 as follows:

$$\text{If } n = 0 \text{ then factorial}(n) = 1$$

This tells how to solve the problem when *n* is equal to 0, but what do we do when *n* is greater than 0? That is the recursive case, or the part of the problem that we use recursion to solve. This is how we express it:

$$\text{If } n > 0 \text{ then factorial}(n) = n \times \text{factorial}(n - 1)$$

This states that if *n* is greater than 0, the factorial of *n* is *n* times the factorial of $n - 1$. Notice how the recursive call works on a reduced version of the problem, $n - 1$. So, our recursive rule for calculating the factorial of a number might look like this:

$$\text{If } n = 0 \text{ then factorial}(n) = 1$$
$$\text{If } n > 0 \text{ then factorial}(n) = n \times \text{factorial}(n - 1)$$

Let's see how this might be implemented in Alice. On the Student CD you will find a world named *MathRobot*. As shown in Figure 8-18, the world contains a `mad_scientist` object (from the *People* collection) and a `robot` object (from the Web gallery's *SciFi* collection).

Figure 8-18 The *MathRobot* world

If you select the `robot` and look at its functions, you will see the `robot.factorial` function shown in Figure 8-19. This function has a Number parameter named n. The figure points out the following three items:

1. This instruction sets the local `factorialValue` variable to 1, and is executed if the parameter n is equal to 0. This instruction is the base case.
2. This instruction sets the local `factorialValue` variable to n times the factorial of $n - 1$. This instruction is the recursive case, and is executed if n is not equal to 0.
3. This instruction returns the `value` variable.

Figure 8-19 The `robot.factorial` method

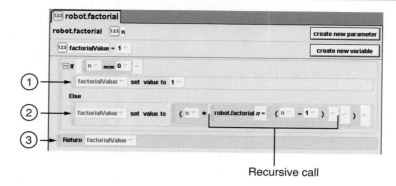

Recursive call

The `robot.factorial` function is called in the `world.animation` method, which is shown in Figure 8-20. Figure 8-21 shows the world running. In the figure, the user enters 4 when asked for a number. The `mad_scientist` tells the `robot` to give him the factorial of 4.0, and then the `robot` says 24.0.

Figure 8-20 The `world.animation` method

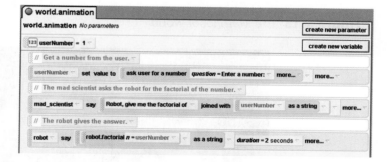

In the example run of the world, the `robot.factorial` function is called with the argument 4 passed into n. Because n is not equal to 0, the `if` statement's `else` clause executes the following instruction:

factorialValue.set value to (n * robot.factorial(n − 1))

This instruction sets the value of `factorialValue`, but it does not set the variable's value immediately. To determine the value to store in the variable, the value of `robot.factorial(n − 1)` must be determined. The `factorial` function is called recursively until the fifth call, in which the n parameter will be set to zero. The diagram in Figure 8-22 illustrates the value of n and the return value during each call of the function.

Figure 8-21 Running the *MathRobot* world

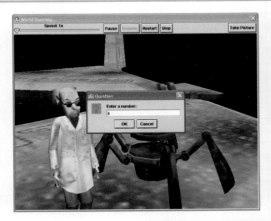

This diagram illustrates why a recursive algorithm must reduce the problem with each recursive call. Eventually the recursion has to stop in order for a solution to be reached.

If each recursive call works on a smaller version of the problem, then the recursive calls work toward the base case. The base case does not require recursion, so it stops the chain of recursive calls.

Usually, a problem is reduced by making the value of a parameter smaller with each recursive call. In our `robot.factorial` function, the value of the parameter n gets closer to 0 with each recursive call. When the parameter reaches 0, the function returns a value without making another recursive call.

In Tutorial 8-3 you will write another recursive mathematical function for the `robot`.

Figure 8-22 Recursive calls to the `factorial` function

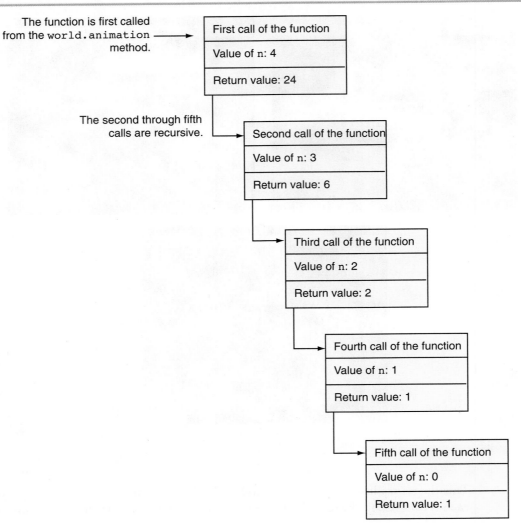

The function is first called from the `world.animation` method.

First call of the function

Value of n: 4

Return value: 24

The second through fifth calls are recursive.

Second call of the function

Value of n: 3

Return value: 6

Third call of the function

Value of n: 2

Return value: 2

Fourth call of the function

Value of n: 1

Return value: 1

Fifth call of the function

Value of n: 0

Return value: 1

Tutorial 8-3:
Writing a recursive mathematical function

In this tutorial you will write a recursive function named `multiply`. The function will have two parameters named a and b. It will use recursion to calculate and return the value of a times b. Remember, multiplication can be performed as repeated addition as follows:

$$7 \times 4 = 7 + 7 + 7 + 7$$

To keep our algorithm as simple as possible, we won't worry about negative numbers or zero. Let's assume that both a and b are positive whole numbers. Given that assumption, here are the rules that we can use to develop our algorithm:

$$\text{If } b > 1 \text{ then multiply}(a, b) = a + \text{multiply}(a, b - 1)$$
$$\text{If } b = 1 \text{ then multiply}(a, b) = a$$

Given these rules, here is the pseudocode for the `multiply` function:

```
Function robot.multiply(a, b)
   If b > 1
      set product variable to (a + robot.multiply(a, b-1))
   Else
      set product variable to a
   End If
   Return product variable
End Function
```

Step 1: Start Alice and load the *MathRobot* world from the Student CD.

Step 2: Select the `robot` object, and then select the *functions* tab in the Details Panel. Click the *create new function* button. Name the function `multiply`, and select *Number* as the function's type.

Step 3: Complete the function by creating the instructions shown in Figure 8-23. (Note that the function has two Number parameters named a and b, and a local Number variable named `product`.)

Figure 8-23 The completed `multiply` function

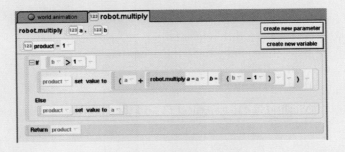

Step 4: Test the function by calling it from the `world.animation` method, as shown in Figure 8-24. The instruction in the figure calls the function to get the value of 5 times 3. You can use other values if you wish.

Step 5: Save the world and play it. Verify that the function returns the correct value.

Figure 8-24 Calling the `robot.multiply` function

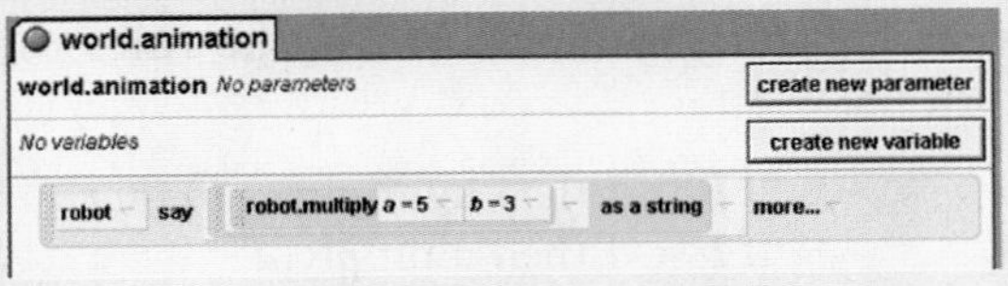

world.animation	
world.animation *No parameters*	create new parameter
No variables	create new variable

robot | say | robot.multiply *a* = 5 | *b* = 3 | as a string | more...

This chapter has given you a brief introduction to recursion and how it is used to solve problems that require repetition. Although we've only scratched the surface of this topic, you now know what recursion is. If you plan to continue your education in computer science, you will study recursion in greater detail in future courses.

 Checkpoint

8.1 What is a base case?

8.2 What is a recursive case?

8.3 What causes a recursive algorithm to stop calling itself?

Review Questions

Multiple Choice

1. This is what a recursive method does.

   a. It calls a different method
   b. It abnormally halts the program
   c. It calls itself
   d. It can only be called once

2. Method *A* calls method *B*, and then method *B* calls itself four times. The depth of recursion is which of the following?

   a. One
   b. Four
   c. Five
   d. Nine

3. This is the part of a problem that can be solved without recursion.

   a. Base case
   b. Solvable case
   c. Known case
   d. Iterative case

4. This is the part of a problem that is solved with recursion.

   a. Base case
   b. Iterative case
   c. Unknown case
   d. Recursion case

5. This is what we must do in the recursive case.

   a. Solve the problem without recursion
   b. Reduce the problem to a smaller version of the original problem
   c. Acknowledge that an error has occurred and abort the program
   d. Enlarge the problem to a larger version of the original problem

6. This is what we must do in the base case.

   a. Solve the problem without recursion
   b. Reduce the problem to a smaller version of the original problem
   c. Acknowledge that an error has occurred and abort the program
   d. Enlarge the problem to a larger version of the original problem

Short Answer

1. In the *Recursion* world presented in this chapter, what is the base case in the `world.boyAskQuestion` method?

2. In this chapter the rules given for calculating the factorial of a number are:

$$\text{If } n = 0 \text{ then factorial}(n) = 1$$
$$\text{If } n > 0 \text{ then factorial}(n) = n \times \text{factorial}(n - 1)$$

   If you were creating a function from these rules, what would the base case be? What would the recursive case be?

3. Is recursion ever required to solve a problem? What other approach can you use to solve a problem that is repetitive in nature?

4. When recursion is used to solve a problem, why must the recursive method call itself to solve a smaller version of the original problem?

5. How is a problem usually reduced with a recursive method?

VideoNote
Creating the
Recursive
Weightlifting
Jock World

Exercises

1. **Recursive Weightlifting Jock**

   Create a world with an instance of the `Jock` class (from the *High School > Students and Teachers* collection) and an instance of the `Barbell` class (from the *Objects* collection). Position the `barbell` and the `jock` as shown in Figure 8-25. Create a method named `curl` that makes the jock curl the barbell. (To curl the barbell, the jock simply raises it up to about the level of his chin.) The method should have a Number parameter that indicates the number of times that the jock is to curl the barbell. Use recursion to make the jock curl the barbell the specified number of times.

Figure 8-25 Weightlifting jock

2. **Recursive Sailing**

Create a sea world with a boat and an island. Position the island some distance away from the boat, as shown in Figure 8-26. Write a method named `sailTo`, which has an `Object` parameter. The method should cause the boat to move one meter toward the object and then recursively call itself until the boat has reached the object. Test the method by calling it and passing the island as the argument.

Figure 8-26 Sailboat and island

3. **Recursive Power**

Add a new function to the robot object in the *MathRobot* world that was presented in this chapter. The function should be named `power`, and it should have two parameters named a and b. The function should use recursion to calculate and return the value of a raised to the power of b. Here is the pseudocode for the function:

```
Function robot.power(a, b)
    If b == 0
        set powerValue variable to 1
    Else
        set powerValue variable to (a * robot.power(a, b-1))
    End If
    Return powerValue variable
End Function
```

Modify the `world.animation` method so it demonstrates the function.

4. **Sum of Numbers**

Add a new function to the robot object in the *MathRobot* world that was presented in this chapter. The function should be named `sumNumbers`. It should have a Number parameter and return the sum of all the numbers from 1 up to the value passed as an argument. For example, if 50 is passed as an argument, the function should return the sum of 1, 2, 3, 4, . . . , 50. Use recursion to calculate the sum. Modify the `world.animation` method so it demonstrates the function.

5. **Fibonacci Numbers**

Some mathematical problems are designed to be solved recursively. One well-known example is the calculation of Fibonacci numbers. The Fibonacci numbers, named after the Italian mathematician Leonardo Fibonacci (born circa 1170), are the following sequence:

$$0, 1, 1, 2, 3, 5, 8, 13, 21, 34, 55, 89, 144, 233, . . .$$

Notice that after the second number, each number in the series is the sum of the two previous numbers. Here are the rules for calculating the nth number in the Fibonacci series:

If $n = 0$ then Fibonacci(n) = 0
If $n = 1$ then Fibonacci(n) = 1
If $n >= 2$ then Fibonacci(n) = Fibonacci($n - 1$) + Fibonacci($n - 2$)

Add a new function to the robot object in the *MathRobot* world that was presented in this chapter. The function should be named `fibonacci`. It should have a Number parameter named n, and should return the nth number in the Fibonacci series. Here is the pseudocode for the function:

```
Function robot.fibonacci(n)
    If n == 0
        result = 0
    Else If n == 1
        result = 1
    Else
        result = robot.fibonacci(n — 1) + robot.fibonacci(n — 2)
    End If
    Return result
End Function
```

Modify the `world.animation` method to demonstrate the function.

A Installing Alice

Alice is free software, made available as a public service from Carnegie Mellon University. You will find a copy of Alice 2.2 on the CD that accompanies this book. You can also download Alice 2.2 from http://www.alice.org.

This appendix gives you brief and detailed instructions for installing Alice. If you are a proficient computer user, you will probably find the brief installation instructions sufficient. If you need step-by-step guidance, detailed instructions are provided for installing the software in Windows.

Brief Installation Instructions

The Alice software is compressed in a file named *Alice.zip*. There is no installation wizard with Alice; you simply copy this file from the CD or download it from the Alice Web site to your system, and then extract its contents to the location where you want to install the software. After you extract the contents of *Alice.zip* you will see a folder named *Alice*. Inside this folder you will find an executable file named *Alice.exe*. Double-click this file to run Alice. If you wish, you can create a shortcut to this file on your desktop.

Detailed Installation Instructions for Windows

> **NOTE:** These instructions and screen images were prepared using Windows 7. If you are installing on Windows Vista or Windows XP, the screens will look different from those shown here, but the steps will be similar.

Step 1: Copy the *Alice.zip* file from the accompanying CD or download it from http://www.alice.org.

Step 2: Right-click the *Alice.zip* file. As shown in Figure A-1, select *Extract All...* from the pop-up menu. The dialog box, shown in Figure A-2, will appear next.

Figure A-1 Extracting the contents of *Alice.zip*

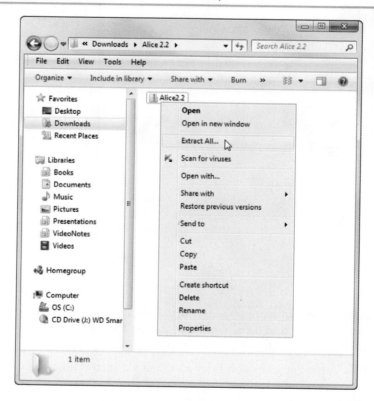

Figure A-2 *Extraction Wizard* dialog box

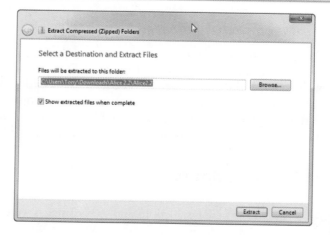

Step 3: Click the *Browse...* button and select the location where you want to extract the contents of the file. (A folder named *Alice 2.2* will be created in the location that you choose. The *Alice* folder will contain all of the Alice software files.)

Step 4: After you have selected a location, click the *Extract* button to extract the contents of the file.

Step 5:   A folder named *Alice 2.2* will appear in the location that you selected in Step 3. Inside this folder you will find a file named *Alice.exe*. This is the file that runs Alice. For convenience, you should create a shortcut to the *Alice.exe* file on your desktop. As shown in Figure A-3, right-click the *Alice.exe* file and then select *Send To>Desktop (create shortcut)* from the pop-up menus. After doing this a shortcut to the *Alice.exe* file will appear on the desktop.

Congratulations! You have installed Alice on your system. To start Alice, double-click the shortcut that you created on your desktop.

Figure A-3 Creating a shortcut on the desktop

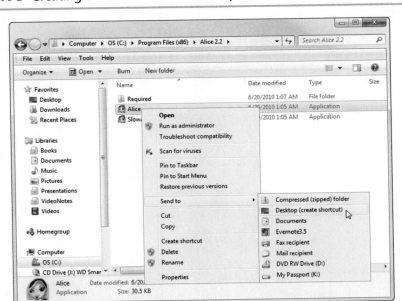

B Answers to Checkpoints

Chapter 1

1.1 A computer is a device that follows instructions for manipulating and storing information.

1.2 A computer program is a set of instructions that the computer follows to perform a task.

1.3 An algorithm is a set of well-defined logical steps that must be taken in order to perform a task.

1.4 Machine language is the only language that computers understand.

1.5 Because computers only understand machine language (which consists of binary numbers), programming languages were invented to make programming easier. Programming languages consist of words, which are easier for people to understand.

1.6 You use the *speed slider* control on the *World Running...* window.

1.7 The World View window

1.8 The Object Tree

1.9 A tile is simply a small rectangular icon. In this section we discussed the use of tiles to represent objects in the Object Tree.

1.10 Properties are values that specify an object's characteristics.

1.11 The `color` property determines an object's color. The `opacity` property determines whether you can see through an object.

1.12 A method is a set of programming statements that an object can execute.

1.13 An example is the `snowman` object that we discussed in the *snowLove* world. The `snowman` object is made of a head section object, a middle section object, and a bottom section object.

1.14 A class is a description of a particular type of object.

1.15 A class is similar to a blueprint, and instances of the class are similar to houses built from the blueprint. The blueprint itself is not a house, but it is a detailed description of a house. When we use the blueprint to build an actual house, we can say that we are building an instance of the house that is described by the blueprint. If

347

we want, we can build several identical houses from the same blueprint. Each house is a separate instance of the house that is described by the blueprint.

1.16 Classes are stored in the Alice galleries.

1.17 Alice goes into scene editor mode.

1.18 Click the class thumbnail, and then on the *information* window for the class, click the *Add instance to world* button. Or click and drag the class thumbnail from the gallery into the world.

1.19 Click the object in the World View window. Or click the object's tile in the Object Tree.

1.20 A yellow bounding box appears.

1.21 It would be the name of an object because by convention the names of objects begin with a lowercase letter and the names of classes begin with an uppercase letter.

1.22 The Details Panel

1.23 Two-dimensional objects have height and width; three-dimensional objects have height, width, and depth.

1.24 An object in a two-dimensional world can move up, down, left, and right; an object in a three-dimensional world can move up, down, left, right, forward, and backward.

1.25 Move Freely, Move Up and Down, Turn Left and Right, Turn Forward and Backward, Tumble, Resize, and Copy

1.26 Because an object rotates around its center point

1.27 The green axis points in the object's up direction, the blue axis points in the object's forward direction, and the magenta axis points in the object's right direction.

1.28 World View, Top, Right, and Front

1.29 The *Move Up and Down* button is not displayed in quad view mode because the right and front viewing windows support up and down movement. If you want to move an object up or down while in quad view mode, simply select the *Move Objects Freely* button and then move the object up or down in the right view or the front view.

1.30 They indicate a position, using the X, Y, and Z axes. The first number (5) is the X coordinate, the second number (0) is the Y coordinate, and the third number (1) is the Z coordinate.

Chapter 2

2.1 `hare.move`

2.2 The method name is specified in the event tile that reads `When the world starts, do`.

2.3 A primitive method is a built-in method for performing basic actions. All objects in an Alice world have primitive methods.

2.4 First select the object. Then, in the Details Panel, select the *methods* tab to display a list of tiles representing the object's methods.

2.5 When you select *other...* the custom number keypad appears. You would use this selection when you need to specify a distance that does not appear on the menu.

2.6 She means that it executes another method.

2.7 An argument is any piece of information that a method requires in order for it to execute.

2.8 A custom method is a method that only objects of a specific class have. Not all classes provide custom methods.

2.9 If a class provides custom methods, you can see a list of those methods in the class's information window. Also, when you add an instance of the class to the world and then select that object, tiles representing its custom methods (if it has any) appear above the tiles for the primitive methods in the Details Panel.

2.10 An object's name should reflect the object's purpose or role in the world. As a result it's easier for anyone reading your code to understand the purpose of the object.

2.11 No

2.12 The camelCase convention is a way of writing multi-word names without spaces. In camelCase you begin the name with lowercase letters. Then the first character of the second and subsequent words is written in uppercase. You use camelCase convention for object and method names.

2.13 PascalCase is the same as camelCase, except in PascalCase the first character is written in uppercase. PascalCase is used for class names.

2.14 Design the program, write the methods, test the methods, and debug the methods.

2.15 Pseudocode and flowcharts

2.16 A logical error is a mistake that does not prevent the program from running, but causes it to produce incorrect results.

2.17 It does its intended task, it doesn't have any logical errors, and it works efficiently, without performing unnecessary steps.

2.18 They help anyone reading the program's code to understand the instructions.

2.19 No

2.20 Two forward slash characters (//) were chosen because comments begin with two forward slashes in many traditional languages, including Java and C++.

2.21 You place the instructions inside a `Do together` structure.

2.22 By placing those instructions inside a `Do in order` structure, which is placed inside the `Do together` structure

Chapter 3

3.1 A variable is a named storage location in memory.

3.2 The variable's name, the variable's type, and the variable's initial value

3.3 The variable area

3.4 That the variable's type is Number

3.5 You drag the variable tile and drop it into the Method Editor at the point where you want the instruction to occur. You select *set value* from the menu that appears. Another menu appears that allows you to specify the value you wish to store in the variable. As a result, a set instruction is created.

3.6 A function returns a value to the instruction that called it.

3.7 You select the object and then you select the *functions* tab in the Details Panel.

3.8 The functions are as follows:

- `ask user for a number`
- `ask user for yes or no`
- `ask user for a string`

3.9   The `distance to` function returns an object's distance from another object, measured in meters. (Precisely, it returns the distance between the two objects' center points.)

3.10   + is the addition operator, − is the subtraction operator, * is the multiplication operator, and / is the division operator.

3.11   It performs a calculation and returns a value.

3.12   7

3.13   A collision occurs when two graphical objects come into contact with each other.

3.14   A string is a sequence of characters.

3.15   `ask user for a string`

3.16   String concatenation is joining two strings together.

3.17   You must use the `world` object's `what as a string` function to convert the variable to a string. You pass the variable as the *what* argument and the function returns a string.

Chapter 4

4.1   *True* or *false*

4.2   The function returns *true* if the user clicks the *Yes* button or *false* if the user clicks the *No* button.

4.3   A sequence structure is a set of instructions that are executed in sequence, in the order that they appear.

4.4   A decision structure is a structure that can execute a set of instructions only under certain circumstances.

4.5   The `If/Else` instruction tests a condition, which is anything that gives a Boolean value. If the value is *true*, then one set of instructions is executed. If the value is *false*, then a different set of instructions is executed.

4.6   A dual-alternative decision structure has two possible paths of execution—one path is taken if the condition is *true* and the other path is taken if the condition is *false*. A single-alternative decision structure has only one alternate path of execution, which is taken if the condition is *true*. If the condition is *false*, the path is skipped.

4.7   You create an `If/Else` instruction with an empty `Else` part.

4.8   A nested `If/Else` instruction is an `If/Else` instruction that is inside of another `If/Else` instruction.

4.9   Equal to, not equal to, greater than, greater than or equal to, less than, less than or equal to

4.10   In the `world` object's function list, under the math category

4.11   In the `both a and b` operator, both *a* and *b* must be true in order for the complex condition to be true. In the `either a or b, or both` operator, the complex condition is true if either *a* or *b* is true, or both are true.

4.12   It reverses the truth of its operand *a*. If *a* is true, then `not` *a* is false. If *a* is false, then `not` *a* is true.

4.13   The `Loop` instruction is a repetition structure.

4.14   By clicking the *show complicated version* button

4.15   An infinite loop is a loop that repeats an infinite number of times.

4.16   `index`

4.17 The `While` instruction is considered a conditional loop because it is controlled by a condition.

4.18 When the condition is tested and found to be false

4.19 The `While` loop is called a pretest loop because it tests its condition before it performs a repetition.

Chapter 5

5.1 You should save the object to a new class.

5.2 It will have the same name as the object, except that the first character will be changed to uppercase.

5.3 You click *File*, then *Import*.

5.4 The specialized class inherits methods and properties from the general class.

5.5 A class-level method in one object should not call a class-level method in another object. If the other object does not exist, an error will occur, and you cannot be sure that the other object will always exist in every world.

5.6 Sometimes an algorithm does not have enough detail to be translated into programming instructions.

5.7 If the method is too long it will be hard to understand. A better approach is to break it into multiple methods.

5.8 An argument is a value that is passed into a method.

5.9 A parameter is a special variable that holds the argument being passed into the method.

5.10 You open the method in the Method Editor and then click the *create new parameter* button.

5.11 An argument will be required.

5.12 A property is really a class-level variable.

5.13 You create a class-level variable in an object by selecting the object and clicking the *create new variable* button in the Details Panel, under the *properties* tab.

5.14 A function is a method that returns a value back to the instruction that called the function.

5.15 You are adding to the value in the property or variable.

5.16 A `Return` instruction is required in all functions. It returns a value back to the instruction that called the function.

5.17 A world-level method is a method written in the `world` object.

5.18 Instead of writing one long world-level method, you can write several smaller methods that each performs a specific part of the task. These smaller methods can then be executed in the desired order to perform the operation.

5.19 You can write a method to perform a task once and then call it (reuse it) each time you need to perform the task.

5.20 A world-level variable is a variable that belongs to the `world` object. Just as class-level variables act as properties for an object, world-level variables act as properties for the world. A world-level variable exists as long as the world is running, and is available to all methods in the world.

Creating a world-level variable is similar to creating a class-level variable. You take the following steps:

1. Select the `world` object in the Object Tree.
2. Select the *properties* tab in the Details Panel.
3. Click the *create new variable* button in the Details Panel.

4. The *Create New Variable* dialog box will appear. In the dialog box you enter a name for the variable and select a type. When you click *OK*, the variable will be created and you will see its tile in the Details Panel, under the *properties* tab.

5.21 You make a billboard and load the file that contains the graphic image.

5.22 You set object a's vehicle property to object b.

5.23 Object a will turn around object b's center point.

5.24 A pose is an object's position that is captured, and can then be restored when the world is played.

5.25 A dummy object is an invisible object that you place at a location in the world. You can then move the camera to the dummy object.

Chapter 6

6.1 An event is an action that takes place while a program is running.

6.2 `When the world starts`

6.3 In the event tile for the `When the world starts` event, click the down-arrow that appears next to the method name and select a different method.

6.4 You click the *create new event* button at the top of the Events Editor. A menu of available events will appear. You select the event that you want to handle from this menu. A tile for the event will then be created in the Events Editor.

6.5 An event handler is a method that is executed in response to an event.

6.6 The `While a key is pressed` event occurs as long as the user holds down a key. This is different from the `When a key is typed` event, which occurs only when the user releases a key.

6.7 First create a tile for the `When a key is typed` event. Then right-click the tile and from the menus that appear select *change to*, and `While a key is pressed`.

6.8 Begin, During, and End

6.9 The `While the mouse is pressed on something` event occurs as long as the user holds down the mouse button. This is different from the `When the mouse is clicked on something` event, which occurs only when the user clicks the mouse button.

Chapter 7

7.1 A data structure is a mechanism for storing data and organizing it in some way.

7.2 0

7.3 The size of a list is the number of items stored in the list.

7.4 The `For all in order` instruction steps through the list, one item at a time, performing the same operation on each item. The `For all together` instruction performs the same operation on all the items in a list simultaneously.

7.5 The `Insert <item> at beginning of list` method inserts an item at the beginning of a list, which is position 0. The other items are shifted toward the end of the list.

The `Insert <item> at end of list` method inserts an item at the end of the list.

The `Insert <item> at position <index> of list` method inserts an item at a specific position, indicated by `index`. The item currently at that position, and all subsequent items, will be shifted toward the end of the list.

7.6 The `remove item from beginning of list` method removes the item at position 0 from the list. (This item is not removed from the world, only from the list.) The remaining items are shifted toward the beginning of the list.

The `remove item from position <index> of list` method removes the item at a specific position, indicated by `index`. (This item is not removed from the world, only from the list.) The subsequent items are shifted toward the beginning of the list.

The `remove all items from list` method removes all items from the list. (The items are not removed from the world, only from the list.)

7.7 Some of the list functions; the list functions that will appear in the menu will be those with a return type that is compatible with the placeholder

7.8 The items in an array and a list are stored in a sequence. Each item's position in both data structures is numbered, with the first item at position 0, the second item is at position 1, and so forth.

7.9 One difference is that an array has a fixed size. While the world is running, the size of an array cannot be changed. Consequently, you cannot add more items to an array than it can hold. Another way that an array is different from a list is that the items stored in an array do not automatically shift their positions when an item is inserted into the array. When you insert an item into an array at a specific position, it replaces any item that was previously stored there. In addition, you can only replace an item that is currently in an array by replacing it with some other value.

7.10 The `For all in order` and `For all together` instructions that work with lists do not work with arrays.

7.11 You would create a `Loop` instruction that executes once for each item in the array. You use the complicated version of the loop, and you use the loop's `index` variable to specify an array item.

7.12 An `ArrayVisualization` object is used to visualize how an array works. It has numbered squares that represent the elements in the array. You can add other objects to the elements in the `ArrayVisualization` and they will appear in the squares. This gives you a way of seeing how an array works.

7.13 To select an item in an array randomly you generate a random number to use as an index. You use the world-level `random number` function to do this. The minimum value of the random number should be 0 and the maximum value should be the size of the array. Also, the random number should be an integer. You can use the random number function's *more... editing* tag to set these constraints.

Chapter 8

8.1 A base case is a case in which the problem can be solved without recursion.

8.2 A recursive case is a case in which the problem must be broken down into a smaller problem and solved with recursion.

8.3 Reaching the base case causes a recursive algorithm to stop calling itself.

Index

Symbols and Numbers

`*` (multiplication) operator, 130

`+` (addition) operator, 130

`<=` (less than or equal to) operator, 164

`<` (less than) operator, 164, 165

`==` (equal to) operator, 164

`!=` (not equal to) operator, 164

`/` (division) operator, 130

`–` (subtraction) operator, 130

`//` (two forward slashes), 88

`>=` (greater than or equal to) operator, 164

`>` (greater than) operator, 164

2D graphics, 31–32

3D objects, 32–33

    illustrated, 32

    modifying, 35–37

3D text

    creating, 142–143

    illustrated, 142

    in Object Tree, 143

    properties, 144

    thumbnail, 143

A

`a joined with b` function, 139

AccountantBob world, 141–142

Add 3D Text dialog box, 143

Add Objects button, 19, 20, 40, 43

algorithms

    breaking into smaller methods, 205

    conversion to statements, 4

    defined, 2

    steps, 2–3

    stepwise refinement, 203–209

Alice

    concept, 6

    defined, 5

    installing and running, 6–11

Alice environment

    defined, 11

    Details Panel, 11, 25–26, 65, 67, 120, 270

    Events Editor, 11, 12, 58, 251, 255–256

    illustrated, 12

    Method Editor, 11, 12, 57–58, 115

    Object Tree, 11, 22–23, 25, 28–29, 96

    toolbar, 11

    World View window, 11, 12

Alice worlds. *See also* worlds

    adding instructions to, 62–64

    adding objects to, 19–30

    creating, 19

    events, 249

    exporting to video, 105–106

    illustrated, 5

    loading, 8–9

    moving objects to center, 94

    as object, 16

    opening and playing, 6–11

    playing, 59, 67

    programming objects in, 6

    saving, 29–30

animation

    recursive problem solving in, 331–332

    tips, 230–241

arguments

    `asSeenBy`, 235

    defined, 64

    duration, 70

    passing, 64, 209–215

    passing incorrect values to, 81

    `style`, 234

arms, positioning, 93–94

arrays, 308–318. *See also* data structures

    concept illustration, 308

    creating, 309–313

    defined, 308

    elements, 308

    last item position number, 309

    lists versus, 308, 314

    `Loop` instruction, 310–311, 312–313

    randomly selecting items in, 316–318

    stepping through, 310

    tiles, 309, 311

`ArrayVisualization` object, 314–316

ArrayVisualization world, 315–316, 317
ask user functions, 121–125
  ask user for a number, 121
  ask user for a string, 121, 138
  ask user for yes or no, 121
  calling, 122–125
asSeenBy argument, 235
assignment, variable, 117
audio, 270–271
axes, 48–49

B
base case, 330
BDE event, 258, 263
billboards, 230–232
  defined, 230
  as objects, 232
  uses, 231
Bird world, 214–215
Boolean functions, 152–153
Boolean values, 151–153
Boolean variables, 224
  creating, 152
  defined, 115
  tile, 152
both *a* and *b* operator, 172
bounding boxes
  camera, 239
  defined, 23
  empty, 24
  in object rotation, 37
bugs, 81

C
calling methods, 64, 137, 228
camelCase names, 74, 327
camera, 33–35
  bounding box, 239
  clicking/dragging, 46
  controls, 33–34
  dummy objects for, 239–240
  moving in 3D space, 34–35
  moving to object, 96
  programming, 237–239
  viewpoint, 33
CameraPointAtCar world, 238–239
capturing poses, 235–236
center points. *See also* objects
  defined, 37
  determination, 39
  illustrated, 38
character builders, 271–273
  characteristics selection, 272
  hebuilder, 271–273
  interface, 272

shebuilder, 271–273
  starting, 271
Circles world, 331–332
circling
  invisible objects, 235
  objects, 233–234
classes
  defined, 16
  example, 17
  information window, 22, 71
  instances, 17, 24
  names, 25, 75
  saving objects to, 199–203
  thumbnails, 22
classes
  AliceLidell, 82–83, 232
  ArrayVisualization, 314, 315
  BlueBird, 214
  Chair, 41
  Cinderella, 93
  Circle, 127
  Coach, 73
  ExerciseGirl, 220
  FlyingPterodactyl, 202–203
  Frog, 71
  GrayJumpJet, 258
  HappyTree, 83
  Hare, 60
  IceSkater, 327
  Lion, 270
  Man, 264
  Monkey, 91, 98
  Motorboat, 232
  Penguin, 98, 103, 118, 127, 195
  Pterodactyl, 196
  Snowman, 134
  ToySoldier, 235
  WhiteRabbit, 82
class-level functions, 220–226
class-level methods, 195–199. *See also* methods
  creating, 196–198
  defined, 195
  independent of other objects, 203
  trial-and-error experimentation, 199
class-level variables
  creating, 216, 217
  defined, 114, 216
  as properties, 215–219
clipboards
  defined, 229
  icons, 230
  number available, 230
  using, 229–230
ClockLoop world, 175–177
code

defined, 4
exporting for printing, 104–105
reuse, 227
Collection Editor, 283–284
in adding array items, 309
in adding list items, 288
defined, 283
displaying, 288, 309
collisions, 132
color property, 13, 169–171, 215
comments, 88–89
default, 88
defined, 88
examples, 90
inserting, 89, 102
tile, 88
compilers, 3
computers
defined, 1–2
operations, 2
programs, 2
conditional loops, 180
constrain to face method, 66
constrain to point at method, 66
coordinates, in object location determination, 48–50
Copy button, 36, 37
count-controlled loops, 179
counter variable, 179
Create New List dialog box, 304, 306
Create New Local Variable dialog box, 114, 115, 152
Create New Parameter dialog box, 210, 211
Create New Variable dialog box, 216, 283, 286, 309
curvature property, 144
custom methods, 71, 72
Custom Number Keypad, 85

D

data structures
arrays, 308–318
defined, 281
dynamic, 282
lists, 281–307
debugging
with print statement, 273–274
programs, 81–82
decision structures
defined, 154
dual-alternative, 160
flowchart, 155
If/Else, 153–163
nested, 162, 163
single-alternative, 160–161
depth of recursion, 325

Details Panel
defined, 11
functions tab, 120, 123, 128, 222
methods tab, 65, 67, 76, 196, 254
properties tab, 25–26, 217, 221
sounds, 270
diagnostic messages, 273
distance to function, 220
divide and conquer, 227
Do in order structures, 102–103
Do together structures, 186, 221
creating methods containing, 98–102
defined, 97
dropping tiles onto, 100
example, 97–98
tile, 97, 99, 101
dollar amounts, entering, 142
dot notation, 58, 196
dual-alternative decision structures, 160
dummy objects
for camera, 239–240
defined, 239
placing, 239–240
tile, 240

E

editing tags, 70
either *a* or *b*, or both operator, 172
elements, array, 308
EndlessRecursion world, 323–324
Enter a string dialog box, 124
errors
logical, 81, 103
syntax, 6
event handlers, 252
event tiles, 85, 251–252
completing, 256
creating, 253, 255
Let the mouse move <objects>, 304, 305
When a key is typed, 253–254, 262
When something becomes true, 267
When the mouse is clicked on something, 261, 263, 266
While a key is pressed, 258, 259–260
While the world is running, 266
events, 249–279
BDE, 258, 263
defined, 249
key press, 253–260
Let the arrow keys move <subject>, 250
Let the mouse move <objects>, 250, 303–306
Let the mouse move the camera, 250
Let the mouse orient the camera, 250
menu of, 251
mouse, 261–263

events (*continued*)
  multiple, handling of, 257
  responding to, 249–253
  specialized, 252
  in traditional programming languages, 252
  `When a key is typed`, 250, 253–254, 262
  `When a variable changes`, 250
  `When something becomes true`, 250, 252, 267
  `When the mouse is clicked on something`, 250, 261, 262–263
  `When the world starts`, 249, 250, 266
  `While a key is pressed`, 250, 252, 257–260
  `While something is true`, 250
  `While the mouse is pressed on something`, 250, 252
  `While the world is running`, 250, 252, 266
Events Editor
  defined, 11, 58
  illustrated, 12, 58, 251, 255
  tiles in, 256
executable programs, 5
Export to HTML dialog box, 104
exporting
  Alice worlds to video, 105–106
  code for printing, 104–105
extrusion property, 144

F
`factorial` function, 333–335
factorial of numbers, 332
Faeries world, 254–257
Fan world, 174–175
`fillingStyle` property, 37
`first index of` function, 298
`first item from list` function, 298, 299
Fish world, 296–297
flowcharts
  decision structure, 155
  defined, 78
  illustrated, 79, 80, 83
  `Loop` instruction, 179–180
  nested decision structure, 163
  as outline, 79, 80
  processing symbols, 78
  pseudocode/instructions comparison, 80
  single-alternative decision structure, 161
  stepwise refinement, 203–209
  terminal symbols, 78
  `While` instruction, 181
fog, 232
font property, 144
`For all in order` instruction, 285, 288–289
`For all together` instruction, 285, 290
FourSkaters world, 285–291
FourSkatersArray world, 311–313

Fridge world, 261–262
functions, 120–130
  `a joined with b`, 139
  `ask user`, 121–125
  `ask user for a number`, 121
  `ask user for a string`, 121
  `ask user for yes or no`, 121
  Boolean, 152–153
  class-level, 220–226
  defined, 120
  empty, 223
  factorial, 333–335
  `first index of`, 298
  `first item from list`, 298, 299
  `is list empty`, 298
  `ith item from list`, 298, 299
  `last index of`, 298
  `last item from list`, 298, 299
  `list`, 120, 297–299
  `list contains`, 298
  methods versus, 120
  `multiply`, 337–338
  point of view, 126
  primitive object, 126
  proximity, 126, 127–129
  `random item from list`, 298, 299
  `random number`, 268–269, 316
  size, 126
  `size of list`, 298
  spatial relation, 126
  tile, 123, 124

G
galleries
  classes, 16–18
  defined, 16
  local, 16
  Web, 16, 30
games, 264–274
  audio, 270–271
  debugging, 273–274
  events in, 264–267
  random numbers, 268–269
  tips for, 268–274
generalization, 202–203
Gilbert world, 169–171
Globe world, 263
GreetingNerd world, 139–140
GumdropBigfish world, 165–168
Gym world, 211–212

H
HamletList world, 306–307
HareWorld world, 67

HawkAndTree world, 233–234
hebuilder tool, 271–273
Hollywood world, 142

I
identifiers, 73
If/Else decision structure, 153–163
If/Else instruction
  condition testing, 154
  creating, 156–159
  defined, 154
  as dual-alternative decision structure, 160
  empty, 155, 156
  execution, 154
  nested, 162, 163
  tile, 155, 156
Import dialog box, 200, 201
indexes, 282
infinite loops, 178
inheritance, 202–203
Initialize array dialog box, 315
Insert <item> at beginning of list method, 297
Insert <item> at end of list method, 297
Insert <item> at position <index> of list method, 297
instances. *See also* objects
  creating, 24, 44, 216
  defined, 17
instructions
  adding to Alice worlds, 62–64
  conditionally executed, 154, 160
  copying, 70–71
  deleting, 70
  in Do in order structure, 102–103
  executing simultaneously, 97–104
  flowchart/pseudocode comparison, 80
  For all in order, 285, 288–289
  For all together, 285, 290
  If/Else, 154–163
  list processing, 285
  Loop, 174–180, 310–311, 312–313
  multiple conditionally executed, 160
  for poses, 237
  print, 273–274
  Return, 224
  set, 117, 118–119
  tiles, 68, 69
  Wait, 219
  While, 180–188
is list empty function, 298
IslandRescue world, 264–267
isOn property, 217, 219
isShowing property, 215

isTired function, 220, 222, 223, 224
ith item from list function, 298, 299

K
KarateClass world, 291–296
key press events, 253–260
keywords, 3
kick method, 292, 295

L
last index of function, 298
last item from list function, 298, 299
Let the arrow keys move <subject> event, 250
Let the mouse move <objects> event
  defined, 250, 303
  tile, 304, 305
  using, 303–306
Let the mouse move the camera event, 250
Let the mouse orient the camera event, 250
LionArray world, 309–311
list contains function, 298
lists, 281–307. *See also* data structures
  adding items to, 284, 287
  arrays versus, 308, 314
  complex processing, 291–296
  concept illustration, 282
  creating, 283–284
  defined, 281
  as dynamic data structure, 282
  example world using, 300–303
  first index of function, 298
  first item from list function, 298, 299
  fishList, 297
  function menu, 299
  functions, 297–299
  indexes, 282
  Insert <item> at beginning of list method, 297
  Insert <item> at end of list method, 297
  Insert <item> at position <index> of list method, 297
  is list empty function, 298
  item types, 283
  ith item from list function, 298, 299
  last index of function, 298
  last item from list function, 298, 299
  list contains function, 298
  modification methods, 296–297
  myList, 298
  non-visual data storage, 306–307
  processing instructions, 285
  random item from list function, 298, 299
  remove all items from list method, 297
  remove item from beginning of list method, 297

lists (*continued*)
  `remove item from position <index> of list` method, 297
  `script`, 307
  size, 282
  `size of list` function, 298
  `studentList`, 295
  tiles, 297
  uses, 281–282
local gallery, 16
local variables. *See also* variables
  creating, 114–115
  defined, 113
  initial value, 115
  names, 114–115
  types, 115
logical errors, 81, 103
logical operators, 171–173
  defined, 171
  illustrated, 172
  list of, 172
  methods with, 173
`Loop` instruction, 174–180
  for arrays, 310–311, 312–313
  complicated version, 178–179
  defined, 174
  empty, 175, 176
  flowcharting, 179–180
  illustrated, 175
  `index` variable, 179
  integers and whole numbers, 177
  tile, 174, 312
  using, 175–177
loops
  conditional, 180
  count-controlled, 179
  defined, 174
  infinite, 178
  modifying, 212
  pretest, 182
  repetitions, predicting, 225
  `While`, 181

M

math expressions
  creating, 130–132
  defined, 130
  menus for building, 132
  operands, 130
  operators, 130
  variables in, 130
MathRobot world, 333–336
method calls, 64–65
  defined, 64
  illustrated, 65
  recursive, 326

Method Editor
  availability, 59
  defined, 11
  dragging tiles into, 57, 58, 61, 67, 79
  illustrated, 12
  location, 58
  variable area, 115
methods
  arguments, 64–65
  breaking algorithms into, 205
  calling, 64, 137, 228
  class-level, 195–199
  creating, 57, 196–198
  custom, 71, 72
  defined, 14, 57
  design, trial-and-error experimentation, 199
  empty, 57–58
  functions versus, 120
  instruction tiles, 59
  list of, 59
  logical error, 103
  names, 73
  opening in Method Editor, 198
  parameters, 210
  primitive, 59–62
  recursive, 323, 327–330
  renaming, 76–77, 83–84, 99, 201
  tiles, 60
  world-level, 226, 227–228
  writing, 79–80
methods. *See also* primitive methods
  `animate`, 288, 312
  `faceEachOther`, 228
  `flapWings`, 197–198, 199
  `fly`, 255–257
  `flyCircles`, 331–332
  `foottap`, 71
  `getTogether`, 228
  `haveConversation`, 228
  `headnod`, 71
  `jump`, 117
  `kick`, 292, 295
  `leftLegDown`, 207, 208
  `leftLegUp`, 206, 207, 208
  `rightLegDown`, 206, 207
  `rightLegUp`, 206
  `runInPlace`, 204–205, 208–209, 212–213
  `skaterSpin`, 327–329
  `spin`, 195–196
  `turnOnOff`, 218–219
  `updateCamera`, 266
more... editing tag, 70, 102
mouse events, 261–263
  handling, 261–262
  tile, 261, 262

mouse mode buttons, 35–37
  illustrated, 37
  location of, 36
  purpose of, 36
MovableFurniture world, 305–306
`move at speed` method, 66
`move away from` method, 66
Move Freely button, 36, 37, 41
`move` method, 60, 62, 65, 209
`move to` method, 66, 213
`move toward` method, 66
Move Up and Down button, 36,
    37, 43
`multiply` function, 337–338

N
names
  camelCase, 74, 327
  class, 25, 75
  as identifiers, 73
  meaningful, 73
  method, 73
  naming conventions, 73–77
  object, 25
  PascalCase, 75
  spaces in, 74
  variable, 114–115
nested `If/Else` instructions,
    162, 163
New Function dialog box, 223
New Method dialog box, 207, 218
not *a* operator, 172, 173
Number variables
  converting to strings, 141–142
  defined, 115

O
object parameters, 213–215
Object Tree, 11, 22, 23, 25
  expanding, 28–29
  object selection, 96
  tile display, 28, 83
Object variables, 115
objects, 13–16
  3D, 32, 35–37
  3D text, 142–144
  adding to Alice worlds, 19–30
  billboards, 230–232
  center point, 37, 38, 39
  circling, 233–234
  creating, 17
  with custom methods, 71
  dummy, 239–240
  function list, 120
  inner, 28
  invisible, circling, 235

location determination, 48–50
manipulating in 3D space, 40–43
methods, 14
moving camera to, 96
moving to center of the world, 94
moving together, 232–233
moving with camera, 238
moving with `While` instruction, 186–188
names, 25
orientation, 38–39
from other objects, 14–15
pitch, 40
positioning a specified distance, 94–96
properties, 13–14, 25–27, 168–171
renaming, 75–76, 200
repositioning, 99
roll, 40
rotating, 37
saving to classes, 199–203
selecting, 23
subparts, 14–15, 37
tiles, 22, 44
vanishing with `While` instruction,
    182–186
visibility determination, 215
world as, 16
yaw, 40
Office world, 216–219
`opacity` property, 13, 26, 27, 168,
    182–184, 215
operands, 130, 167
operators
  defined, 4
  logical, 171–173
  math, 130
  relational, 163–168
`orient to` method, 66
orientation, object, 38–39

P
parameter variables, 113
parameters
  creating in method, 210–211
  defined, 210
  object, 213–215
  `times`, 327, 328, 331
  `who`, 294
PascalCase naming convention, 75
passing arguments, 64, 209–215
  defined, 209
  incorrect values, 81
  to methods, 211–213
  object parameters, 213–215
  objects, 214
Pause button, 10
pitch, 40

placeholders, 122, 141, 158, 167, 184
  list tiles dropped on, 297
  tile slots, 258
Play button, 9, 59, 61, 62, 64, 67
`play sound` method, 65, 271
`point at` method, 66
point of view functions, 126
`pointOfView` property, 49, 50
poses
  capturing, 235–236
  instructions to set, 237
  restoring, 235
  saving objects and, 236
pretest loops, 182
primitive methods, 59–62
  `constrain to face`, 66
  `constrain to point at`, 66
  defined, 59
  `distance to`, 220
  `move`, 60, 62, 65, 209, 210
  `move at speed`, 66
  `move away from`, 66
  `move to`, 66, 213
  `move toward`, 66
  `my first method`, 76–77
  `orient to`, 66
  `play sound`, 65, 271
  `point at`, 66
  for positioning character arms, 93–94
  `resize`, 65
  `roll`, 65
  `roll at speed`, 66
  `say`, 65
  for scene setup, 90–92
  selecting, 91
  `set point of view to`, 66
  `set pose`, 66
  `stand up`, 66
  `think`, 65
  `turn`, 65, 67, 234
  `turn at speed`, 66
  `turn to face`, 66, 127, 213
primitive object functions, 126
`print` instruction, 273–274
printing, exporting code for, 104–105
PrintingRandomBee world, 274
problem solving, with recursion, 330–338
problem statements, 78, 82
processing symbols, 78
programming languages
  defined, 3
  keywords, 3
  operators, 4
  syntax, 4
programming statements, 4–5

programming the camera, 237–239
programs
  algorithms, 2–3
  comments, 88–90
  defined, 2
  designing, 78–79
  development cycle, 77
  executable, 5
  testing and debugging, 81–82
properties, 13–14
  adding to objects with class-level variables, 215–219
  changing, 26–27
  changing with set instructions, 119
  class-level variables as, 215–219
  color, 13, 215
  creating, 221
  `curvature`, 144
  defined, 13
  displaying, 25–26
  `extrusion`, 144
  `fillingStyle`, 37
  `font`, 144
  incrementing, 220
  `isOn`, 217, 219
  `isShowing`, 215
  `opacity`, 13, 26, 27, 168, 182–184, 215
  `pointOfView`, 49–50
  `text`, 144
  tiles, 26
  value, setting, 26–27
  value, testing, 168–171
  `vehicle`, 232–233, 238
proximity functions, 126, 127–129
pseudocode
  defined, 78
  flowchart/instructions comparison, 80
  illustrated, 80
  as outline, 80
  stepwise refinement, 203–209

Q
quad view mode, 47–48

R
`random item from list` function, 298, 299
`random number` function, 268–269, 316
random numbers, 268–269
RandomBee world, 268–269, 274
Record button, 105
recursion, 323–341
  base case, 330
  defined, 323
  depth of, 325
  introduction to, 323–326
  in mathematical problems, 332–338

problem solving with, 330–338
recursive case, 330
warning, 328
recursive case, 330
recursive methods
calls, 326, 328–329, 335
creating, 327–330
defined, 323
functioning of, 330
relational operators, 163–168
as binary, 164
defined, 163
illustrated, 164
list of, 164
steps for using, 165
using, 165–168
remove all items from list method, 297
remove item from beginning of list method, 297
remove item from position <index> of list method, 297
RepeatingNerd world, 139
repetition structures
Loop instruction, 174–180
While instruction, 180–188
RescueAtSea world, 186–188
Resize button, 36, 37
resize method, 65
Restart button, 10, 62, 64
Resume button, 10
Return instruction, 224
reuse, code, 227
roll, 40
roll at speed method, 66
roll method, 65
rotating objects, 37
runInPlace algorithm, 204–207

S

SalutingSoldier world, 236
Save Object dialog box, 200, 201
Save? dialog box, 30
saving
Alice worlds, 29–30
objects to classes, 199–203
poses and, 236
say method, 65
scene editor mode, 21, 43, 239
scenes
primitive methods for, 90–92
setting up, 90–96
Scroll View button, 47
sequence structure, 153–154
set instructions, 134–136
changing properties with, 119
creating, for variable, 117, 118–119

defined, 117
with function call, 122
illustrated, 118
menus for, 131
modifying, 125
with specified value, 122
set point of view to method, 66
set pose method, 66
set values, 117, 122
shebuilder tool, 271–273
simulations, 264–274
audio, 270–271
debugging, 273–274
events in, 264–267
random numbers, 268–269
starting, 265
tips for, 268–274
single view mode, 47
single-alternative decision structures, 160–161
size functions, 126
size of list function, 298
snowLove world, 13–15
SnowWorld world, 228
SoccerGoal world, 177–178
SoccerPractice world, 300–303
sounds
importing, 271
object, 270
playing, 270–271
recording, 271
SpaceJet world, 258–260
spaces, name, 74
spatial relation functions, 126
specialization, 202–203
specialized events, 252
Speed Slider control, 9
stand up method, 66
statements
problem, 78, 82
programming, 4–5
stepwise refinement, 203–209
defined, 204
runInPlace algorithm, 204–207
Stop button, 11, 62, 129
Stop Recording button, 106
strings
concatenation, 139
converting non-strings to, 140–142
defined, 138
joining, 139–140
user entering, 138–139
style argument, 234
subparts, 14–15
defined, 14
manipulating, 43–46
object modifications to, 37

syntax
   defined, 4
   errors, 6

T

Take Picture button, 11
templates, selecting, 19
Tennis world, 180–181
terminal symbols, 78
testing
   programs, 81–82
   property values, 168–171
text, 3D, 142–144
text console, 273, 274
text editors, 4
text property, 144
think method, 65
three-dimensional worlds, 32–33
   degrees of freedom, 32
   movement in, 33
   as virtual worlds, 32
tiles
   array, 309, 311
   Boolean variable, 152
   comment, 88
   defined, 6
   Do together, 97, 99, 101
   dragging into Method Editor, 57, 59, 61, 67, 79
   dummy object, 240
   event, 85, 251–252, 253
   For all in order instruction, 288
   For all together instruction, 290
   function, 123, 124
   If/Else instruction, 155, 156
   illustrated, 12
   instruction, 68, 69
   Let the mouse move <objects> event, 304, 305
   list, 297
   Loop instruction, 174, 312
   method, 60
   mouse event, 162, 261
   object, 22, 44
   Object Tree display, 28
   property, 26
   random number function, 268
   variable, 115, 116
   When a key is typed event, 253–254
   When the mouse is clicked on something event, 261, 262
   While a key is pressed event, 258, 259–260
   While instruction, 180, 187
times parameter, 327, 328, 331
toolbar, 11
trash can, 70

truncating numbers, 178
Tumble button, 36, 37, 42
turn at speed method, 66, 67
Turn Forward and Backward button, 36, 37, 42, 45
Turn Left and Right button, 36, 37, 45
turn method, 65, 67, 234
turn to face method, 66, 127, 213
TurnCamera world, 237
two-dimensional graphics, 31–32

U

Undo button, 46

V

Vanishing Cookie world, 183–186
variable area, 115
variables, 113–120
   assignment, 117
   Boolean, 115, 152, 224
   class-level, 113, 215–219
   counter, 179
   creating and using, 116–117
   creating set instructions for, 117, 118–119
   declaration, 115
   defined, 113
   initial value, 115
   lists as, 283
   local, 113, 114–115
   in math expressions, 130
   names, 114–115
   Number, 115, 141–142
   Object, 115
   parameter, 113
   tile, 115, 116
   types, 115
   values, 119
   world-level, 113, 226, 229
vehicle property, 232–233, 238
video, exporting Alice worlds to, 105–106
video capture window, 106
viewpoint, camera, 33
virtual worlds, 32
visual effects tips, 230–241

W

Wait instruction, 219
Web gallery, 16, 30
Welcome to Alice! dialog box
   Examples tab, 8
   illustrated, 7
   Open a world tab, 8
   Recent Worlds tab, 8
   Templates tab, 8, 19
   Tutorial tab, 8
When a key is typed event

defined, 250
tile, 253–254, 262
When a variable changes event, 250
When something becomes true event, 250, 252, 267
When the mouse is clicked on something event
  defined, 250
  handling, 262–263
  tile, 261, 263, 266
When the world starts event, 249, 250, 266
While a key is pressed event. *See also* events
  defined, 250, 252
  handling, 257–260
  tile, 258, 259–260
  When a key is typed event versus, 257
While instruction, 180–188
  creating, 182
  defined, 180
  empty, 182
  flowchart, 181
  in making object vanish, 182–186
  in moving object, 186–188
  placeholder, replacing, 187
  as pretest loop, 182
  tile, 180, 187
While something is true event, 250
While the mouse is pressed on something event, 250, 252
While the world is running event, 250, 252, 266
who parameter, 294
WorkOut world, 204–209
world.my first method method, 57–58
  automatic creation of, 57, 76
  defined, 57
  dot notation, 58
  execution, 59
  renaming, 76–77, 99, 135, 327
world object, 120
World Running... window, 9–11
  illustrated, 63
  opening, 9
  text console, 273, 274
  toolbar, 9–11
World View window, 11, 12
world-level methods, 227–228
  calling, 228
  defined, 226, 227
  divide and conquer, 227
  example, 228
world-level variables, 114, 226, 229
worlds. *See also* Alice worlds
  AccountantBob, 141–142

ArrayVisualization, 3
Bird, 214–215
CameraPointAtCar, 23 5, 317
Circles, 331–332
ClockLoop, 175–177
EndlessRecursion, 323, 32
Faeries, 254–257
Fan, 174–175
Fish, 296–297
FourSkaters, 285–291
FourSkatersArray, 311–313
Fridge, 261–262
Gilbert, 169–171
Globe, 263
GreetingNerd, 139–140
GumdropBigfish, 165–168
Gym, 211–212
HamletList, 306–307
HareWorld, 67
HawkAndTree, 233–234
Hollywood, 142
IslandRescue, 264–267
KarateClass, 291–296
LionArray, 309–311
MathRobot, 333–336
MovableFurniture, 305–306
Office, 216–219
PrintingRandomBee, 274
RandomBee, 268–269, 274
RepeatingNerd, 139
RescueAtSea, 186–188
SalutingSoldier, 236
snowLove, 13–15
SnowWorld, 228
SoccerGoal, 177–178
SoccerPractice, 300–303
SpaceJet, 258–260
Tennis, 180–181
TurnCamera, 237
Vanishing Cookie, 183–186
WorkOut, 204–209

X
X axis, 48, 49

Y
Y axis, 48, 49
yaw, 40

Z
Z axis, 48, 49
Zoom button, 48

defined, 250
tile, 253–254, 262
When a variable changes event, 250
When something becomes true event, 250, 252, 267
When the mouse is clicked on something event
defined, 250
handling, 262–263
tile, 261, 263, 266
When the world starts event, 249, 250, 266
While a key is pressed event. *See also* events
defined, 250, 252
handling, 257–260
tile, 258, 259–260
When a key is typed event versus, 257
While instruction, 180–188
creating, 182
defined, 180
empty, 182
flowchart, 181
in making object vanish, 182–186
in moving object, 186–188
placeholder, replacing, 187
as pretest loop, 182
tile, 180, 187
While something is true event, 250
While the mouse is pressed on something event, 250, 252
While the world is running event, 250, 252, 266
who parameter, 294
WorkOut world, 204–209
world.my first method method, 57–58
automatic creation of, 57, 76
defined, 57
dot notation, 58
execution, 59
renaming, 76–77, 99, 135, 327
world object, 120
World Running... window, 9–11
illustrated, 63
opening, 9
text console, 273, 274
toolbar, 9–11
World View window, 11, 12
world-level methods, 227–228
calling, 228
defined, 226, 227
divide and conquer, 227
example, 228
world-level variables, 114, 226, 229
worlds. *See also* Alice worlds
AccountantBob, 141–142

ArrayVisualization, 315–316, 317
Bird, 214–215
CameraPointAtCar, 238–239
Circles, 331–332
ClockLoop, 175–177
EndlessRecursion, 323, 324
Faeries, 254–257
Fan, 174–175
Fish, 296–297
FourSkaters, 285–291
FourSkatersArray, 311–313
Fridge, 261–262
Gilbert, 169–171
Globe, 263
GreetingNerd, 139–140
GumdropBigfish, 165–168
Gym, 211–212
HamletList, 306–307
HareWorld, 67
HawkAndTree, 233–234
Hollywood, 142
IslandRescue, 264–267
KarateClass, 291–296
LionArray, 309–311
MathRobot, 333–336
MovableFurniture, 305–306
Office, 216–219
PrintingRandomBee, 274
RandomBee, 268–269, 274
RepeatingNerd, 139
RescueAtSea, 186–188
SalutingSoldier, 236
snowLove, 13–15
SnowWorld, 228
SoccerGoal, 177–178
SoccerPractice, 300–303
SpaceJet, 258–260
Tennis, 180–181
TurnCamera, 237
Vanishing Cookie, 183–186
WorkOut, 204–209

X
X axis, 48, 49

Y
Y axis, 48, 49
yaw, 40

Z
Z axis, 48, 49
Zoom button, 48